LUMSDALE

THE INDUSTRIAL REVOLUTION IN A DERBYSHIRE VALLEY

ALAN & CHRISTINE PIPER

BANNISTER PUBLICATIONS LTD

First published in Great Britain in 2019 by
Bannister Publications Ltd
118 Saltergate, Chesterfield, Derbyshire S40 1NG

Copyright © 2019 by Alan Piper & Christine Piper

The moral rights of the authors have been asserted.

ISBN: 978-1-909813-64-9

All rights reserved.
No part of this book may be reproduced in any form or by any electronic or mechanical means, including information storage and retrieval systems, without written permission from the authors, except for the use of brief quotations in a book review.

Cover illustration of the Upper Bleach
Works Copyright © Sarah Burgess

Typeset in Palatino
Cover design by Design Kabin, Chesterfield, Derbyshire
Printed and bound in Great Britain

CONTENTS

Dedication	vii
Preface	ix
Acknowledgments	xi

Chapter 1: The Lumsdale Valley and its Mills

The context for our story	1
The Mighty Bentley Brook	3
The mill ponds	6
The mills above the waterfall	9
The mills below the waterfall	15
A microcosm of the Industrial Revolution	19

Chapter 2: Why Lumsdale, why 'Lums' and why Derbyshire?

Introduction	23
Why here? Resources and investors	24
Why is it called Lumsdale	30
The context of interest in Derbyshire: science and industry	37
Interest from visitors and artists	40

Chapter 3: Early lead smelting

Introduction	45
Why in Lumsdale?	46
Using water power: the ore hearth	50
Lummes Mill	53
Other early smelters	56
The lower smelting mills	58

Chapter 4: Lead: new technology and diversification

The latest technology - the cupola	61
The Pond Cottage cupolas	64
The 'Paint Mill' site	69
Slag mills	71
The strange case of the Offspring Mill	73
Red lead	78
The decline of the lead smelting industry	80

Chapter 5: Corn and fulling mills

Introduction	85
The Bown(e)s and the fulling mill(s)	86
Two fulling mills	88
Fulling and corn grinding	92
The site(s) of the corn and fulling mills	95
The end of the 'old' industries	101

Chapter 6: Cotton spinning

What has Arkwright got to do with Lumsdale? 103
Watts, Lowe & Co, Lumsdale 105
The Cotton Mill and Arkwright's patent 112
The history of the business 115
The other cotton mill 119
The end of cotton spinning in Lumsdale 121

Chapter 7: Bleach, barytes and bone - the Gartons

The bleaching process 123
John Garton, bleacher and landowner 129
John Garton the businessman 133
Barytes 136
Bone 138
End of the John Garton era 141
Edward Hall Garton 142
The sale of the Gartons' Lumsdale Estate 147

Chapter 8: The end of bleaching - the Farnsworths

Richard Farnsworth 149
John Farnsworth 151
Richard Farnsworth junior 152
A diversion to the Wragg saga 154
Acquiring the Garton business: George (Harry) and Ernest Richard 157
The purchase of 'Lumsdale' by Ernest Richard Farnsworth 1907 159
George (Harry) Farnsworth 161
The fifth generation of Farnsworths 165

Chapter 9: A fragile valley

What happened next? 173
Mrs Mills's legacy 177
No longer secret 182
Woodland management – flora and fauna 184
Conserving the industrial heritage 186

Chapter 10: Concluding thoughts

Introduction 191
The workers 191
The First Industrial Revolution 196

List of Plates 199
References 201
Newspapers 212
Maps 213
Index 214

DEDICATION

This book is dedicated to the memory of Mrs Marjorie Mills who loved the Lumsdale Valley and bequeathed it to the Arkwright Society for the benefit of future generations.

PREFACE

One of us was brought up in Lumsdale from the age of three. She went to university to study history and there met a law student. In due course we married and brought up our own family in Harrow. We were often in Lumsdale during the next forty years but, looking back, were woefully ignorant of the history and significance of the valley. In 2014 we retired here and became involved in the Lumsdale Project. We had a tour with Julian Burgess who for over thirty years has kept the story of Lumsdale alive through countless tours and talks. We started leading tours, armed with half a dozen pages of notes written by Christopher Charlton, and began to realise that there was a much greater story to tell. We have found material everywhere from local papers to the Derbyshire Record Office and the Royal Collection. The staff and volunteers at Cromford Mill, in particular Doreen Buxton and Rosemary Annable, have been immensely helpful. Friends and neighbours have kindly lent us priceless deeds and other documents and this book is the result.

In Lumsdale we find the Industrial Revolution in miniature. Because of its small scale there are a few individuals who play a large part in each generation and we have come to know them in (sometimes quite intimate) detail.

They all help to piece together the story but the jigsaw is far from complete. There are many omissions, reflecting the current state of our knowledge, but we hope there are few errors. If you can add to the story please write to us at the Lumsdale Project, The Arkwright Society, Cromford Mills, Mill Lane, Cromford DE4 3RQ.

Readers are very welcome to come to Lumsdale but we ask all visitors to understand that it is private property, owned and maintained either by the Arkwright Society or by residents. Please respect the privacy and quiet enjoyment of residents and do not trespass on those parts of the valley which are private land or which are restricted for the protection of the site. Much of the valley is protected as a Scheduled Monument. It is all vulnerable to damage, decay and erosion and its conservation for future generations is mainly the responsibility of volunteers. For current information visit www.cromfordmills.org.uk/lumsdale

Enjoy Lumsdale as much as we do. We trust this book will add to your pleasure.

All profits from the sale of this book will be donated to the Arkwright Society for the benefit of the Lumsdale Project.

Christine & Alan Piper
1st July 2019

ACKNOWLEDGMENTS

We are grateful to all the owners, authors and publishers of copyright material which appears in this book. In particular we thank the following people or organisations for permission to reprint or use material and photographs from the sources listed below:

The Arkwright Society: Deeds and other documents in the Arkwright Society archive at Cromford Mills including Plates 14 and 16, the postcard view of Garton's and other mills, and photograph of Garton's Mill.

Sarah Burgess: drawing of the Upper Bleach Works 1999 © Sarah Burgess.

Julian Burgess: Map of Lumsdale, Plate 1 © Julian Burgess.

Derbyshire Record Office for an extract from George Sanderson's Map of the Country 20 Miles Round Mansfield (Ref D1037Z/P1), Plate 2.

Sally Goodall for the photograph of Marjorie Mills (© Mrs Sally Goodall) and for the loan and use of other materials.

Helmshore Mills Textile Museum (Lancashire County Council) for consent to photograph the Arkwright water frame in their collection, Plate 17.

Picture the Past for licence to use the postcard view of the Upper Pond, Plate 5 © picturethepast.org.uk

Royal Collection Trust for the drawing by J.C.Nattes of Lumsdale Mill near Matlock Derbyshire 17th September 1798 © Her Majesty Queen Elizabeth II 2019.

TuckDB Postcards (https://tuckdb.org) for the postcard view of Lumsdale, Plate 12.

University of Manchester for permission to transcribe a letter in the Oldknow Collection, John Rylands Library and Glynn Waite for the postcard view of Garton's Mill, Plate 15.

We also wish to thank The British Newspaper Archive for access to the following publications:

Bath Chronicle and Weekly Gazette
Belper News
Bristol Mercury
Bristol Mirror
Chesterfield Herald
Derby Daily Telegraph
Derby Mercury
Derbyshire Advertiser and Journal
Derbyshire Courier
Derbyshire Times
Dundee Evening Telegraph
Hartlepool Northern Daily Mail
Lancashire Evening Post
London Gazette
Manchester Mercury
Nottingham Evening Post
Nottingham Review & General Advertiser for the Midland Counties
Pall Mall Gazette
Sheffield Daily Telegraph
Sheffield Independent

and to acknowledge our use of the Wirksworth website on www.wirksworth.org.uk.

The authors have made every effort to trace and contact owners of copyright material but if you let the publisher know of any errors or omissions we will rectify them at the earliest opportunity.

1

THE LUMSDALE VALLEY AND ITS MILLS

The context for our story

This book is about the history of the Upper Lumsdale Valley, on the outskirts of Matlock in Derbyshire. More specifically it focuses on the area which since 1996 has been owned and managed by the Arkwright Society, the charity which was formed to care for the mills at Cromford where Sir Richard Arkwright built his first water powered cotton mill. Mrs Marjorie Mills had bequeathed the valley to the Arkwright Society which had been helping to protect it for some years before that. We tell that story in more detail in Chapter 9.

We will discuss the industrial history associated with the Bentley Brook as it flows from a point opposite the entrance to Highfields Upper School, through three large mill ponds, passing the sites of mills and lead smelting works dating back to the sixteenth century or earlier, and dropping over a dramatic waterfall. The brook then goes on to power more mills sixty metres below. We will chart the place of these mills in the industrial revolution and tell the story of the families who owned the mills and some of the people who worked for them.

All this happened within a stretch of some 800 metres, lying north-south between the Chesterfield and Alfreton roads out of Matlock and protected as the Lumsdale Conservation Area and a Scheduled Monument. At the north end the dominant features now are Highfields School, which opened as a comprehensive in 1982, and housing estates built in 2017-2019. The tarmac road down the valley passes stone cottages from the eighteenth and also early and later twentieth centuries and by-passes the ponds, a waterfall and earlier mills, taking a route at a lower level of the valley. The brook finds its own way along the edge of the valley, flowing over underlying gritstone rock and bordered on the east by green fields. Beyond the fields is a gritstone ridge quarried for centuries for its very fine building stone. The quarry tips are covered with pine woods. The paths along the western side of the brook to the waterfall are a popular route for local residents and dog-walkers and for thousands of visitors who have themselves contributed to the changes in Lumsdale since 2014.

The industrial history of Lumsdale also features a very early cotton mill using Arkwright's invention, the water-powered spinning frame, but its industrial history is more complicated and much longer than that connection suggests. The valley has seen evolving and ever-changing patterns of industrialisation for more than four centuries, with mills and factories for lead smelting, fulling, the grinding of minerals as well as corn and bones, cotton spinning and cotton bleaching. In addition the valley was often in the forefront in pioneering new industrial techniques before their use was widespread. It does, indeed, appear incredible that so much of importance could have taken place in so small a valley and one which - even now - is relatively isolated and seemingly not on major access routes. Chapter 2 will, consequently, begin to explain why it all happened in Lumsdale.

Yet it would be wrong to see Lumsdale as a small area cut off from the rest of the world. For two reasons this area of Derbyshire came to a much wider notice: first as part of what we now call the Peak District and, secondly, as part of the Midlands Enlightenment. The 'houling wilderness' described by Daniel Defoe (1724-27) and the visitors' love of the 'sublime' beauty of this area made it 'the' place to visit whilst the Midlands became a powerhouse for new ideas and inventions. So in the next chapter we will also look at that in more detail.

However, this chapter will concentrate first on what was, in practice, the most important feature of the valley - the Bentley Brook, the stream which powered so many mills. We will take the opportunity to point out features which remain visible to the visitor today.

The Mighty Bentley Brook

> *'Water-falls ... Lumsdale, N.E. of Matlock, on 1st grit, high and romantic'*
>
> — (FAREY 1811: 489).

When John Farey wrote this two hundred years ago he identified the attraction which brings many people to Lumsdale today. However, the waterfall, albeit very beautiful, was not of itself what led to the industrial development of Upper Lumsdale, which ended when the last bleaching mill closed in 1929. That development covered many industries but, with one possible exception, they all depended on their proximity to a never-failing source of water, notably to turn mill wheels by water power but also to provide a source of water for washing textiles and minerals. They also depended on holding ponds to store water and ensure a good head of water when needed by the various mills which operated in the valley.

So in this chapter we focus on the all-important issue of managing the water supply to power the mills. It will, therefore, seek to establish, not always successfully, where the watercourses went, when the ponds were built and what mills they served. It will be helpful in this chapter to bookmark Plate 1 which is a map of the valley, for which we are grateful to Julian Burgess, Chair of the Lumsdale Project Group, with the stream, ponds and the surviving ruined mills with the names by which they are currently referred.

In 2014 the Lumsdale Project Group of the Arkwright Society chose 'the Mighty Bentley Brook' as the heading for the first of the interpretation boards at the top of the valley because it is indeed a powerful stream. It has never been known to dry up and can come down the hillside with considerable force after storms. It is at other times a deceptively quiet stream for most of its journey down from Cuckoostone Dale to Matlock Green.

Its importance as an impetus for wealth-creating industry is evident from the comments of Henry Moore who saw the valley on his descent from Riber in 1818:

'After amusing myself with surveying the different views from this elevated station, and making a sketch, I began to descend; when turning my eye to the right across the valley, I discovered a cascade pouring its silvery waters down the dark rocks of a glen, in a region where dusky sterility seems to hold an everlasting reign; not a tree, nor a patch of green is seen, to cheer the gloom of the savage waste, yet several dwellings are there. Curiosity induced me to visit this place, merely to ascertain the motive human beings could have for fixing their abode on such a forbidding spot: I found that great ruler of the actions of man, interest, had prompted them to reside here; it cheers the gloom by dispensing that part of happiness we may term worldly: the stream being admirably calculated for turning over-shot wheels, several bleaching mills are established upon it. The cascade makes a tolerable good sketch; the rocks that it runs over are extremely rugged, and of a brown gritstone; but the want of verdure and trees renders the colouring monotonous' (Moore 1818: 60-61).

'Interest' is of course not curiosity but profit. Clearly, apart from noting the cascade, Moore was not impressed!

Bentley Brook rises at Matlock Moor, flowing south through Cuckoostone Dale, under the A632 - once the Matlock-Chesterfield Turnpike - into Lumsdale. In Lumsdale it enters a series of mill ponds. It then flows over a waterfall and passes several mill ruins. Lower down, the Bentley Brook is joined by the Knabhall

Brook, flowing out of Tansley, itself dammed and supporting large mills. Finally, it runs through control gates into a bend of the River Derwent, just beyond Matlock Green and by Hall Leys Park in Matlock. Daniel Defoe's description of the Derwent was 'a fury of a River' and 'a frightful creature when the hills load her current with water' (1724-27: 40) and the Bentley Brook, though much smaller, has some of those characteristics. The amount of water in the stream can increase tremendously in a short time because it draws its water from a wide expanse of moorland above Lumsdale. It also has a significant drop. It was, therefore able to provide constant power.

Although small in width and only about five miles in length, Bentley Brook is classed as a 'main river' by the Environment Agency south and west from the boundary of the Lower Bleach Works; it is an 'ordinary watercourse' as it runs down through the mills. Appearances are deceptive, however, and the power of this gentle brook is immense. William Adam summed it up in his book of 1861:

'We cannot help remarking on the terrible effects produced by this stream, when swollen into a mighty torrent, on the night of the 25th June, 1835, when George the Fourth died. That ever-memorable night, when the whole heavens seemed crashing and rending to atoms – a scene, every instant of intense light, and profound darkness, that might be felt – this little stream, swollen into a mighty torrent, thundered along, carrying everything in its course near it. Walls and bridges were swept away throughout its course. In Matlock Town the gardens were completely destroyed, and many of the heaviest stones were carried by the force of the torrent considerable distances. But of how much utility is this little busy stream in its gentleness, in turning so many mills, giving employment to so many busy hands, and thus in many ways contributing its quota of benefit to the well-being of man' (1861: 101).

The date 1835 is a mis-print; the King died in 1830 and the *Nottingham Review* of 1 July 1830 confirms that date and the damage to several bridges and weirs.

Earlier maps (for example, Burdett's c.1767) show that in the

Matlock area, apart from the much larger river Derwent, the Bentley Brook was the only other water course of any significance. The nearest other streams with Bentley Brook's characteristics are the Bonsall Brook, which comes down the Via Gellia valley to the Derwent at Cromford and which powered several mills (see, for example, Smith 2018) and, to a lesser extent perhaps, the Warney Brook powering a corn mill (now DFS) or Sydnope Brook in Two Dales (formerly Toad Hole), Darley Dale, which powered the late-eighteenth century cotton and flax mills in Ladygrove, Sydnope Dale (for a brief history see www.ladygrovemill.co.uk/about- ladygrove-mill).

Nevertheless, as the number of mills in the valley increased, the water needed to be managed. This was done by a series of holding ponds and goits (elsewhere called leats) to divert water to the mill wheels (the mill head race). Also needed were channels to bypass and isolate the mill or regulate the flow on to the mill wheel, as well as the tail race to take water away from the mill wheel and back to the stream. In Lumsdale however, when several mills were operating down the hillside the tail race of one mill became a 'mid race', in effect the head race of another. Where the valley drops steeply there was also a wooden launder built on stone pillars to take water down to the bottom mill (Plates 11, 12 and 15).

The mill ponds

The Little Dam and the Upper Dam

It has proved extraordinarily difficult to date the construction of the mill ponds and the various channels taking water from one mill to another. What is clear is that the earliest exercise in water management was the capture of water from the Bentley Brook (no doubt by means of a weir) some 75 metres above Ivy Cottage.

This was then channelled by a goit which ran under the wagon way which crossed a stone bridge and gave access to the quarries.

The surface of the wagon way was uncovered and hacked through when a sewer connection to the Thornberries estate was made in October 2017. Some of the road stones and part of the cover of the goit were rescued and can be seen in front of *Pinecroft* nearby.

The goit continued, parallel with the lane, to the site of the Bone Mill, although grinding bone was not then its function. The goit is shown on the Enclosure Map of 1780 and on many later maps. Burdett's map of 1767, though of small scale, shows no ponds along the course of the Bentley Brook and only one building, on the site of Pond Cottages, which we know was a cupola – see Chapter 4. The goit was then broadened into a long narrow pond which held a supply and created a head of water for the Bone Mill. It is the only expanse of water shown on Sanderson's map of 20 miles around Mansfield, surveyed in 1830-1834 and published in 1835, a map notable for the accuracy of the field boundaries recognisable today (Plate 2). It is called Little Dam on the 1848 Tithe Map. The site of this pond is shown on OS and other maps distinguished by its own outline, though apparently silted up, as late as 1899. On the 1922 map it appears to have been incorporated into the larger Upper Pond.

It is inferred that the supply of water to the Bone Mill was at high level from the top of the dam wall to the top of the wheel so that the wheel was over-shot. The mill and its white-gabled cottage are shown in a postcard, undated but probably late nineteenth century (Plate 5). A tail race carried the spent water in a culvert beneath the path and back into the brook.

The Little Dam was later augmented by construction of a larger dam with a high stone wall across the valley floor so that the sheet of water stretched back to the causeway, just north of Ivy Cottage, which doubled as the wagon way to the quarries.

The date of that expansion is not clear. Mel Morris in her Lumsdale Conservation Area Appraisal notes that the dam walls of the two largest ponds, the Upper and Lower, share the same heavy engineered construction and says they were built in 1850 (Morris 2010: 10). However, Gratton's Tithe Map shows that the

Upper Pond - called the Upper Dam, beside and separate from the Little Dam - was in existence in 1849 and the plan on a deed of 1859 shows that the Lower Pond and its wall were not yet built.

There is evidence in the form of a small sluice in the southern corner of the Upper Pond to suggest that water from here was used to power the Bone Mill at some stage. The principal outflow from the Upper Pond was however further to the north and only served to allow water to continue its flow along the Bentley Brook (Plate 4). The stub of a cast iron pipe seen protruding from the wall is only an aid to draining the pond, not connected with any other structure.

The Middle Pond

Following the Brook southwards, the next feature was a small clapper bridge, made of large slabs of stone supported on stone piers (Plate 6), a kind of bridge often associated with Dartmoor and Exmoor. It is shown on Sanderson's map in 1835 (Plate 2) and gave access up the hill to the quarries. It is now ruined and both the piers and parts of the deck slabs can be seen re-used as stepping stones.

The bridge marks the northern limit of the area which became the Middle Pond. Again the date is obscure. Sanderson's map shows the footprint of the pond with a track along its west edge but also the stream passing to the east of it. The first edition 1"-to-the-mile OS map of 1840 shows a similar footprint but no clear sign that there was a pond. We know however from references in deeds that Watts, Lowe & Co. (see Chapter 6) built a large reservoir or dam and this is one of only two candidates. The Middle Pond was certainly in existence by 1846 when Gratton surveyed for the Matlock Tithe Map and, then being one of two, was called the Lower Pond, with a sluice at its southern end dropping the flow beneath a bridge which led to the fields on the hillside.

The brook then passes in a culvert behind and well below the ground level of Pond Cottages and we have found no evidence that there was ever a mill wheel here. That is consistent with the first use of the site after 1749 for a pair of lead-smelting cupolas but there were probably slag mills associated with the cupolas which would have required water power for the bellows.

The Middle Pond now looks much as it did a century ago thanks to the de-silting in 2014 described in Chapter 9.

Lower Pond

The Lower Pond presents more problems. When Gratton surveyed in 1848/9 and as late as 1859 it was not there, nor was the bridge across the stream adjacent to Pond Cottages. The lane from Tansley, called by several variations of 'Oakstage' Lane, reached Lumsdale Farm and then turned sharply south and then south-west to cross the stream, possibly by a ford, somewhere below the line of the present dam wall. On both sides of the stream were plantations and there were two small ponds, one just below the future site of the Sawmill and one in the field just above the Chimney. It is suggested that the latter was a settling pond associated with lead smelting and the 1880 OS map indicates that it was fed by a spring from the north-west rather than from the Bentley Brook. A small square on the 1848 map may indicate the Chimney but it is not identified as such and its date is uncertain.

The mills above the waterfall

There does not appear to have been any mill on the Bentley Brook to the north of the Arkwright Society estate. A building shown on maps close to the brook at Bentley Bridge is shown in the Historic Environment Record as 'a 19th century farmstead of a linear plan. The farmhouse was attached to the agricultural range. The site was in an isolated location. All traditional buildings have been lost' (Derbyshire HER ref. MDR22387). The most northerly mill is therefore the Bone Mill and its ruins survive.

The Bone Mill

In Chapter 3 we deal with the history of this site as a centre of lead smelting. The site of what was referred to in 1657 as the 'New Mill' was named as White's Mill, the only feature identified on the first edition 1" OS map in 1840. On an 1880 map and an 1886 mortgage plan it is labelled Bone Mill. By the time it was sold in 1906 it was a plantation with cottage, 'formerly used as a Bone Mill'. The buildings have been robbed of much of their stone but the wheel pit, about 8 metres long and with central blocks to support the wheel hub, is still impressive. Between the mill and its cottage was a yard, at the lower end of which is a substantial pair of gateposts. The tail race is visible beyond the path.

Another mill?

The Enclosure Map and the Tithe Map both show there was a small building close to the west bank of the stream, before the Lower Pond was built, which may have been another mill. It was about where the outfall from the Lower Pond is now. Indeed the Enclosure Map appears to show a water course through that structure to another mill on the site of the Paint Mill or Grinding Mill. Salford Archaeology recently observed in relation to this location:

'In the south-west corner of the [Lower] dam wall, a large pipe projects through the external face of the wall between three and four courses from its top. It is approximately 15" (0.38m) in diameter and formed a water feed to the Saw Mill to the immediate south-west. To the east, a sluice was placed at the base of the wall possibly representing an earlier headrace for the Saw Mill.

It has a dressed kerbing to a channel to the south, which appears to have formed a headrace leading into a void with vertically cut bedrock, aligned with its eastern side, and possibly representing a disused wheel pit with a possible blocked tailrace beyond, although this could not be established without intrusive vegetation clearance and excavation' (Wild 2017: 28 and plates 36 - 39).

So we have several indications that there may have been another mill in Lumsdale not previously recognised and now lost. If this was a mill it was on land which, until it was awarded to Peter Nightingale on Enclosure in 1780, was manorial waste. Unlike the Bone Mill there is no evidence we have found either confirming that the Lords of the Manor had any right to let it after Enclosure or identifying its owner or tenant. It is possible that it was in the 1780s the Offspring Mill discussed in Chapter 4 but that remains another area for speculation.

Saw Mill

The water management which makes Lumsdale very special, if not unique, begins with the outflow from the Lower Pond wall. It provided power direct to the wheel of the Saw Mill which must have been built not long after 1859. The same water was then retained and channelled to the Paint Mill, the Grinding Mill, and the mill in the Upper Bleach Works. Whether it also powered the Lower Bleach Works is a matter of conjecture.

The Salford investigation quoted above suggested that the large pipe protruding from the Lower Pond wall was not the original headrace to the Saw Mill and that is consistent with the OS map of 1880 which shows a channel branching off the earlier Paint Mill headrace (see below). The later maps show no such features however and we have to rely on observation and other documents. The Saw Mill wheelpit is about 7.8m long and 1.6m wide. John Ruddy, assessing the buildings as a specialist conservation and structural engineer before a conservation project in 017, considered it likely that hidden below the debris in it (a combination of soil and fallen masonry) would be 'a spectacular semi-circular gritstone base to the waterwheel pit' (Ruddy 2017: 11). The auction particulars in 1906 referred to a saw mill here but the 1929 particulars only referred to the lot containing 'a range of ruined Buildings, formerly used as Paint Mills with Old Wheel House'. Access to the Saw Mill was apparently through a gateway now blocked and replaced with a stile (although this gateway might have been made originally for the 'lost' mill mentioned above). This gateway would not have had room for manoeuvring any substantial tree trunks but maybe John Garton had no requirement for that. It could, instead, have been sawing stone from the nearby quarries, with access across the bridge by Pond Cottages built after creation of the Lower Pond. Maybe its last use was for grinding minerals for paint - the proximity of a French burr stone grinding wheel beside the path is consistent with that.

The tail race from the Saw Mill is clear, leading beneath the current path and out from the south-west corner of the building, draining bright orange water through a stone-lined culvert beneath the building. There was an out-flow into the brook through a hole in the retaining wall. The 1880 OS map shows the tail race joining the old head race of the Paint Mill and feeding the wheel. The Salford report says:

'Following the construction of Saw Mill to the north, the headrace was apparently remodelled to comprise a timber launder from the tailrace of the new mill, although it would originally have led directly from Bentley Brook, to the immediate north-east of the wheel pit, using the pool below the short waterfall as a natural reservoir. However, this area has been heavily remodelled, obscuring any evidence for either headrace, although two parallel stone walls, visible in plan, and aligned with the northern edge of the wheel pit, may relate to the support for a timber launder' (Wild 2017: 40).

The Paint Mill (Plate 9)

The head-race to the Paint Mill before the construction of the Lower Pond and the Saw Mill is unfortunately not shown clearly on the Enclosure or Tithe Maps and the earliest plan we have is attached to a conveyance in 1859 (DRO D858/T/17). That shows a channel leaving the stream near the point of the possible ford (across the brook near the current dam wall) and leading straight to the mill. The same channel is shown on the 1880 OS map. The ground has been covered since with spoil and waste from later industry and the route of that channel is no longer visible.

The Paint Mill wheel pit is about 8m long and 1.3m wide. Ruddy again considered it likely that there would be 'a spectacular semicircular gritstone base to the waterwheel pit' (2017: 25). The north wall of the wheel pit today does not show how water fed the wheel so we infer that it came in at or above ground level. At one time it was enclosed by buildings on both sides as photographs and beam slots in the eastern gable show.

The site is conspicuously labelled Paint Mill on the 1880 OS map and 1886 mortgage plan but not later. By the time of the 1906 auction it was in ruins. The contemporary postcard (Plate 12) shows the eastern extension roofless. Limited excavation in 1987 confirmed that the room to the west of the wheel had a heated floor for drying barytes, quantities of which remained.

On the east bank of the brook are what may appear to be two bridge abutments, one at high level and one opposite the end of a passageway or tunnel descending from the level of the Paint Mill yard. Two cast iron fittings at the mouth of the tunnel have been mistaken in the past as evidence of a bridge but John Boucher has identified them as two 'plummer blocks' holding small vertical wheels which supported a turntable device common in Victorian factories and quarries. The footprint of a third block is visible and the fourth, completing the circle, may be under a gritstone block which has fallen into the brook. The purpose of such turntables was to enable four-wheeled skips to be turned in confined spaces and here the turntable made it possible for skips to be turned to and from the mouth of the passageway and on to the bank of the brook (Personal communication now included in Wild 2017: 43).

If the device was Victorian in date it probably related to the time when the Paint Mill was active as such and grinding barytes.

John Ruddy was able to access the next part of the water channel, a mid-race between the Paint Mill and the Grinding Mill. He found that the culvert was formed in gritstone masonry throughout and had a flat bottom, vertical walls and a horizontal soffit. The soffit (or underside of the roof) was formed primarily by stone slabs spanning between the sidewalls. 'It began as being 1m high by 0.8m wide, with increase in height towards the centre, with the soffit abruptly rising to being 2.5m above the base' (Ruddy 2017: 59).

The Grinding Mill (Plate 10)

The visitor today is discouraged by iron railings from falling into a pit just outside the north wall of the Grinding Mill.

Ruddy notes:

'This holds high significance as it is where the subterranean culvert from the Paint Mill wheel pit appears. Evidence suggests there was a penstock here, and there is a further subterranean culvert which runs from here to the stream. Also buried below debris will be the entrance for the watercourse into the Grinding Mill' (2017: 57).

'Penstock' carries various meanings but presumably here it is a pipe or other restricted channel directing and perhaps regulating the flow of water to the wheel.

Wild, commenting on the same features notes that several phases of the headrace appear to have survived and he sets out what he thinks was the latest phase:

'[This] appears to have comprised a leat directly from the tailrace of the Paint Mill, immediately to the north, entering the wheel house within a stone culvert. An open channel below may represent an overflow, or bypass channel, directing water around the outer edge of the wheel house and into the central section of the adjacent waterfall. Internally, a cast-iron pipe within a remodelled rectangular aperture marks the position of the stone culvert headrace. However, the opening of a further headrace leat survives to the east, within a retaining wall to the north of the wheel house, demonstrating that water was originally supplied from directly above the waterfall within Bentley Brook' (2017: 50 and pl. 72,75,76).

Our own recent observation is that after heavy rain water flows out of the brook through a small stone-lined culvert close by and emerges through the eastern aperture, though whether this would provide enough volume of water to power a wheel is open to speculation.

Wild also says that 'the Grinding Mill, appears to have been erected as a corn mill, but was used subsequently as a mineral grinding mill' but does not cite evidence. He does, however, identify the remains of the original mill which, he says, was placed at right angles to the Bentley Brook, and comprised a rectangular two-storey structure through which the present path passes by means of a doorway.

'The mill would have been powered by a waterwheel placed on its eastern side, although the extant wheel pit is placed within a later structure, placed perpendicular [i.e. at right angles] to the original mill, and of almost equal size. This not only housed the deep wheel pit but also grinding wheels on a platform to the west, the curved stone housing for one such wheel still extant. It was erected directly onto the bedrock, which is exposed along the edge of a waterfall' (2017: 46-48, pl. 66-74).

The Grinding Mill wheel pit is the largest in Lumsdale measuring 10m by 2.9m although the wheel would have been narrower as the trench in the bottom of the pit indicates. The Tithe Map seems to show a wall between the building and the waterfall which would be consistent with, originally, an external wheel. The name 'Grinding Mill' does not appear on any maps nor in the auction particulars for the sale of the Garton estate in 1906 when it fell within lot 6 and was included in 'ruins of Paint Mill' (DRO D504/131/4). Remnants of more French burr stones in the area of the Grinding Mill would be consistent with grinding barytes there.

The mills below the waterfall

The ravine

The path which today leads from the Grinding Mill down steps, along a more level section and then down more steps to the road was constructed by the Arkwright Society in the 1980s for the benefit of visitors. From at the latest 1798 until at least 1905 this was the route of a wooden launder carrying water. The tail race from the Grinding Mill survives for the first few metres as a row of dressed sandstone blocks with some iron fittings still in situ. These and a row of masonry pillars supported a wooden launder which carried the water along the west bank of the brook to the mill in the Upper Bleach Works. It is illustrated in somewhat different forms both in the drawing by Jean Claude Nattes in 1798 (Plate 11) and in several postcards published around 1900 (Plates 12, 14, and 15).

The stone pillars on which the launder rested are still visible beside the level section of the modern path on the valley side. The postcards show the launder turning away from the brook and forming the head race for the Upper Bleach Works mill.

Jean (or John) Claude Nattes (c1765-1839) was an English watercolourist and a founder member of the Society of Painters in Water Colours in 1804, although he was expelled three years later for exhibiting other people's work as his own. He was however a prolific artist, commissioned in 1789 by Sir Joseph Banks (and paid £709) to record for him the buildings of Lincolnshire (Hoppit 2018: 403). Some seven hundred of his illustrations are in the Lincolnshire Archives (www.lincstothepast.com). His connection with Banks may well have brought him to Overton Hall at Ashover and even to Tansley, where Banks had property. He toured Derbyshire in 1798 and several of his sketches are in the Royal Collection. His drawing of Lumsdale dated 17 September 1798 is one of the most detailed. One would expect his depiction of the buildings in the ravine to be reasonably accurate although he has exercised considerable licence in the drawing of distant hills and the machinery below the launder has been the subject of some controversy.

Nattes's drawing, the search for the precise location of the smelting mills given by Elizabeth Turnor to Bonsall School in 1734 (see Chapter 4) and the conundrum of the 'north-east-south-west' description of land acquired by Wilson and Barton (see Chapter 5) lead us to wonder about the buildings shown by Nattes on the west side of the ravine. Were they the Turnor/Bonsall mills? If so, did they have their own internal succession of channels turning water wheels?

The Upper Bleach Works Mill

A hundred years later than Nattes there is no doubt that the launder supplied water to the mill in the Upper Bleach Works. The age and function of this mill are uncertain. In his *Sketch of a tour into Derbyshire and Yorkshire* published in February 1783 (but not in the earlier edition) Bray describes the Lumsdale falls and adds:

'At the bottom [of the Lumsdale Falls] is a little mill, turned by a small branch of the stream, which is conducted by a channel made for that purpose. A little above this mill is the station for seeing the fall' (Bray 1783 2nd edition: 128).

This pre-dates the construction of the 1783 cotton mill in the Lower Bleach Works site and so is likely to refer to the corn mill which preceded it. However, Bray's description of the purpose-made channel as 'a small branch of the stream' does not seem to be the wooden launder illustrated by Nattes in 1798 which leads to the machinery in the foreground of his sketch.

The Upper Bleach Works site appears to be on two levels with the remains of the water mill at the higher level. Wild investigated that site:

'The wheel house was placed in the north-eastern part of the complex, forming the western [*eastern?*] room of a north/south-aligned building, and housing a central narrow wheel pit. This is heavily overgrown, but retains ironwork related to the framing of the wheel on its western edge' (Wild 2017: 56, pl.85-90).

He notes that at the southern end of the wheel house there is an arched opening above the tail race, which appears to have run between the mill block and a detached rectangular structure and that the tail race passes below a low lintel at the western end of the detached structure (ibid).

There has been so much re-building and destruction in this area that interpretation is difficult. The tail race below the wheel pit is partially blocked by a later wall and the site is full of fallen stone and overgrown. The 1929 plan included by Wild on page 7 appears to show a tail race from the wheel pit turning east at right angles and discharging the spent water back into the brook. A thorough archaeological investigation is needed.

The Lower Bleach Works Mill

There is no clear evidence of how the early mills on the Lower Bleach Works site received and discharged their water. Wild suggests that one of the openings beside the road, the one to the east of the stone tramway, may be the water course between the mills in the Upper and Lower Bleach Works (55, pl.84) but it is difficult to see how this could be a continuation of the tail race described above. He also says of the surviving cotton mill in the Lower Bleach Works:

'The early mill was placed at an approximate 45° angle to Bentley Brook, but parallel to its course slightly further to the north, suggesting that the original headrace for the mill was taken from the bend in the water course' (62).

That suggestion, based on observation, is remarkably like Bray's description that we quoted earlier but Watts, Lowe & Co. did not buy the land for the cotton mill until early in 1783 (see Chapter 5). They may however have copied the idea.

'The water wheel [of the 1783 cotton mill] was placed externally against the western gable, within what appears to have been an open wheel pit, unlike those enclosed within wheel houses to the north. A large central aperture in the gable wall has a dressed semi- circular arch, and would have transferred power from the wheel into the mill. A slightly projecting aperture with stone surround high in the gable wall at the northern end of the wheel pit probably represents the course of the original headrace, with a timber chute probably projecting the water directly onto a backshot wheel' (Wild 2017: 64 and pl. 99 to 103).

Precisely how the water reached that aperture is not explained but there is another potential source from a spring to the west of the mill feeding two storage tanks, one under the garden of Lumsdale House and one closer to the mill. These are specifically referred to, and the benefit of them included, in the lease of the Bleach Works by Edward Hall Garton to the Farnsworths on 14 June 1905. Also mentioned for the first time is the right to use the water of a spring on the eastern bank of the brook, shown on plans, carried across on a bridge prominent in a postcard photograph (Plate 12). Pure spring water would have been more valuable for bleaching purposes and for the boilers than for turning a wheel and more investigation is required to prove the source(s) of power for the mill.

The Lower Bleachworks site, both when powered by a wheel and when engaged in bleaching, will have generated a lot of waste water and there are channels below the surface to discharge it underground into the brook as it passes below the site.

So much we do not know!

We are still left with questions of chronology. The Little Dam above the Bone Mill (in an earlier use) was undoubtedly the earliest pond. The Lower Pond was the last to be built, sometime after 1859. When Edward Hall Garton defined his estate in 1886 for the purpose of mortgaging it he compared old descriptions of its various parts with current field and plot numbers. He set out the old description of the fifty-two acres awarded to Peter Nightingale on Enclosure referring to 'a large pond or reservoir ... erected and made by or at the expense of Messrs Watts Lowe & Co.'. That dates one of the two upper ponds between 1784 and about 1807 - but which one? It does not seem an appropriate description of the Little Dam. Construction of the Middle Pond would have involved much less cost and labour than the more elaborate extension to the Upper Pond with its massive stone wall. Until more documents come to light or there is some major archaeology we can only speculate.

A microcosm of the Industrial Revolution

Our aim is that our account of the industrial development of the Lumsdale Valley will also contribute to a clearer idea as to how and why the industrial revolution occurred. There are various aspects of the story which seem to us very important in this process so we will mention them here.

The pre-industrial revolution

As Brewer has noted, 'For a hundred years the Industrial Revolution was given credit for many of the advances which were made much earlier' (Brewer 1981: 27) until Nef – and others – argued that 'it can be more properly regarded as a long process stretching back to the middle of the sixteenth century' (J U Nef (1934) quoted in Deane (1965)). That is indeed borne out by developments in Lumsdale where water power had been used for lead smelting and utilising what was then the latest technology of the ore hearth long before the various dates of the 1750s, 1760s and 1770s when the 'First Industrial Revolution' is deemed to begin.

The importance of family networks

The lead smelting, cotton spinning and bleaching, and the grinding businesses - over several centuries - all reveal the importance of family ties in the setting up of business partnerships and consortia to finance and/or run the different mills which resulted. The consortium which set up the first cotton spinning mill in Lumsdale on first sight appears to be an unconnected and somewhat motley group of men who did not all live in Matlock but, as Chapter 6 reveals, there were family links between several of them and to future generations of Lumsdale businessmen.

Lynn Willies (1986: 267) notes of Derbyshire lead mining and smelting that 'Capital from outside the region on any scale was rare, except for the London Lead Company, though even in the seventeenth century the field was well enough known to attract capital to Dovegang [mine]'. It would appear, however, from the experience of Lumsdale that there were usually links between the investors.

The 'flexibility' of partnerships and consortia

Many of the same family names can be seen throughout large parts of the story. Consortia were set up, subdivided, reformed in order to invest in what at the time was seen as the most likely way to make money. This flexibility may at times have been to the detriment of the work force but, in terms of kick-starting an industrial revolution, it was what was needed. That flexibility also showed a willingness to seek out and invest in new inventions, new machinery or new ways to carry on whatever was the core business at the time. Similarly, as markets changed, there was flexibility in moving to different aspects of the business, such as bleaching, rather than spinning cotton.

The crucial importance of access to raw materials and distribution networks

Lumsdale was small but it could access lead and minerals which could be found only in this area and, for a while, it could access raw cotton competitively. And, as we shall see in the next chapter, the valley was well placed for distribution networks for its lead in earlier centuries, and its bleached cotton in the later nineteenth century.

Sadly the demise of the valley as an important cog in the first industrial revolution also shows that, with sustained success, as in the Lumsdale bleaching industry, can come a weakening of the desire to modernise machinery and be cognisant of global economic change. Given that the Second Industrial Revolution - the technological revolution - witnessed the expansion of, for example, electricity, petroleum and steel it is perhaps significant that Mr Farnsworth had not yet introduced electricity to his works in 1920 (see Chapter 8). But the rise as well as the demise of industries in Lumsdale also reveals that people do matter in this process.

We will comment on the above aspects as we deal with the different stages of industry in the valley.

2

WHY LUMSDALE, WHY 'LUMS' AND WHY DERBYSHIRE?

Introduction

This small valley has seen so much industry over the centuries and, consequently, visitors often ask why it all happened in Lumsdale. So this chapter will start by reviewing those resources – natural and human – which enabled the industrial revolution to take place in Lumsdale. We will also deal with a different question which visitors to Lumsdale have in mind when they ask 'Why Lumsdale?'. They want to know why Lumsdale is called Lumsdale when the stream which runs through it is called Bentley Brook. Unfortunately there is no clear answer to that question. There are many theories about the origins of 'the Lums' or Lumsdale and we will explain our preferred theory. However, this chapter will also seek to place Lumsdale in a much wider context, that of the eighteenth century Midlands 'powerhouse' as well as the early focus on Derbyshire, rather than other parts of the country, by geologists, artists and early writers of guide books.

Why here? Resources and investors

Rich in resources

Though a small area and seemingly off the beaten track, Lumsdale became an important centre of industry because it has been a valley rich in resources, or at least had access to resources, to support several different industries over at least three centuries. In this section we will discuss the raw materials and minerals, together with the stone and wood needed to build the mills and the fuel for the smelters. We will also touch on the important issue of the investors although we shall deal with them in much more detail throughout the book.

Gritstone

The most obvious resource is the gritstone in the ground. Farey describes the attributes of '1st or Millstone Grit Rock' – 'which by its thickness and its hardness, and truly indestructible properties, gives rise to the greater part of the Silicious Rock Scenery in Derbyshire … easily worked, considering the extreme hardness of its particles, and its great durability, which appears to me superior, to that of any Free-stone which I have seen in England.

… Some of the beds of this 1st Grit Rock, which have usually spherical stains in them of light Red colour, are perfectly infusible, and form the best Fire Stone which is known, for lining the Hearth of Iron-Furnaces and others where intense heat is kept up. [T]hese Fire Stones … are also got at Lums Dale in Matlock … As this Rock is one of the finest and best marked features of the great Derbyshire Denudation, I shall mention in order the places [where it is found] … Riber-Hill, Tansley, Lums Dale, Matlock-Bank' (Farey 1811: 220- 223).

The 1848 Tithe Map shows Parish Quarries near the Wishing Stone and on the hillside to the east. The OS maps from 1879 onwards show the progression of the quarries along the hillside from Tansley towards the Chesterfield Road.

There are several 'old quarries' in a line to the north on Tansley Moor and one small 'old quarry' north of the Oakstage nearer Lumsdale. Lumsdale Quarry, to the east of the Upper and Middle Ponds, covers about five acres. Access was by the wagon ways which are now Footpaths 33 and 35 along the northern edge of the Upper Pond and leading uphill from the 'stepping stones'. By 1899 the Bentleybrook Quarry of similar size had been opened up to the north with access from Quarry Lane and what is now Footpath 7 through the Thornberries Estate. Both were later extended into the hillside to the east. Lumsdale Quarry is shown as 'disused' by 1922 but the quarry on the Oakstage had been re-opened and extended. Quarrying at Bentleybrook (later called Lumshill) Quarry continued until late in the 1900s. One of us recalls the sound of the warning whistle and the bang of the explosion as fresh rock was brought down.

An advertisement placed by G.S. Drabble 'quarry owner and stone merchant' in Kelly's Directory of 1891 notes that he supplies the best stone from three quarries including the Old Bentley Brook Quarry which overlooks Lumsdale. The advertisement explains that public and private bodies near and far buy the stone and that 'Select Beds of Stone in the Bentley Brook and Farley Hill Quarries are used in Stairs for Public Buildings, as Hotels, Theatres etc., in London, Brighton, etc.' (see www.andrewsgen.com/matlock/stone.htm#inf). In similar vein Famous Derbyshire Health Resorts stated that 'no stone known to modern engineers equals that quarried at Farley Quarries, Darley Dale and the Old Bentley Brook Quarries' (compiler unknown 1893: 23).

Thus there was ample fine-quality material for building the mills, dams, watercourses and dwelling houses needed in Lumsdale. Moreover the Fire Stone described by Farey was perfect for the hearths of the lead smelters operating before 1750.

Wood

Matlock Moor was a good place for growing trees. When Joseph Smith (who was 'leaving his situation') sold up in 1815 he offered for sale 'upwards of 400,000 trees, consisting of Black Italian Poplars, Alders, Elms, Scotch, Spruce, Larch and Yew Firs, Beech, Ash, Sycamore, Etc. ... fit for Forest Planting' (*Derby Mercury*, 5 October 1815). We can infer that in earlier times of less methodical planting there was plenty of timber available. The 1848 Tithe Map shows a number of 'plantations' in close vicinity to the Bentley Brook and the 1880 OS map shows woodland along the ridge to the east before the development of the quarries. When the Lumsdale estate was sold in 1907 the purchasers paid extra for the timber on their lots.

Brick

The 1876/1880 OS map shows a brick field with a kiln just north of where the (later) Brickyard Cottages stand on the Chesterfield Road. It was 'disused' by 1899 (OS 1:2,500 map).

Coal

A current Coal Authority on-line search reveals an outcrop of coal on the line of the Bentley Brook running from about the middle of the Upper Pond to the northern edge of the Middle Pond. Farey includes it in his list of collieries as 'Lumsdale 1 m NE of Matlock, 1st coal (lately)' (Farey, 1811: 203). There is no evidence of any large-scale mining but the outcrop would have been useful for fuel in the furnaces of lead smelting cupolas and slag hearths.

Lead

As we note in Chapter 3 the nearby limestone areas of Derbyshire were rich in lead, notably around Winster, Wensley, and Ashover. Although there was none in Lumsdale, it was near enough to make it economical to transport it (even up hill and down dale) to the place where it could be efficiently processed.

Barytes

Lumsdale was very close to the sources for a useful, and still economically important mineral.

'Barite, also called barytes or heavy spar, the most common barium mineral, barium sulfate (BaSO4). Barite occurs in hydrothermal ore veins (particularly those containing lead and silver), in sedimentary rocks such as limestone, in clay deposits formed by the weathering of limestone, in marine deposits, and in cavities in igneous rock. ... Commercially, ground barite has been used in oil well and gas well drilling muds; in the preparation of barium compounds; as a body, or filler, for paper, cloth, and phonograph records; as a white pigment and as an inert body in coloured paints.' (www.britannica.com/science/barite accessed 4.4.2019)

In this area the deposits are limited mainly to a line along the eastern edge of the limestone around Matlock, Cromford, Wirksworth and Brassington. In 1858 8,000 tons were produced in Derbyshire compared with 13,337 tons for the whole of the UK. The next largest amount was nearly 2,000 tons from Northumberland (Hunt 1860: 376). This by-product of the lead mining industry enabled John Garton to introduce barytes grinding for paint production (and possibly also in his bleaching processes) to Lumsdale.

Wool, flax and cotton

All the resources for the various textile processes carried out in Lumsdale would have been useless without the materials to make the fabrics. We know little about the sources of wool and the flax to make linen except that there was flax grown at Ashover (Farey 1813: 168) and there were clearly sheep to provide wool for fulling mills and supplies for the flax mill at Matlock Green are documented (referred to in a conveyance of 1869) (DRO D856/T/17).

Until the eighteenth century cotton made-up goods were imported from India but during the 1700s the import of raw cotton or cotton wool increased first gradually and then dramatically. From 1771 to 1781 the average weight of cotton imported was around 5.5 million lbs (2.5 million kilos). That figure doubled in the next three years to 1784 when cotton spinning had begun in Lumsdale and increased to 39 million lbs (17.7 million kilos) by 1789. Across the century the quantity increased from about 2 million lbs in 1701 to 56 million lbs in 1800. The increase is attributed to the invention of mechanical processes for production in the mid-century and corresponding increases in exports (Baines 1835: 215).

In 1772-74 64 per cent came from the West Indies, and 28 per cent from the Levant (Turkey) and southern Europe. That continued during the period of the American War of Independence but when that ended in 1783 - and the Napoleonic wars interrupted supplies from the West Indies - America became the primary supplier until the American Civil war in the 1860s again disrupted imports (Price, 1998: 84).

Workers

No industry is possible without workers. The very large profits made by owners of lead mines - especially in the seventeenth century - had given many labourers employment as miners, albeit a wretched and dangerous job. It also gave employment to many in the lead smelting trades as an alternative to quarrying and farm work.

Smelting could be carried on anywhere sufficiently near to make transporting lead worthwhile and with a good source of water power. Hence Lumsdale was ideal.

However, the decline of the lead industry meant that workers became available for work in other water powered trades such as cotton spinning and bleaching. Again Lumsdale was ideally placed to employ those who had previously worked in the nearby limestone hills where there was lead. For instance, Obadiah Allen married Hannah Boden at St. Giles' Matlock in 1812. Their first child was born in 1814 when Obadiah was a miner and they lived on Matlock Bank. They were still there until at least 1820 but by 1827 they had moved into Lumsdale and Obadiah had then become a bleacher. He was still bleaching when their ninth child, Elizabeth, was baptised in 1835.

Investors

Another critical resource was land and finance. We will show in Chapters 5 to 7 how the Lumsdale estate was created - in part from land which had been owned by families for generations, in part allotted from manorial waste in the Enclosures - and put together by investors who collected parcels of land for development and added to it for their own practical benefit and pleasure. Old family money was joined later by investors who saw their chance to profit from traditional industries, new technical developments and new industries. Without such people willing and able to invest there could have been no industrial revolution. It meant, however, that investors wanted good returns for their money: if conditions and markets changed then they moved their investment elsewhere or to other industries where more profitable opportunities arose. We will see throughout the book how that accounts for changes in the uses of mills, their remodelling or the building of new mills.

There were other influences on investors. The Midlands came to be a very important area for the development of a widespread interest - by manufacturers, investors, landowners and the growing middle class - in the new sciences and technology. Derbyshire in particular became the focus of interest in minerals and geology. It was also of great attraction to the early, intrepid visitors and artists who brought the 'wild' scenery of the area into the public gaze. Matlock and Lumsdale were therefore most definitely on the map as a result. We will deal with those influences in a later section but first we will try to establish why it is called 'Lumsdale'.

Why is it called Lumsdale?

Lums Mill

The first problem for those who have tried to find an answer to this question is that 'Lums' is spelt in all sorts of different ways. The spellings are interchangeable and the differences do not seem to signify anything. Also there are many references to the Lums Mills and they are clearly different mills over time and place.

Crossley and Kiernan in their article say that it was in the first half of the seventeenth century that 'the mills came to be described as in Lumsdale rather than on Matlock East Moor' and that 'the first known occasion was in 1637, in the inventory of William Woodiwis of Bonsall' (Crossley and Kiernan 1992: 39). In fact the references are to a Lums Mill rather than to Lumsdale: Woodiwis 'had waste (slag) "at Over Lummes smiltinge mill"' and 'Lumbs Mill, according to a note in the Wolley Manuscripts, was leased by Edward Gill and others to William Wolley in 1657' (ibid, citing LJRO B/C/11 and Wolley Mss. 6671 respectively). Nevertheless, it is significant that there appears to be a place - 'Lums' - and that the dale in which it is to be found is no longer seen as just part of the much larger East Moor.

The Wolley Manuscripts are an invaluable collection of documents and other information compiled by Adam Wolley (1758- 1827) a distant cousin, descended from William's uncle John Wolley of Allen Hill. Adam Wolley the Younger was an attorney and antiquarian who collected historic documents, eventually filling fifty-three volumes which he bequeathed to the British Museum and which are now in the British Library. The Derbyshire Record Office has copies on microfilm and they are a vital reference. They are the source of much of the information in Chapter 5 and Adam himself features in Chapter 6.

Then in 1716 there was an arbitration award relating to ownership of the Manor of Matlock which, as related by Benjamin Bryan, rather confusingly refers to 'Lomas's (Lumb's) Mill' (Bryan, 1903:11). A decade later there is a reference to 'Lumms' in a manuscript covering the period 1724-1728 where there is a list of 7 local smelting mills supplying lead to (probably) the Wingerworth red lead mill. One entry is 'Lumms 996' indicating that the mill in Lumsdale was supplying 996 out of total 1756 pigs of lead (Edwards, 1994: 40). The smelting was still going on when William Bray was writing his *Sketch of a tour into Derbyshire and Yorkshire* but the spelling has changed: 'Take the road to Chesterfield and at the turnpike go off on the right … when a smelting house called The *Lumbs* is soon seen' (Bray, 1778: 128, italics in original).

In an advert in the *Derby Mercury* in 1781 the spelling is again 'Lumms' and now someone has either assumed that the mill must have got its name from the stream or at least associated the area with the name of the stream: 'The Lease (of which two Years were unexpired at Lady-Day last) of the Lumms Smelting Mills, situate upon the Lumms Brook, in the Parish of Matlock' (18 October 1781). In 1818 another travel writer uses the 'Lumbs' spelling: 'Between two and three miles from Matlock is the Lumbs smelting house where red lead is made' (Walford, 1818: D).

By the 1810s, however, the assumption was being made that the place with the Lums mills must be Lumsdale. John Farey, for example, in his *General View of the Agriculture and Minerals of Derbyshire* lists 20 lead smelting cupolas, one of which is 'Lumsdale in Matlock (formerly)' (1811: 366) and on page 489, in his list of waterfalls, he includes 'Lumsdale, N.E. of Matlock, on 1st grit, high and romantic'. Similarly, Ebenezer Rhodes heads section XI of the relevant page of his *Excursions in Derbyshire* with 'Approach to Matlock – Visit to Lums-Dale' (Rhodes, 1824 ed: 246) and Stephen Glover in *The History of the County of Derby,* referring to bleaching houses, says that 'One of the most eminent in the county is that of Mr. John Garton, at Lumsdale near Matlock' (1829: 253) and 'At Lumsdale there are extensive bleach works, and a bone mill, the property of Mr. Garton' (Glover,1830: 104).

Some years later William Adam, in his *Dales, Scenery, Fishing Streams and Mines of Derbyshire,* having looked at the waterfall, states that 'From this point down to near the Messrs Radford's mills, is called Lumsdale.' (1861: 102).

The Lumms Brook

We noted above that the *Derby Mercury* in 1781 had an advert relating to 'Lumms Brook' but, as Chapter 1 pointed out, the stream which flows through Lumsdale is now known as the Bentley Brook. However, if we look for more eighteenth century instances of Lumms Brook we see that the spelling of the name of the stream changes almost as often as that of mills in the valley.

A lease of 1749, for a most important acre of land at the head of the valley (see Chapter 4) had also described the boundary of the land as 'the River brook or rivulet called the Lumbs brook' (DRO D858/T/1), albeit with a different spelling. A similar phrase was used when the lease was transferred on several occasions up to 1790 so the assignments in 1769 and 1771 (DRO D858/T/5 and /6) also refer to the 'River Brook or Rivulet called the Lumbs Brook', in 1789 to 'the Brook or Rivulet called the Lums Brook' and in 1790 to 'the Lumbs Brook' (DRO D858/T/8 and 9).

The 1762 transfer of lease for that same plot of land is even more intriguing: it refers to the 'Cupola situate and being on a place called Lumbs Hill' and a surveyor's plan of the same cupola in 1761 calls it 'Lombs Cupola' (DRO D858/P/1). Lums Hill or Lumshill is often used later, for example as the name of what are now Beech House (auction particulars 1906), Lumsdale Road (auction particulars 1929) and the quarry at the top of Quarry Lane (OS 1967). We have however found no other use of 'Lombs'.

The brook

However, deeds in 1772 and 1782 conveying land below the waterfall refer to 'a brook called the Lums Mills Brook' (both in AS archive) and an advertisement in the *Derby Mercury* on 24 October 1781 also included this: 'The Lease (of which two Years were unexpired at Lady-Day last) of the Lumms Smelting Mills, situate upon the Lumms Brook, in the Parish of Matlock'.

In the early part of the nineteenth century we find other variations. In the 1820s Rhodes called it a river: 'The fall of water includes the whole of the little river Lums' and 'The River Lums is, however, in general but a penurious stream, which is dammed up a little above the cascade' (Rhodes, 1822 ed: 99; 1824: 247-8). In Glover's *History of the County of Derby*, however, it is referred to as the Lumsdale Brook (Glover, 1829: 258) in the lists of bridges and their rivers, referring to 'Bentley Bridge in Matlock' (at the top end of Lumsdale) over the 'Lumsdale Brook'. One year later, in his 1830 *Peak Guide* Glover refers to it rather differently: 'When the stream (called Bentley Brook or the Lums) is swollen with rain, the river rushes over the top of the rock through a narrow cleft' (Glover 1830: 107). So the name Bentley Brook is being used in 1830 and yet in 1861 Adam, in a passage headed 'The Lums' refers to 'the Lums, a small stream' (Adam 1861: 99).

The early Ordnance Survey (OS) maps write in the name Bentley Brook in different places. The OS map of 1880 puts Bentley Brook opposite Drabble's Mill (Tansley Wood Mills at the bottom end of Lumsdale) whilst the OS map of 1899 puts the name Bentley Brook between Bailey's Mill (Matlock Corn Mill) and Hunt Bridge (now the area from lower Lumsdale to Matlock Green). There is a mention in the eighteenth century Manorial rolls for Matlock Manor of 'The Towne Brook' and that name is used as late as 26 May 1897 when the *Derby Mercury* wrote about the plans for the Queen's Diamond Jubilee which included 'throwing a bridge across the town brook at Knowlestone Place'. However that suggests that the Town Brook was an old name for the part of Bentley Brook which runs from Matlock Green and into the Derwent.

All of this raises two questions: could the old name have been the Lums Brook - and Lumsdale is named after it - and, if so, when and how and why did the name Bentley Brook evolve?

The origin of the name Bentley Brook is obscure but the Chesterfield Road follows the line of the Roman Hereward Street and there is sometimes (but not always) a link between 'Bentley' and a bend in a Roman road (Dodd and Dodd, 1980: 23, 26). In relation to a place in a Lancashire valley J. G. Shaw states that 'The Bent is from Anglo-Saxon *bent*, meaning coarse grass, such as grows on cold, wet land' (Shaw 1889: 16). That would describe the upper part of the brook in Cuckoostone Dale but not Lumsdale.

However, the evidence suggests that the old Lums mills did not get their name from the stream, nor did the stream get its name from the mills or from a miller but, we will argue, from the place where the mills were situated. We will summarise below the other explanations that have been provided for the name Lums or Lumsdale and explain our preferred answer.

Chimneys and pools

Given that the word 'lum' or 'lums' seems to be associated with a mill then one might expect the mill to belong to Mr Lum or Lumb (or even Mr Lomas) but George Wigglesworth notes that 'A search of registers has yielded no reference to persons using the surname Lum[b] locally although it is common both as a surname and place name in the West Riding' (2011: 8). Whilst there are families called Lomas in the Matlock and Wirksworth Parish Registers none is associated either with Lumsdale or with milling.

Instead it has been suggested that the name originates from the Anglo-Saxon or Celtic word 'lumb' or 'lum' which meant 'pool' but the difficulty with this is that, as we have shown above, one or more mills was referred to as Lums Mill (in whatever spelling) before the current holding ponds were created in the eighteenth and nineteenth centuries and there is no other indication that pools were a feature of the valley.

However, the writer of the website of the Church of St Michael at Lumb in Rossendale, Lancashire, states more precisely that 'The Celtic meaning of Lumb is 'Deep Pool or Wooded Valley'; the Anglo Saxon is 'Deep Pool in the bed of a river'' (www.lan-opc.org.uk/Rossendale/Lumb/stmichael/index.html ©Lancashire OnLine Parish Clerks). It is possible that the spot to which the waterfall fell may once have been a deeper pool and Eilert Ekwall (author of The Concise Oxford Dictionary of English Place-Names 1936), in *The Place Names of Lancashire* states that 'lum' is an English dialect word which means 'a deep pool in the bed of a river', particularly in the Lake District and Lancashire. Later, in relation to Lumb or Lumn Mill near Walmersley he says it can refer to be 'a woody valley, a deep pool' (Ekwall 1922: 15) although deep pools are not a feature of Lumsdale valley.

Another suggestion is that lum relates to the Scottish word for chimney - as in the Hogmanay greeting 'Lang may your lum reek' (long may your chimney smoke) - with (in Edinburgh, it is said) 'other folks' coal'. Again the difficulty is that the word appears to have been used first in relation to Lumsdale mills at a time when the only chimneys were associated with relatively small lead smelters' hearths and before the development of the long chimneys of the cupolas and the surviving nineteenth century one. And why should any Derbyshire man or woman use a Scottish word?

Cleft or fissure

Instead, we think the answer lies partly in Ekwall's reference to a woody valley although we are aware that at some points in its history parts of the valley have been denuded of all vegetation as a result of the industries working in it. Significantly - given the nature of the Lumsdale valley - the word 'lum' has been used in reference to certain geological features. Further, those features have given rise to the use of Lum or Lumb as place names in other parts of Derbyshire and further afield.

In its feature 'Town and County Gossip' the *Derby Daily Telegraph* in 1925 included the following about a place near Milford: 'There recently appeared in this column a reference to the Depth-o-Lumb, a delightful dell belonging to Lumb Grange. This place-name has frequently perplexed visitors to the district as to its meaning. From information since obtained it is gathered that a lumb is a deep cleft, down which a stream flows' (3 January 1925).

The paper goes on to say that in a deed of 1584 (from Norton near Sheffield where there is such a gorge-like wooded valley to this day with a stream, waterfalls and ponds, see (www.gravespark. org/history.html) it was spelt Lume and, later, Lum and that 'In addition to our own Depth-o'-Lumb, there is

Lumsdale, near Matlock and Lumsdale or Lumford Mill ... a little beyond Bakewell'. (We can find no other reference to that mill, Arkwright's third mill, being called 'Lumsdale'.) The gorge - the deep cleft - of Depth-o-Lumb has also been known as the 'Depths of Lumb' (Peakdistrictonline).

For Lumbs and Lums in Derbyshire, John Palmer's place name index (Palmer 2006) also gives Lumb Wood at Eckington and The Lumb at Norton. There is also Robinson's Lumb (Robinson Lumms Wood in a map of 1795), an ancient woodland near Barlborough; Black Car Lumb near Holmsfield; Lumb Hole Mill in Kettleshyme near Whaley Bridge; Godbers Lumb near Denby; Lumb Farm Country Club near Marehay; Lumb Lane in Northwood at Darley Dale; Goodwins Lumb near Hazelwood and The Lumb in the copper mines on Ecton Hill. There are no doubt more. Clearly not all those places are deep valleys.

To confuse matters further, *A Glossary of Words used in the Neighbourhood of Sheffield* says in relation to the Limb Valley at Whirlow, 'The stream itself was formerly called a lim, or torrent, and the word is still found in the neighbourhood of Sheffield as lumb or lum. In Anglo-Saxon the word is found as *hlimme*'. The Glossary says, however, that a Lum is 'a narrow valley containing a stream of water', followed by evidence of various other local lumbs, limbs, and lums which are either 'a narrow valley' or a 'woody hollow' (Addy 1888: 141). The listed Lumb Clough Lead Smelting Mill in North Yorkshire is also clearly in a narrow, wooded and steep sided valley (Historic England; see also Dickinson et al 1975).

Geology

However, Lum also appears to be a technical term in geology. So, for example, Farey in his treatise for the Board of Agriculture includes the following: 'China-Clay ... is procured in small quantities ... in a *Lum or fissure* in the 4th lime ¼ mile E. of Newhaven House, also in a similar Lum at Milkhill-Gate ... and perhaps in other places on this same stratum' (Farey 1811: 447, italics added). In the *Derbyshire Miners Glossary* under the heading 'Lumb' it says:

'For water; a term used by the Miners, sometimes for those holes which they make at the foot of their Shafts, in Mines troubled with water, in order to collect the water in masses, and draw it out.

In Sumps the same method is used, teeming and drawing it from Lumb to Lumb. The falls of water, or the cavity into which they fall, are in some places called Lumbs' (Mander, 1824: 40-41).

Whilst these instances are in relation to the strata and lead mining in the limestone area of the Dales - and Lumsdale is gritstone - they all imply the same feature: that of a cleft with falling water.

So our conclusion is that the lum in Lumsdale is a classic narrow wooded valley, gorge or fissure in the ground with a stream and waterfall. It is therefore no surprise that at least until the 1950s people who lived in Upper Lumsdale talked about 'going down the Lums' when referring to the valley. It also follows that any reference to 'the Lumsdale Valley' is a double tautology – the same thing said three times over!

The context of interest in Derbyshire: science and industry

As noted above, it has become very clear to us in researching this book that Derbyshire was really important in the seventeenth and eighteenth centuries: it was not off the beaten track but an important place for both the industrial revolution and new thinking more generally. This section will explain why.

Scientists and Inventors

From the middle of the seventeenth century what has come to be known as the Enlightenment - the Age of Reason - led to new ways of thinking and new ways of understanding the world. In particular there developed the study of 'natural philosophy', later to be called science, with its roots in earlier ideas such as those of Galileo (1564- 1642). The writings of Francis Bacon (1561-1626) together with William Harvey (1578-1657) and William Gilbert (1544-1603) 'kick-started the scientific revolution in England' (Jardine 2011), with many others, such as Isaac Newton (1642-1726) to follow. Yet there were many other lesser-known people using the new technical instruments and 'reason' to advance knowledge: Jardine talks of their 'crowded, motley lives, in which conversation in the coffee- house and vigorous correspondence with like-minded individuals in other countries figured as importantly as strenuous private study and laboratory experiment' (Jardine 1999: Introduction).

So what has all this to do with Lumsdale? For an assortment of reasons Derbyshire was of particular interest to these early scientists. First, it contained the natural phenomena - stemming from the early studies in chemistry, geography and geology - which were of interest to the new philosophers. Indeed, 'the earliest recorded geological tour was made to Derbyshire in 1626 by the Enlightenment philosopher Thomas Hobbes' (Cope 2016: 738). One result was the poem he wrote *De Mirabilis Pecci, Being the Wonders of the Peak in Darby-shire.* Other geologists followed.

John Farey, for example, was land steward for the Duke of Bedford's Woburn estates where he learnt skills in geology and later became a consulting geologist. He wrote many articles but his major work was a report in three volumes (Farey 1811-17), commissioned by the Board of Agriculture, on the agriculture and minerals of Derbyshire (see Ford and Torrens 2001). So as a pioneer geologist it was Derbyshire which was of interest both to him and the Board of Agriculture which commissioned the survey.

He pointed out that there had been 'no elementary Mineral or Geological work published' so that he would have to explain the importance of 'Terrestrial *Stratification*' [italics in the original] so as to make clear the consequences resulting from 'the admirable and regularly stratified structure of the planet we inhabit' (Farey 1811: 105). The Matlock area in particular had strata and minerals and a topography which fascinated early geologists so one of Farey's plates was 'Section of Strata at Matlock High Tor' (1811: 129) and Matlock is mentioned specifically on numerous pages of his work.

Lums Dale is mentioned twice in the work, once about a 'lum' (see above) and another in relation to 'Fire Stones' which are found in the valley (see *Gritstone* above; Farey 1811: 220-21).

Secondly, with Cromford and Belper at the forefront of the industrial revolution, there were inventors and entrepreneurs who were themselves interested in new sciences. Consequently, the people interested in all the new scientific ideas and inventions developed an informal network where the early industrialist and the natural philosopher - sometimes the same person - could exchange ideas which had practical and industrial uses. The result was that by 1700 there was 'a commitment to science as the firm basis for success in commerce and industry' (Jardine 2011). Derbyshire was clearly not without such people, indeed the Midlands were very important in the Enlightenment – a Europe- wide interest in 'reason' and philosophy. However the new thinking in the English 'Midlands' was particularly important.

The Midlands Enlightenment

The introduction to a special journal issue on the Midlands Enlightenment claimed that it 'dominated the English experience of enlightenment' and that its representatives 'through their attention to the application of science shaped the course of industrial development for the following half century' (Budge 2007a: 157). Members of the Lunar Society, originally Lunar Circle and named because their meetings were timed for the full moon (to light the way home), were leading lights in this movement which met in and around Birmingham from about 1765 to 1813. The three founder members were William Small, a Scottish physician who had been a professor in the USA, Matthew Boulton, the Birmingham manufacturer and inventor, and Erasmus Darwin, physician, poet (see Budge 2007b) and grandfather of Charles Darwin (Ritchie-Calder 1982: 136).

This society was important:

'The members of the Lunar Society were brilliant representatives of the informal scientific web that cut across class, blending the inherited skills of craftsmen with the theoretical advances of scholars, a key factor in British manufacturing's leap ahead of the rest of Europe' (Uglow 2017).

One of the links with the Matlock area is Erasmus Darwin who also founded the Derby Philosophical Society (see Elliott 2009). 'Darwin became embroiled in one of the many disputes about patenting during this period: he and James Watt appeared as witnesses on behalf of the cotton manufacturer Richard Arkwright in 1785' (McNeill 2013). Indeed, Sir Richard Arkwright was a visitor and corresponding member of the Lunar Society. Joseph Wright of Derby, who painted the well-known portrait of Arkwright and picture of Arkwright's Mills at Cromford, had connections with members of the Lunar Society and produced several paintings which were at the very least inspired by their gatherings, for example, 'An Experiment on a Bird in an Air Pump' (1768).

Interest from visitors and artists

This growing interest in science and nature, together with interest in new technologies, brought Derbyshire - and the early industries there - to a wider public through the writing of records of travels, the early guide books for visitors. We have already referred to some of those above. But these early tourist guides were also enthused by the ideas of the enlightenment. They wanted to observe, categorise, to record in detail - especially details of the topography, minerals, mills and mines - and to note where industry was encroaching on nature. These travel books not only reveal how important Derbyshire was on the sought-after 'visitor routes' but they have also proved immensely useful in writing this book! So for example, Thomas Walford produced *The Scientific Tourist through England, Wales, & Scotland, in which the traveller is directed to the principal objects Antiquity, Art, Science and the Picturesque*, noting, for example, that 'Between two and three miles from Matlock is the Lumbs smelting house where red lead is made' (1818: Vol II).

So whilst these visitors may have no or little link with Lumsdale, the knowledge they conveyed about this area and its industries helped to ensure that investors – local and from further afield – knew about the investment opportunities.

Celia Fiennes

We know, for example, that Celia Fiennes had already visited Derbyshire at the end of the seventeenth century because she left copious diaries of her tours which included Derbyshire in 1697, reprinted as *Through England on a Side Saddle in the Time of William and Mary*. She appears not to have reached Matlock, however, possibly because of the following realisation: 'From Castleton to Buxton is 6 mile, but they are very long. You might go 10 of miles near London as soon as you are going halfe so many here.'

However, she did visit Chesterfield, Bakewell and Chatsworth. While at Chesterfield, immediately following her note that 'In this town is ye best ale in the Kingdom Generally Esteem'd', she commented again on the difficulty of the terrain but also the importance of the minerals in the area:

'All Derbyshire is full of Steep hills and nothing but the peakes of hills as thick one by another is seen in most of ye County wch are very steepe, wch makes travelling tedious and ye miles Long. You see neither hedge nor tree but only Low drye stone walls round some ground Else its only hills and Dales as thick as you Can Imagine, but tho' the Surface of ye Earth Looks barren yet those hills are impregnated wth Rich marble stone metals, Iron and Copper and Coale mines in their bowells, from whence we may see the wisdom and benignitye of o^{er} greate Creator to make up the Defficiency of a place by an Equivolent, and also the diversity of the Creation wch Encreaseth its Beauty' (Fiennes 1697 *Tour Hull to Chatsworth*, reprinted 1888).

After visiting Chatsworth – and being amazed by its splendours – she went on to Bakewell where she was both scathing and admiring of Derbyshire people:

'You are forced to have guides as in all parts of Darbyshire, and unless it be a few y^t use to be guides ye Common people know not above 2 or 3 mile from their home, but they of ye Country will Climbe up and down wth their horses those steep precipices' (1888: 85).

Daniel Defoe

The next well-known visitor was Daniel Defoe who visited Matlock where he described the warm bath at Matlock Bath. He also had mixed feelings about the inhabitants, particularly the lead miners or 'subterranean wretches, who they call Peakrills':

'The inhabitants are a rude boorish kind of people, but they are a bold, daring, and even desperate kind of fellows in their search into the bowels of the earth; for no people in the world out-do them'.

He was also much taken with the wildness of the scenery as were many travellers, poets and artists at that time. 'Travel with me through this houling [sic] wilderness in your imagination, and you shall soon find all that is wonderful about it', he wrote and, when approaching Wirksworth, 'mounting the hills gradually for four or five miles, we soon had a most frightful view indeed among the black mountains of the Peak'.

Yet, in common with all these early travellers he wished to document in detail the industry he saw:

'... to a valley on the side of a rising hill, where there were several grooves, so they call the mouth of the shaft or pit by which they go down a lead mine,...we were agreeably surprized with seeing a hand, and then an arm, and quickly after a head, thrust up out of the very groove we were looking at ... the man was a most uncouth spectacle; he was cloathed all in leather, had a cap of the same without brims, some tools in a little basket which he drew up with him ...For his person, he was as lean as a skeleton, pale as a dead corpse, his hair and beard a deep black, his flesh lank, and, as we thought, something of the colour of the lead itself ... he look'd like an inhabitant of the dark regions below, and who was just ascended into the world of light'.

(All excerpts above are from Defoe 1724-27: Letter 8 part 2 The Peak District).

Later tourist guides

The next important tourist book for our purposes is William Bray's *Sketch of a tour into Derbyshire and Yorkshire*. He saw Mr Arkwright's

Mill at Cromford - 'It employs about 200 persons, chiefly children' (1778: 119) - and Matlock Bath, Matlock Dale, Matlock Bridge, and then Lumsdale where he noted a smelting mill but again it is the 'rudeness' of the scenery that strikes him (1778: 128).

James Pilkington's book, *A View of the Present State of Derbyshire*, published 10 years later in 1789 was also rather offensive about those of us who live in the hills: 'It has been observed, that civilisation does not take place so early in a mountainous, as a champaign *[i.e. flat, open]* country. This may in some degree, account for the rude manners of those, who live in the Peak of Derbyshire'. However, he thinks that their employment is partly to blame: 'Having always been engaged in mineral concerns, and having but little intercourse with the rest of the world, they could not receive that polish, which a free and extensive commerce with neighbouring countries frequently gives' (1789: 57).

By 1802 when the Rev'd Richard Warner published *A Tour through the Northern Counties of England and the Borders of Scotland* purple prose was evident when he extolled the beauties of the Matlocks: 'Here a scene burst upon us at once, impossible to be described - too extensive to be called picturesque, too diversified to be sublime, and too stupendous to be beautiful; but at the same time blending together all the constituent principles of these different qualities' (p166 quoted in Ainley, 2012: 16). Chapter 3 of *A New Historical and Descriptive View of Derbyshire* by the Rev D.P. Davies (1811) is more interested in the minerals: it is entitled 'Subterraneous geography - mines - and minerals etc'.

Artists

Another group of visitors - artists - also brought Derbyshire to the attention of a wider world and in turn brought ideas and contacts to those interested in the new industries. Joseph Wright of Derby was of course local but others came from far afield. As Ainley says,

'Derbyshire was one of the first locales for landscape artists in Britain. Stephen Daniels cites engravings of the Peak District in the 1740s after Thomas Smith of Derby "...showing sublime crags and magnificent caves, and describing the mineral wealth of the region" that "promoted a taste for British scenery"' (Ainley 2012: 6-7, referencing Daniels 1999: 61-62; Thomas Smith of Derby was a landscape painter who died 1767).

For example, John Robert Cozens sketched '39 studies of Matlock, largely of cliff and rock scenes' (Ainley 2012: 6) and in fact made drawings, two sketches entitled 'At the Smelting Mills near Matlock' in 1772 though they lack detail. The National Library of Wales has been unable to locate the originals and the copies reveal little. However, as Ainley commented of these drawings, they are 'notable for the fact that he seemingly turned his back on any evidence of the industry, let alone any signs of laboring, but for a whisp of smoke' (Ainley 2012: 17).

Similarly Jean Claude Nattes, visiting Derbyshire in September 1798, sketched scenes of rocks and bridges from Derby through Dovedale and to Chee Tor and Blackwell Mill. In Lumsdale he ignored the recent cotton mill just to his left, preferring the picturesque rocks, colour-coded with numbers for future reference, and the interesting launder and machinery with a background more reminiscent of Edale than Matlock Bank. (Drawings among 500 in the Royal Collection accessible on-line). His picture (Plate 11), though fascinating, raises more questions than it answers.

So, whilst so many artists came to the area they have not been of great use for our book!

What have been immensely useful are the documents which we have accessed and we will rely on them in the following chapters, the next of which focuses on the early lead smelting industry.

3

EARLY LEAD SMELTING

Introduction

In 1994 David G. Edwards had the chance to examine a handwritten notebook containing the records of production of some 280 tons of red lead (lead oxide) at a Derbyshire mill, probably Wingerworth, in the period from April 1724 to July 1728. Among the information was a record of the supplies of lead to the mill for re-processing. Out of a total of 1756 pigs more than half, 996 pigs, came from the 'Lumms' smelting mill – 6 miles from Wingerworth, the other main supplier (at 476 pigs) being 'Olermill' (Owler Mill) at Holymoorside (Edwards 1994: 40).

So what was a pig of lead? On the title page of his 'Attempt to establish An Universal Weight and Measure' in 1794 William Martin quoted Deuteronomy: 'Thou shalt have a perfect and just weight. A perfect and just measure shalt thou have'. Unfortunately that did not yet apply to the weights of a pig or a fother of lead - or of a hundredweight (cwt) for that matter - even throughout Derbyshire. Martin explained that 'Derbyshire lead is generally accounted for by the fodder; 16 pieces, or half pigs, are called a fodder' but that 'The weight of a fodder is different at different places' and set out comparisons:

'at the furnaces or mills where it is smelted 24cwt of 112lbs
Derby   22½cwt of 112lbs
Gainsbro' and Stockwith   21½cwt of 112lbs
Hull   19½cwt of 120lbs
London   19½cwt of 112lbs'

— (MARTIN, 1794: 24)

Earlier in the eighteenth century John Worlidge had also written about the variations:

'FODDER, or FODER of LEAD; is a Weight containing eight Pigs, and every Pig one and twenty Stone and a half, which is about a Tun, or a common Wain or Cart-Load: I find also in the Book of Rates, mention of a Fodder of Lead, which is there said to be 2000 Weight [i.e. 20cwt]; at the mines 'tis 2200 Weight and an half; among the Plumbers at London, 1900 and an half' (Worlidge 1703).

If we take the first of Martin's figures, the lead supplied from 'Lumms' to just this one local processor thus amounts to almost exactly 150 tons.

So where in Lumsdale were the mills smelting lead ore and what were these mills like? First, however we need to answer another question: why were smelters built in Lumsdale?

Why in Lumsdale?

Easy access to lead

To smelt lead there needs to be a local source of galena (lead ore) and yet Lumsdale is a gritstone valley and lead is found in limestone. However, Matlock is on a boundary of the millstone grit - the Dark Peak - and the limestone layers - the White Peak (see English Heritage 2011: 1 for a detailed map). Limestone cliffs can clearly be seen in Matlock Bath whilst the lead workings in Masson Hill (between Matlock and Bonsall) in the eighteenth and nineteenth centuries have now been well documented (see Warriner et al 1981). North-west of Masson - the area around Winster and Wensley Hill – and around Wirksworth (see Slack 2000) are perhaps the best known lead mining areas, where the large houses and other buildings and church monuments bear witness to the riches amassed by those who owned mines, notably the Gells and the Dukes of Devonshire and Rutland. The deeper and much larger mines constructed from the seventeenth century onwards 'required investment capital for drainage and haulage and thus such mines were often controlled by the landed gentry and an emerging group of wealthy industrialists' (Barnatt et al 2013: 8).

Those new investors could also be found developing another source of lead for Lumsdale - at nearby Ashover where the presence of a geological anticline made mining possible. One of John Farey's unpublished papers included a sketch of the Ashover anticline (see Ford 1967) - an arch-like fold of strata which is akin to the Peak District 'Derbyshire dome' but in miniature. In such anticlines the newer gritstone layers are eroded making the underlying limestone visible or accessible. So the Nether Sough Company was formed in 1734 to exploit the vein owned by the Gregory family and the Gregory mine near Overton Hall became a very important lead mine in the second half of the eighteenth century:

'The Gregory mine was once one of the most productive lead mines in England, said to produce 1511 tons annually and provided employment for 300 people. Operations started in 1758 and ended in 1804 when it finally closed' (www.mindat.org/loc-818.html accessed 28.2.2019).

Easy access to water power and fuel

Ore hearth smelters needed power to operate the bellows for the fire and Lumsdale had a steady source of readily manageable water. And, as Crossley and Kiernan (1992: 8) point out, such lead smelting mills 'did not require a large quantity of water to power their bellows'. 'Normally a weir was built upstream, forming a diversion into a head-race, which fed the smelting-mill directly or by means of a pond'. These mills also needed access to woodland for fuel however and, as they did not need large ponds to maintain the water supply, they 'could be sited on the upper reaches of streams adjacent to the coppice woodlands on which they relied for fuel' (ibid). We shall see that some of the Lumsdale smelting mills were sited higher up the valley on the flat land where the old maps show woodland plantations.

This was important because the ore hearth smelting mills depended on 'white-coal', kiln dried wood, rather than charcoal for fuel as charcoal burnt at too high a temperature for this purpose. The white-coal used in the ore-hearth consisted of wood which had been de-barked and dried. The remains of white-coal kilns - circular hollows approximately 3-4 metres across - can often be found at smelting-mill sites and in nearby woods. Originally the kilns used a wood fire to dry the white-coal, but seventeenth-century accounts show mineral coal in use (Crossley and Kiernan 1992: 8). However, if there was another hearth to re-smelt slag then charcoal would be used because a higher temperature was then needed. Both clearly depended on sources of wood nearby.

The early smelters would have been more like blacksmiths' shops and were often housed in barn-like structures needing wood and stone (and gritstone for the hearth) in their construction and when a more permanent building material was needed for the larger mills Lumsdale had, on the gritstone edge to the east, a plentiful supply of stone.

Routes

Businesses smelting lead also needed a relatively easy route to home and overseas markets for their products. The first place on the route out of the Peak District was probably Chesterfield: Farey, who did most of his survey in 1807, said that 'Chesterfield was always a great Mart for Lead, but particularly so, since the opening of the Chesterfield Canal to the Trent, in 1776' (1811: 382). So after that time lead could be taken down the Trent but otherwise Bawtry, a significant staging post on the Great North Road, had been the next important place, such that 'In 1622 a group of Derbyshire merchants jointly purchased land at Bawtry to build wharves to facilitate the dispatch of their lead' (Crossley and Kiernan 1992: 10). From Bawtry the lead could be carried to Hull in barges.

Joseph Whitfield, whom we will meet in Chapter 4, 'made considerable grants towards the costs of improving roads along that line', the route from Kelstedge to Bawtry (Raistrick 1988: 83). He was also, together with other officials of the London (Quaker) Lead Company, a promoter in 1766 of a turnpike road from Ashover to join the Chesterfield to Mansfield turnpike (ibid: 84).

Roger Burt says of this route:

'The lead was shipped to Hull, in the form of ore, pig, manufactured sheet, and oxides (e.g. red lead) by two routes: either northwards through Chesterfield and overland to Bawtry on the Idle, or southwards through Derby and Nottingham and then down the Trent. The former route was probably the more important during the period, helping to support the turnpiking of several roads in the district between 1756 and 1766, as well as the Chesterfield to Stockwith-on-Trent canal in the 1770's' (Burt 1968: 251).

G. G. Hopkinson says, however, that the Matlock-Chesterfield turnpike was not achieved until 1778 'largely through the efforts of Thomas Holland of Ford Hall, Higham, who did much to raise an interest in the scheme and to solicit subscriptions for it from local landowners and lead merchants' (Hopkinson 1971). Two branch roads across the East Moor were also constructed down to the bridges at Rowsley and Darley, 'thereby improving communications between the lead mining areas to the west of the Derwent and the smelting plants at Kelstedge and Bowers Mill' (ibid). And possibly Lumsdale.

Howard and Knight (2015: 2, referencing Riden, 1987) refer to the 'substantial and long-standing Pb [lead] export trade to the Low Countries, the Baltic and Scandinavia' from Derbyshire via Hull and Amsterdam but Wood points out other markets to which the lead went:

'From there, it could be exported to the Amsterdam markets, or shipped on to London or Bristol. It might then pass across

Europe to the Mediterranean; to "the Indies"; to the Americas; or to trading ports on the African coast' (1999: 70).

If lead was being delivered more locally, then the area around Matlock had many ancient trackways:

'A possible Roman road from Chesterfield to Ashbourne, and perhaps Rocester, was called Hereward's Street (c.1275); it ran through Matlock and Wirksworth, the lead-mining area, and passed close to Ashover ... and Okeover ... The Old Portway ran from Milford near Belper, through Wirksworth to Winster, close to Birchover ... another lead-mining area, and to Alport' (Cole 2010: 121).

In the early days of exporting lead it was carried by packhorse trains across the moors. Carriers were then paid by the sack or pack and 'in many cases are accused, and often rightly, of using small sacks and shallow baskets', a situation remedied by the later use of the 'checkweighman' (Raistrick 1988: 83).

However, Burt says that 'with the improvement of the Derbyshire Derwent after 1719, the more circuitous southern route offered the advantage of nearly continuous water carriage, and experienced a great increase in traffic. Together with the successive extensions of the navigable limits of the River Trent, this also greatly facilitated internal shipments to the midland markets, and correspondingly reduced the percentage of output handled by Hull' (1968: 251).

What is clear is that throughout the time that lead smelting was happening in Lumsdale there were good - for the time - routes out of the valley to significant markets. As the profit from lead mining and lead smelting decreased, however, the fact that the mines near Matlock were far from major ports became much more significant.

Using water power: the ore hearth

Traditionally lead ore had been processed near where it was mined, by means of a fire on the open hillside in a hollow referred to as a bole. Richard Watson noted these: 'There are several places in Derbyshire called Boles by the inhabitants, where the lead has been anciently smelted, before the invention of moving bellows by water' (1785: 265). He goes on to explain that there was no 'certain tradition concerning the manner in which the ore was smelted' but says that 'In Derbyshire as well as in Peru [sic] they seem chiefly to have relied on the strength of the wind for the success of the operation' (1785: 265-66). Given that much of Lumsdale is an enclosed valley and boles were usually used very near a lead mine it is very unlikely that there were ever boles on the hills round Lumsdale.

Because the bole depended on a natural draught, the invention of the ore hearth which allowed smelting in very different places was extremely important – and certainly for Lumsdale. As Crossley and Kiernan (1992: 6) explain, in the 1570s 'lead-smelting in Derbyshire was transformed by new technology' and by the time Watson was writing the bole method of smelting was 'universally disused' (1785: 270). Crucially for Lumsdale the ore hearth needed a water supply to power the bellows.

Lynn Willies describes the new ore hearth:

'The smelting mill was a fairly simple structure. It required only a small dam and waterworks, and a barn like building to contain the hearth. This was usually constructed of gritstone blocks so as to form an oblong cavity and perhaps three by two feet and just over a foot in depth. An air nozzle, or tuyere, from the bellows entered at the rear, blowing the ore/fuel mixture, whilst smelted lead overflowed into the pot at the front. It was thus not unlike a blacksmith's hearth. Fumes were removed by an arched stone hood surmounted by a chimney' (Willies 1971: 384-394; 1980: 186).

There is evidence that by the 1580s or 1590s this new technology was being used in two smelting mills in Lumsdale.

Two mills on manorial waste

These two mills 'appear to have been built by Adam Wolley of Riber, a member of a bole-smelting family whose status had risen from that of "yeoman brenner" to "gentleman brenner" over the sixteenth century', a brenner being someone who smelted lead

(Crossley and Kiernan 1992: 38, referencing PRO PROB 11/58 q.31). In other words, the Wolley family had moved socially from being people who owned their own land but were 'commoners' to becoming members of the gentry. However, he became involved in a dispute which has provided the evidence of what was going on in Lumsdale.

That dispute led to a claim by the Duchy of Lancaster in 1609-10 that Wolley had failed to gain the Duchy's permission to build the mills on manorial waste (uncultivated land held by the Lord of the Manor of Matlock) half a mile from the town. At that point the Crown was lord of the manor as Charles I was also Duke of Lancaster (as, of course, is Her Majesty Queen Elizabeth II).

'The commission was appointed when Wolley and William Walker refused to vacate the mills after the Duchy had leased them to John Carpenter in 1608 (PRO DL1/238/13). Depositions in the case differ over the date of building: William Walker, who had shared in the construction of one of the mills, said they had been up for 10 years; Anthony Hopkinson of Bonsall suggested 20 years, i.e. from about 1589' (Crossley and Kiernan 1992: 38).

Crossley and Kiernan found no documentary evidence about the outcome of the case but noted that in 1618 the two mills on 'manorial waste' were in the tenure of Adam Wolley, Thomas Fullwood and John Carpenter. The evidence in this case also provides estimates of yield, a considerable quantity of ore having to be carted in to produce a few fothers: 'Ronald Fritchley of Wirksworth had 27 loads of ore smelted by Wolley, producing two fothers, one hundred-weight and a half, while Hopkinson estimated that a fother took 15 or 16 loads of ore. Wolley smelted ore at 15 shillings a fother, finding wood and labour' (ibid).

Later in 1618 the mills were leased by the Duchy of Lancaster to Richard Gunnard, a London clothworker, and Sir James Oughterloney (ibid). This may have been Sir James Ouchterloney who was a carver - a member of the royal household - in 1604 under Charles I (Randall 1983: 10) and was granted land in Eskrick near York in 1620 (Baggs et al 1976). However, Adam Wolley apparently carried on as a lead smelter because Francis Whitehead described himself as 'smelter to Wolley' in 1618 although when Adam Wolley died in 1619 there was no reference to his lead business in his will or his probate inventory (Crossley and Kiernan 1992: 39).

Adam's eldest son, William, seems to have inherited or otherwise acquired the lease of the mills, however, and sub-let them to local smelters and merchants. Diocesan records, now in the Lichfield Joint Record Office, include the 1637 inventory of William Woodiwis of Bonsall, who had waste (slag) 'at Over Lummes smiltinge mill'. These records unfortunately do not identify or locate the two mills on manorial land but they are important because they show the mills being described as Lums mills rather than mills on Matlock East Moor (see Chapter 2).

Lummes Mill

The 1657 lease

The Wolley Manuscripts do enable us to begin to identify the site of one of these early mills. Wolley refers twice, at 6669 f.256 and 6671 ff.310-313, to a 'Lease of Lumbs Mill within the said Manor for the term of 21 years'. In fact this lease, dated 7 September 1657, is one of the early surviving original documents at the Derbyshire Record Office. The premises comprised in the lease are:

'one Lead mill at Lummes in Mattlocke in the Countie of Derbie aforesd *commonly called the New mill* with all wayes waters watercourses Dame or Dammes Proffitts and Commodities whatsoever to the same belonging or in any wise Appertaining' (DRO D433/1; italics added).

The term was twenty-one years from March 1657 at a rent of one shilling (5p) a year and the lessee - the person taking the mill for the term of the lease - was William Wolley of Riber. The lessors were representatives of the Lord of the Manor and the land which was then within their power to lease was the manorial waste containing what we now know as the Bone Mill below the Upper Pond. Was the New mill the first on the site or does it imply that there had been an older one? Had it been called the 'New mill' (like, for example, 'New Street' in Matlock) for many years?

It was certainly already in existence before 1657. And was it the Bone Mill or an earlier mill on the same site or even somewhere else? Read on!

And who were these representatives of the Lord of the Manor who had granted a lease for Lummes Mill? The history of the Manor is told by Benjamin Bryan (1903) and is complicated. Originally granted to one of the Earls of Derby in the twelfth century, it was confiscated from a supporter of Simon de Montford and was at one time held by John of Gaunt as Duke of Lancaster and forfeited to the Crown on his death. In 1628 the impecunious Charles I granted it to the Corporation of London who sold it the following year to four members of the Derbyshire and Nottinghamshire gentry who held the Manor and its rights as trustees for the copyholders. Although copyholders are best regarded as tenants it is important that in this case they were also entitled to share any profits. However, by the end of the seventeenth century the Manor itself was so unprofitable that the trustees lost interest, vacancies were not filled and by 1699 they had all died.

Another court case allows us to know what happened next when a dispute arose between the copyholders and one Thomas Statham. The copyholders, although formally tenants of the Lord of the Manor, regarded themselves as owners in proportion to the rents they paid. However, the Manor itself was a freehold which could be held by persons who were not copyholders. So, when Thomas Statham, the major shareholder of the Manor's income, appointed new trustees to hold the Manor in trust for the copyholders it prompted an action in the Court of Chancery to resolve the issue. That Court was able to resolve disputes more quickly and equitably but, even so, proceedings dragged on until 1716 when arbitrators appointed to resolve the dispute found for the copyholders. It was confirmed that they had in fact purchased the Manor in 1629 subject to the payment to the Crown of a rent of £16.10s.3½d (£16.51) payable by the copyholders. The arbitrators determined specifically that the profits of Lomas's (Lumb's) Mill were to be paid to the proprietors of the Manor (Bryan 1903: 8-11).

Moving on to 1772, we know that George Norman of Winster, whom we shall meet again in Chapter 4, left to his nephews James Swettenham and George White 'All my Leasehold and other Title Estate and Interest whatsoever with all Benefit and Advantage of the same of in or to the Lumbs Upper Mills'. The use of the plural 'Mills' accurately reflects the transcript at the National Archives (PROB 11/982/79) but begs a question. George Norman also bequeathed to his nephews one of the Lumsdale cupolas (see Chapter 4) but did this really refer to more than one Upper Mill? Or is this, as seems more likely, a casual reference to a single mill or a drafting or transcribing error?

White's Mill

In 1778 George White took a lease in his own right from the Lords of the Manor of the Lumbs Smelting Mills (again plural) for twenty-four years commencing 5 April 1779 at the yearly rent of £6 (Wolley Mss. 6671 f.311). 'White's Mill' is shown on the first edition of the one-inch Ordnance Survey map published in 1840. It stood on the fifty-two acres of freehold land awarded to Peter Nightingale when common land was enclosed and distributed among existing landowners in 1780 and was shown on the Enclosure Map. The right of the Lords of the Manor of Matlock to 'Lumb's Mill, with all the buildings, weirs, goits and appurtenances' had been preserved by the Enclosure Act 1780 (Bryan, 1903: 92).

On the 1:2,500 (25" to the mile) Ordnance Survey map of 1876-80 and the one-inch map of 1884 the same mill is shown as 'Bone Mill'. There is a complete chain of title deeds from Nightingale to John Garton and the Bone Mill formed part of his estate sold at auction to Ernest Richard Farnsworth. The conveyance dated 25 February 1907 included:

'All that Leasehold Cottage formerly a Bone Mill … delineated on the [annexed] Map or plan and thereon marked 'Bone Mill' … subject to the rent of Six pounds per annum payable to the Lords of the Manor of Matlock in respect thereof' (authors' title deeds).

The particulars prepared for the auction explained:

'The Cottage at the Southern end of the Upper Pond, formerly a Bone Mill, is believed to be Leasehold for a long term of years, and for the last fifty years the Lords of the Manor have demanded and received from the late John Garton and Edward Hall Garton the sum of £6 annually as the rent of the said Mill ... In the Lease dated 10th June 1749, the Mill is referred to so that it was evidently in existence at that time' (DRO D504/131/4).

The consistency of references to the owners, tenants and terms of the lease through from 1657 to 1907 and beyond is compelling evidence that the mill referred to is indeed the Bone Mill or its predecessor on the same site.

Other early smelters

George Hodgkinson

What else can we deduce about this particular Lumbs Mill from early documents? In 1657 a George Hodgkinson was summoned to Chesterfield 'on 9 January next' to account for the lead he had smelted since 29 September 1657. On 30 June following (1658) he paid 11s.7d (58p), being the excise on 13 pigs of lead smelted at Lumms Mill from 25 March to 24 June at the rate of 7s.2d (36p) for every 8 pigs (Wolley Mss. 6681 f.425 as told to him by Sir Joseph Banks, Hodgkinson's great, great grandson). This raises the question as to whether this Lumms Mill is one that William Wolley sub-let to Hodgkinson soon after he had acquired the head-lease (i.e. the lease granted by the freeholder) or whether Hodgkinson had another lead mill in Lumsdale. In the light of the transactions described next, the former seems more likely.

William Wolley died late in 1666 and was buried in Matlock on 3 December in that year. He named his brother Anthony and his 'loving friend and neighbour John Statham' as executors but Anthony had died earlier in 1666 and so Probate was granted to Statham (National Archive PROB 11/324/59-116).

The executor's account shows on 20 April 1669 the receipt 'of

Mr George Hodgkinson upon sale of The Reversion of a Lease of Smiltinge Mill in Matlock sould for £050:00:00' (Wolley Mss. 6687 f.41d). The 'reversion' is the landlord's interest in property which is subject to a lease - the right to possession of the land when it reverts to him at the end of the lease. It could itself be a leasehold with a sub-lease and this sale would appear to be of Wolley's lease granted out of the freehold in 1657 but subject to a sub-lease.

The Wolley Manuscripts also refer to an assignment of the same 1657 lease by John Statham as Wolley's executor to George Hodgkinson dated January in '22 Chas. 2' - the twenty-second year of the reign of King Charles II. As the microfiche at the Derbyshire Record Office does not show clearly whether the date is 1, 21 or 31 January and, as King Charles's regnal year runs from 30 January in one year to 29 January in the next, it could have been 1670 or 1671 (Wolley Mss. 6671 f.310). That could have been the deed carrying out the 1669 sale and Hodgkinson could well have been the sub-tenant improving his status by buying out his landlord.

Robert Cliffe

So we know that George Hodgkinson was running a smelting mill in, and probably before, 1657 and probably also in 1670/1. However we also know that in 1674 a smelting mill was occupied by Robert Cliffe. The evidence is the damaged transcript of a bond entered into by one Thomas Shore in 1674 which is among the Wolley Manuscripts. The primary obligation to which Shore was bound is set out in Latin, the microfiche is of poor quality and the top corner of the document is missing altogether but the important part, from our point of view, is in English and intact. It sets out the circumstances in which Shore would be released from his obligation under the bond:

'The Condition of the above written obligation is such that if ye Above bound Thomas Shore his Heires Executors & Administrators or any of them doe or shall well & truly pay and deliver or cause to bee paid & delivered unto ye Above named Thomas Smith or to his certaine Attorney his Executors Administrators or Assignes three ffothers of good pure merchantable pigge lead att or before the ffirst day of May next ensuing the date of ye obligation above written at the Smilting mill called or knowne by the name of Lummes Mill situate or being in the parish of Matlocke in the County of Derby abovesaid now in the tenure or occupation of Robert Cliffe or of his Assignes without any manner of fraud or further delay Then the obligation above written to be voyd and of none effect or else to remaine in full force & vertue' (Wolley Mss. 6681 f.295).

What this means is that if Thomas Shore came up with the goods - the smelted lead - he would be released from his obligations, whatever they were, under the bond. As corroboration of Robert Cliffe smelting in Lumsdale we have evidence in relation to a lead mining tithe dispute in Ashover. Stuart R. Band notes that there appeared to be increased activity at a particular rake because 'By the years 1695/6/7 Robert Cliffe of Tansley, then aged 30, who was probably the same Cliffe who was smelting at Lumms Mill in 1674, bought 100 loads of ore during this period at 27s:6d the load' (Band 1996: 55).

The lower smelting mills

The 1749 lease referred to above, which is critical to the developments described in the next chapter, relates to a plot of land 'lying between the Upper most and the Nether most Lumbs mill' so we know that there were then two mills operating in the valley. We also know, as we shall explain, that the 1749 lease included the site of Pond Cottages so it follows that one smelting mill was above and one below Pond Cottages. So where was the 'Nether most mill' and was there more than one smelting mill below Pond Cottages?

There is evidence in the form of a Lease and Release dated 28 and 29 October 1737 that Elizabeth Turnor of Bonsall conveyed the freehold of two smelting mills to trustees for Bonsall School (Lincolnshire Archives, Tur/X 18/1/11, 12). This was part of a package of properties in Matlock and Tansley to provide them with an income of £40 a year to help finance the running of the school. The site appears to be, by process of elimination, south of the manorial waste granted on Enclosure to Peter Nightingale in 1780 and north of the land which was formerly in the estate of the Bown family (see Chapter 5). The difficulty is knowing precisely where the southern boundary of Nightingale's land was in relation to current landmarks. The Enclosure Map, when compared with later maps, shows the boundary crossing the brook and passing to the south of a mill, possibly but not certainly the Paint Mill. It does not show another mill where the Grinding Mill ought to be but that is not surprising because it would have been outside the Enclosure in any event.

When John Garton made his Will in 1860 he referred specifically to 'the Corn Mill called Lums Mill purchased by me from the Trustees of Bonsall School' but that does not help us much. We are however helped by the exercise Edward Hall Garton carried out in 1886 in relation to a mortgage deed. Garton, who then owned much of the valley, wished to mortgage it as security for a loan from his cousin Henry Edwin Bailey. There was evidently some uncertainty at the time and so the mortgage deed contains a schedule identifying the parcels of land by their numbers on Gratton's Tithe Redemption map of 1846. Unfortunately, the boundary between the land acquired by his father John Garton from Gamaliel Jones in 1821 (see Chapter 7) and the land he bought from Bonsall School in 1828 ran through plot 350 on the Tithe Map. Plot 350 included various pieces of land between the west end of Oakstage Lane and the Paint and Grinding Mills and so we have to ask which bit of Plot 350 included the lower smelting mills.

The 1821 purchase by John Garton was identified as 'part 350 – Dam, Plantation, Lane to Tansley Common and other Road'. The 1886 mortgage deed then identified the premises described in 1828 as 'all that messuage dwellinghouse or tenement heretofore used as a Smelting Mill and also that other Mill heretofore used as a Smelting Mill and afterwards used as a Corn Mill' as being '350 part of – Paint Mill and Brook'. So it was Edward Hall Garton's understanding in 1886 that the Bonsall School site, which had once been smelting mills, were in 1828 a dwellinghouse and corn mill and on the 1846 map called the Paint Mill.

Could the Bonsall School land have been further down the valley? The drawing by Jean Claude Nattes in 1798, (Plate 11) shows a group of buildings at the top of the valley which could be the smelting mills. Their footprint is not unlike the present ruined buildings with an additional building between the Paint and Grinding Mills. There is a short launder above an external water wheel. The function of the buildings lower down is not clear. They are similar in plan to the later buildings of the Lumsdale House stable yard but, if Edward Garton's analysis is correct, this (Plot 353) was not the land given by Mrs Turnor and bought by his father from Bonsall School.

We can therefore reasonably infer that the lower Lumsdale smelting mills were on or near the site of the Paint and Grinding Mills though not necessarily the buildings we can see today. There is an area of woodland above the stable yard still to be explored but encouragement for our conclusion can be had from the amount of slag found not only by Crossley and Kiernan (1992: 39) but also by Lumsdale volunteers recently planting wild garlic to the west of the present mills, the area shown in Plate 10.

So until the middle of the eighteenth century the lead smelting industry in Lumsdale was concentrated in two sites, the upper one around what we now know as the Bone Mill and the lower one - with two mills in 1737 - near the top of the waterfall. Archaeology may one day tell us more.

However, the industrial scene in Lumsdale was soon to be changed quite radically by another technological invention and the differently constructed lead smelting mills to which that led. We will deal with that in the next chapter.

4

LEAD: NEW TECHNOLOGY AND DIVERSIFICATION

The latest technology: the cupola

> *'But lately, some persons at Ashover have again set up a bole, or rather a furnace, which is esteemed the cheapest and best way, and the Oar [sic] is run with pit coal fires instead of whitewood coal used in the smelting mills. 1735'*
>
> — (WOLLEY MSS. 6681 F.393; CITED IN WILLIES, 1980: 179).

The introduction of the cupola

This note in the Wolley Manuscripts refers to the new furnace method of smelting lead. Only fourteen years later this latest technological development - the cupola - was introduced in Lumsdale although it was probably not the first in Derbyshire. Farey, writing in 1811, reported as follows:

'The Cupolas or low-arched reverberatory furnaces, now exclusively used for the smelting of lead ore in Derbyshire, were introduced from Wales by a company of Quakers, about the year

1747, the first of which was erected at Kelstedge, in Ashover; but this is now disused and pulled down' (Farey 1811: 365).

Lynn Willies, acknowledging that the 'prevailing view' was that the first cupola was at Bowers Mill at Kelstedge, stated that the Olda Cupola at Totley had 'a slightly earlier introduction' (1969: 100). However, he said that the cupola at Bowers Mill had been installed earlier than 1747 because it was introduced a few years after the London Lead Company took over in 1734 (ibid: 99). We will come back to a link with Bowers Mill which suggests that Willies's earlier date is the better one. Willies also argues that the 'Bagshaw-Twigg-Barker developments at Totley were responsible for its [the cupola's] popularisation in this area. They appear to have had some connection with at least eight of the cupolas listed, including Totley, Lumsdale and Harewood' (1969: 97). The argument for the importance of the Bagshaw group is also to be found on the website of the Northern Mine Research Society.

Certainly, as we shall see, there was a Twigg active in Lumsdale by 1749. We do know that the cupola at Lumsdale was one of the first five in the county (Willies, 1969: 97) and we know that the London Lead Company's agent in Kelstedge was Joseph Whitfield (Willies 1969: 100, 1980: 215). We shall soon meet him in Lumsdale. We also know where the first cupolas were built in Lumsdale. But, first, what was a cupola?

The reverberatory furnace

'Generally the cupola furnaces were "cased" in a barn-like building with an integral chimney ... or with a short flue leading to a free standing chimney nearby' (Willies 1990: 6). We know that the 'Pond Cottages' cupolas had integral chimneys: there is no indication of any flue leading to a chimney nearby. The roof inside the furnace was arched and the floor (or 'bottom') for the ore was concave. Pilkington explained the process he saw in 1789:

'At one end the fire is placed upon bars under an arched roof ... At the other extremity a perpendicular chimney is built.

When the fire is kindled and every part, excepting the two ends, is closed, the flame is necessarily drawn through the whole length of the furnace, and by its reverberation from the roof the ore is smelted without ever coming into immediate contact with the fuel' (Pilkington 1789 vol 1: 120-121).

Auxiliary buildings would usually include stores for ore and fuel, a counting house, a smithy and, often, an adjoining slag mill (Willies 1990: 6). For a very detailed account of the process with diagrams, see Willies (1990: 6-9). As regards the time that smelting took, Richard Watson noted the following:

'At the great smelting houses in Derbyshire, they put a ton of ore at a time into the furnace, and work it off in eight hours; the ore might be wholly melted in one hour, but the lead, perhaps, is not formed in the greatest possible quantity in eight hours' (1785: 219-220).

Hopkinson notes that 'the cupola could smelt grades of ore impracticable in the smelting mill' and that this 'led to the Barkers [lead smelters] buying ore, discarded by previous generations of miners' in Matlock and Winster (Hopkinson 1958: 11) so that cupolas could use lesser grades of ore, of importance as the best lead veins were being exhausted.

Cupolas for lead smelting were first used in Flintshire in the 1690s and the cupola is sometimes referred to as the Flintshire furnace (Rowe 1983: Chapter 1). The London Lead Company, which we mentioned above, was very important in the commercial development of the cupola. Originally the 'Company for Smelting down Lead with Pit Coal and Sea Coal', it was incorporated by Royal Charter in 1692. After it merged with the Ryton company and the Welsh Company in 1704-5 it was generally referred to as either the London Lead Company or the Quaker Lead Company (Raistrick 1933) as, throughout its history, its trustees and agents were often Quakers (members of the Society of Friends). The company's new Gadlis Smelt Mill in Flintshire (built 1703-4) used Derbyshire ore to test innovative techniques and the company then took out leases of mines around the Derbyshire villages of Winster and Wensley (Raistrick 1988: 137) - which points up the advantage Lumsdale had in being able to access these sources of lead so much more easily.

The 'Pond Cottages' cupolas

The 1749 lease

A lease granted in 1749 by the Lords of the Manor is the crucial next piece of evidence for the development of lead smelting in the upper part of Lumsdale. It is an intriguing document because, as we noted in Chapter 2, it refers to Lumbs Brook but it also confirms the existence of the two existing smelting mills. The lease is to George Wall of Wensley, gentleman, John Wall the younger of Riber, gentleman, and John Twigg of Ashover, gentleman, 'being entered into a partnership with an intent to smelt or refine Lead ore and to manufacture the same into White lead or otherwise' for 999 years at 2s.6d. (half-a-crown or 12½p) p.a. It comprises:

'Soe much & such part (not exceeding in the whole the quantity of one acre of Land statute measure) of That part of the said comon or wast Ground called the East Moor lying between the Upper most and the nether most Lumbs mill within the said Manor or Royalty aforesd the River brook or rivulet called the Lumbs brook being the boundary thereof North or North [——] as they the said George Wall John Wall the younger & John Twigg shall make choice for the purposes aforesd Also full and free liberty power licence & authority to fence in & inclose the same and for the purposes aforesd to set up erect and build such & so many cupolas mills smeltinghouses store houses and other Edifices & Buildings as they... shall think proper... Also so much & such part of all that the said brook or Rivulet called Lumbs Brook as shall happen to be lying within the compass of the said acre of Land with the benefit of the stream thereof for the better carrying on their said undertaking & works with liberty of ingress egress and regress to and for the said George Wall John Wall the younger and John Twigg ... with horses and carriages to and from the same as oft as occasion shall require' (DRO D858/T/1).

In other words, the lease was for an unspecified acre of land on manorial waste, uncultivated land on which they could build as many cupolas as they liked, use the stream and take horses and carts to and from it. This was unusual: lessees were not normally entitled to choose their acre after the grant of their lease. The area was clearly intended to be alongside the brook, though the draftsman appears to have been confused with his compass points. Did he leave the gap in the lease to insert later '-west' or '-east' and did he not understand that the brook flows almost due north-south so the boundary had to be on the west or east side anyway? We can, however, find the general area of the grant by reference to the fifty-two acres which remained common or manorial land until it was granted to Peter Nightingale in the Enclosures of 1780 but we have to look at the later documents of title to identify it precisely.

Hopkinson says that in 1758, Alexander Barker bought 'Lumbs Cupola' from Wall and Twigg and then it was resold to Joseph Whitfield' (Hopkinson 1958: 12). However, Hopkinson gives no source for that statement and it is not confirmed by the deeds at the Derbyshire Record Office. By 1758, of the original lessees, only John Wall of Riber was still alive. He and the widows of the other joint owners, John Twigg and George Wall, then sold the lease for £250 to a consortium of Matthew Sparke Whitfield of Bowers Mill, Kelstedge near Ashover, gentleman, Joseph Boot of Higham, gentleman, and Lydia Woodward of Matlock Bridge.

The property was then described as follows:

'a Building called a Case for two ffurnaces with Two long chimneys cramped with iron, ffour ore houses a compting house and Smithey, one ffurnace with the Bottom and utensils belonging thereto, one hundred and half of new iron unwrought, one anville in the Smithey, twelve Lead weights of half hundred each, some New Bricks and a pair of Slagg-Mill Bellows and other Buildings implements and things in or upon the said premises' (DRO D858/T/2).

Even then the draftsman thought it worth noting that the chimneys were 'long' and 'cramped with iron' - which would be necessary only because they were very tall.

The engraving of a smelting mill at Middleton Dale (Plate 8) shows a very similar pair of cupolas and associated buildings.

The new owners

Matthew Sparke Whitfield, one of the new lessees, was the son of Joseph Whitfield, agent of the London Lead Company and general manager of both mining and smelting in Derbyshire (Raistrick 1988: 137), and Elizabeth Spark - and is therefore an example of a child being given his mother's maiden surname. Joseph and Elizabeth were married at the Quaker meeting in Bournlow, near Haltwhistle in Northumberland in 1735. Matthew was born at Bowers Mill, Ashover in 1736 and his birth was registered by the Quaker meeting in Chesterfield and also in Allendale, Northumberland. Joseph Whitfield arrived at Kelstedge in 1735 (ibid: 153) at about the time when the London Lead Company reconstructed Bowers Mill to install a cupola. The family retained its connection with Allendale, another lead-smelting area. Matthew's children William and Joseph, born in North Wingfield Derbyshire in 1764 and 1769, were also registered in Chesterfield and at the Quaker meeting in Allendale.

We can guess that Joseph had seen the opportunity to use the new cupola technology in Derbyshire in an industry with which he was familiar because there was already a smelt mill at Whitfield in Northumberland (Raistrick 1988: 80-81). In Lumsdale, Joseph's 22-year-old son Matthew also saw an opportunity in 1758; he paid half the purchase price and took half the profits. The other lessees, Joseph Boot and Lydia Woodward, were father and daughter, Lydia Boot having married James Woodward in 1732 and been widowed, and they had one quarter share each.

In 1762 the property was divided and part of it was sold for £92 to George Norman, a wealthy lead merchant from Winster (DRO D858/T/3-4). Helpfully a scaled drawing had been prepared and survives in the DRO (D858/P/1).

It shows 'Lombs Cupola with it's Appurtenances' [*sic*] and includes what we now know as Pond Cottages, the stretch of the Bentley Brook to the east, the site of the property now known as Pinetrees to the west of the lane, and an area of land now partly in the Lower Pond and partly to the west of it stretching down almost to where there is now the Chimney. The area of land has now expanded to 1 acre, 1 rood and 19 perches but Mr. Norman was to have just half an acre (two roods) and, to make up his share, he was assigned a strip at the southern end of the site. Otherwise his share was the northern end of the row of buildings now replaced by Pond Cottages, constituting one of the cupolas, two ore houses and a counting house to the north of it and a smithy on the other side of the lane.

Matthew Whitfield, Joseph Boot and Lydia Woodward retained the other cupola and two 'offices' west of the lane and south of the smithy, one of which survives and is the little building often referred to as a counting house. They were each to pay half the rent, 1s. 3d. (6p) to the Lords of the Manor.

Joseph Boot died in 1766 leaving a daughter Sybilla, born in 1758. On 27 May 1769 Joseph Whitfield, as her surviving guardian, took control of her father's quarter share in the partnership (DRO D858/T/5) and he held it in trust for her until she died. Again the transfer included a furnace with the bottom and utensils, 1½cwt of new unwrought iron, an anvil in the smithy, 12½cwt lead weights, some new bricks and a pair of slag mill bellows. On 20 May 1771 Lydia (acting with her sister Ann Wragg née Boot as representatives of Sybilla's estate) sold both her share and Sybilla's to Joseph Whitfield for £93 9s. 6d. (£93.47) each with 49 pieces of lead, 1 ton 12cwt. of lead ore, one pair of slag bellows, all the slag and waste lead, iron barrows, weighbeams, weights and all other working tools (DRO 858/T/6).

The southern cupola

Having bought the shares held by Lydia and Sybilla in May 1771, Joseph and Matthew Whitfield sold, nine days later, the southern cupola and outbuildings for £350 to William Longsdon, a lead merchant from Eyam who operated the Gang (near Wirksworth) and Orchard (Bradwell) Mines (Willies 1986: 267).

The description of the property and its materials and equipment is similar to that used from 1762 but the building to the west of the lane is described as 'those two orehouses or buildings used as orehouses with a Chamber over the same', a feature which, with its original and heightened roof-lines, is visible in the building today (DRO D858/T/7).

So the Whitfields bow out of our Lumsdale story in 1771. Their Bowers Mill in Kelstedge 'does not seem to have been worked as a cupola after 1778' either; by about 1800 it was used as a rope walk (Willies 1969: 100; Raistrick 1988: 120). Matthew died at North Wingfield in 1774 and again his burial, in the Friends' burial ground in Chesterfield, was also noted in Allendale 'aged near 38 years'. His sons made their way back to the north-east. William returned to Burnlow and Allendale and died in 1803, aged 39. Joseph was in 1788 articled for five years as a clerk to John Kirsopp an attorney in Newcastle. Whether working with lead had anything to do with the early deaths of Matthew and William, father and son, we do not know.

In 1790 Longsdon, who had bought the southern cupola in 1771 for £350, sold it for only £30 to William Milnes of Ashover (DRO D858/T/9). Here there is yet another family connection - this time between the Milnes and Twigg families of Ashover. John Twigge of Bonsall (1728-1758) had a daughter Dorothy who married a William Milnes. They had two sons, John and William (Ince's *Pedigrees* 008d). The Milnes family had been involved in lead smelting for many years but the purchase price for the cupola suggests that it was not bought as a going concern but for another purpose - see below.

The northern cupola

In the meantime the northern cupola had also changed hands. George Norman of Winster, son of Jethro Norman, both lead merchants, died leaving no children but two nephews. His two sisters had married William Swettenham and William White respectively (Ince's *Pedigrees* 086b) and, when he died in 1772, George left to his nephews James Swettenham and George White both 'All that my cupola at Lumb Mills' and also 'All my Leasehold and other Title Estate and Interest whatsoever with all Benefit and Advantage of the same of in or to the Lumbs Upper Mills' - that is the mill on the Bone Mill site (The National Archives PROB 11/982/79).

In 1789 - a year before the sale of the southern cupola - Swettenham and White sold the northern cupola. The sale was also to William Milnes and for the same price of £30 (DRO D858/T/8). The lease still had 959 years to run.

So by 1790 William Milnes owned both cupola sites. He is the same William Milnes who, with his brother John, were partners in the business of Watts, Lowe and Co., already operating their cotton mill lower down the valley. Willies states that shortly after 1790 the cupola was converted into five messuages (1969: 106), said to be accommodation for mill workers which would explain the purchases. That is confirmed by a Release or conveyance (in private hands) of 24 December 1813 which, after setting out details of the two purchases by Milnes, recites that 'soon after[wards] ... the said cupolas or some part or parts thereof were converted into five messuages or dwellinghouses by or at the expense of the said Messrs Watts Lowe & Company'.

The 'Paint Mill' site

The other site in Lumsdale where there is evidence of the more advanced lead smelting was the piece of level ground immediately above the waterfall where the Paint Mill and Grinding Mill now stand (Plate 10). As we noted in Chapter 3, by a Lease and Release in October 1737 Elizabeth Turnor, with the intention of endowing Bonsall School (founded by her grandfather Robert Ferne) with property to produce an income of £40 p.a., transferred to trustees for the School two smelting mills at Matlock, four closes of land on the Tansley side of the Bentley Brook and some other land at Bonsall (Tur/X18/1/11,12 in Lincolnshire archives). We can identify the land in Tansley Parish from tithe maps.

The site of the smelting mills was bought by John Garton from the trustees on 25 December 1828.

Here also the modern technology of the cupola was introduced before 1784. In September that year there was offered for sale:

'the remaining Term of Twenty Years, of the Lease granted by the Trustees of Bonsall School, of all those Premises situate upon the Lumbs Brook, near Matlock, and called the lower Lumbs Mills; consisting of *Cupola and Slagg Mill*, with Furnace, Bellows, and Water Wheel; with necessary Conveniences, all in good Repair, and fit for immediate Work: There are two small Houses close to the Work fit for Workmen. - The Whole are subject to the Payment of Five Pounds yearly' (*Derby Mercury* 26 August 1784; italics added).

These may be the same Lumms Smelting Mills - in the plural because here was a cupola smelter as well as a slag smelting mill - which were advertised in October 1781 with less than two years of a previous lease still to run (*Derby Mercury* 18 October 1781). That would allow for a new twenty-one year lease to start in 1783, as is suggested in the 1784 advertisement.

It is probably the mill which Bray described in his *Sketch of a Tour into Derbyshire* in 1783:

'It stands on a point, from which the water falls a great height over the rudest rocks, and has worn a deep hollow, covered with fragments of stone, some of them very large, between which the current finds its way. ... At this smelting house red lead is made' (2nd ed. 1783: 128).

Bonsall School retained ownership of the site for over 90 years and at least one smelting mill continued in use until sometime before John Garton purchased it for £400 in 1828. The description of the site and its recent occupants contains some familiar names:

'All that Messuage dwellinghouse or tenement heretofore used as a Smelting Mill And also all the other Mill heretofore used as a Smelting Mill but now used as a Corn Mill situate lying and being in the Parish of Matlock in the said County of Derby at or near a place there called the Lums formerly in the tenure or occupation of [——] Whitfield since of Messrs William and John Milnes but now of the said John Garton his undertenants or assigns' (Indenture 25 December 1828 in AS archive).

It is difficult to say which of the Grinding Mill and Paint Mill became the dwelling house or the corn mill but the discovery of strips of decorative marble, thought to be a fireplace surround, in the Paint Mill when some limited excavation was done in 1986-7 suggests that this was the dwelling (SPAS 1987). Although the Whitfields and Milneses had an interest in lead smelting there is no indication that the Gartons were ever so engaged. The same excavation explored, at least superficially, the under-floor heating channels in the Paint Mill that were used to dry barytes, a business which John Garton carried on from, at the latest, 1830.

Slag mills

We have noted above that many of the mills in this area either were slag mills or had a slag mill nearby and that the 1769 transfer of part of the Pond Cottages site business included 'a pair of slag mill bellows'. This raises another issue. As Historic England says in relation to a Yorkshire slag mill, 'An air blast was supplied by bellows, normally operated by a waterwheel; more sophisticated arrangements were used at some 19th century sites' (Historic England List Entry Number: 1016203). However, there is no current evidence of the use of the Bentley Brook at this point to provide water power. Nevertheless, there must have been a slag mill nearby using the 'waste' from the cupola.

Slag-hearths have a long history:

'By the sixteenth century, bole slags were re-smelted at high temperatures, which produced the characteristic black, glassy slags. It is likely that the bellows-blown shaft-furnaces, developed in the sixteenth century, also smelted slags' (Martell and Gill 1990: fn20).

Watson, writing in 1785, said there were probably only one or two ore hearths still operating as smelting mills in Derbyshire because of the move to cupolas but that they were now operating as the means to extract lead from the slag and 'it is then called a slag hearth' (1785: 273). So slag mills continued to be needed even after reverberatory furnaces replaced the ore hearth:

'Though somewhat more effective in extracting the lead from the ore, cupola slag was still fairly rich in metal, and occasionally in the late eighteenth, and almost invariably in the nineteenth century it too was re-smelted in the slag mill' (Willies 1980: 181).

Watson believed the fire in the slag hearth used 'the cinder of pitcoal instead of charcoal' (1785: 273). If that was so, Lumsdale had nearby sources of coal, including possibly from the seam which runs along the line of the Bentley Brook. Aditnow, 'the site for mine explorers and mining historians', suggests a mine on the east side of the stream near the Bone Mill 'where there is evidence of waste slag and clinker mixed in with shale and some hillocks and hollows' (www.aditnow.co.uk/Mines/Lumsdale-Coal-Colliery_20312/#location).

If we move forward to the 1820s there is another contemporary account. Martell and Gill translated *Voyage Metallurgique en Angleterre* which was written after a visit to Britain in 1823 by graduates of the School of Mines in Paris. That document stated that:

'In Derbyshire, slag-hearths are also used to re smelt the rich slags and dross from the reverberatory furnace. They are generally found next to each other [p.584 in original]. They are about 3 ft. high and are very large; they are made of four slabs of cast iron. Some parts of the interior are constructed of refractory bricks; they are surmounted by a chimney. The sole is made of compressed clay and cinders (menu coke). The tuyere is sloping' and 'In general the hearths are fed by wooden bellows' (Martell and Gill 1990: 28).

The tuyere, as in the ore hearth, is a nozzle through which air is forced into the smelter, furnace, or forge. Air or oxygen is injected into a hearth under pressure from bellows or a blowing engine or other devices.

Martell and Gill (1990) also footnote a reference to Dickinson et al (1975) which is about a lead smelting mill at Lumb Clough, Yorkshire. Historic England listed that mill because 'Lumb Clough smeltmill is a good example of the small, simple ore hearth smeltmill typical of the 17th and early 18th centuries'. The listing goes on to say, 'Early sites were typically small and simple buildings with one or two hearths, whereas late 18th and 19th century smelt mills were often large complexes containing several ore and slag hearths' (List entry 1015819, 17 April 1997).

This is helpful because we have so little information about the slag mills in Lumsdale and we have found no clear evidence of a water wheel powering the necessary bellows. The next section deals however with a mill which does appear to have been a water- powered slag mill.

The strange case of the Offspring Mill

There appeared in the *Derby Mercury* in 1783 and 1784 a series of advertisements placed by one Matthew Sanderson for the disposal of a water mill called Offspring Mill or Lums (later Lumbs) Mill. The first, in October and November 1783, by Mr Sanderson of 53 King Street, Manchester, were for the sale or letting of the lease of a mill and read as follows:

'Water Mill, called Offspring Mill, or Lums Mill, now used as a Smelting or Slagg Mill, but capable of being converted into a Mill for Cotton, or various other Purposes, with the Wheel, Cylinder, Bellows, Stampers, and other Machinery and Appurtenances to the same belonging. N.B. The Stream on which the Mill Stands is very powerful, never deficient of Water: The Building and Water-Wheel almost new' (*Derby Mercury* 30 Oct and 6 Nov 1783).

There were just under 12 years left of a twenty-one year lease (so it was granted to run from Michaelmas, 29 September 1774) and the annual rent was £4. Clearly it was being used as a smelting mill and, although it was equipped to smelt slag, it could be converted to other uses and had the advantage of a stream which was 'never deficient of water'.

As we have already said, it is no surprise to find any mill called Lumbs Mill but the identity of an Offspring Mill remains a mystery and so we have tried to find a connection between Mr Sanderson and Lumsdale in the hope that will give us a clue to the whereabouts of his mill and why he was trying to sell it. We have found no direct connection but newspapers and other records do tell the story of a Matthew Sanderson who, if they do all relate to 'our' Mr Sanderson, adds another element to the development of industry in the valley.

Matthew Sanderson

Sanderson first comes to notice in the report of proceedings at York Assizes in 1771 where, after noting that 'none were capitally convicted' (i.e. sentenced to death) at those Assizes, the report goes on:

'A remarkable cause was tried at these assizes, before Mr. Justice Willes, between Benjamin Taylor of Green-lane, near Sheffield, butcher, plaintiff; and Matthew Sanderson, of the same place, chymist, defendant. The action was brought for a nuisance, by making sundry articles, which not only infected the inhabitants, or rather the plaintiff's own family in particular, but also his pastures and gardens, to a degree never before heard of. When, after a hearing on both sides, for nearly eight hours, and many sensible remarks made by the Judge between a real nuisance and disagreeable smell, and how many of his Majesty's subjects might be liable to such prosecutions, from carrying on many necessary trades, the Jury directly concurred with the Judge, and, without going out of the court, declared in favour of the defendant' (Annual Register 1775: 135).

So Mr Sanderson's activities as a chemist were producing obnoxious smells in Green Lane, Sheffield which is close to the Kelham Island, at the centre of the Sheffield iron and steel industry and now home of the museum to all that has been lost. But what had Sanderson been doing to cause such a stink? There is a clue in the patent granted on 27th October 1774, 'unto Matthew Sanderson, of Masbrough, in the parish of Rotherham & county of York, chymist and refiner, of his new invented certain cheap ingredients (never before used for any such purpose), which, being mixed with metallick earths or clays, and poor, flinty, sulphureous, and stubborn ores of lead and copper and slag, and when brought into a state of fusion, occasions the metallick particles thereof to be precipitated, and by the help of a high blast furnace (capable of holding a large quantity of crude materials), blown with two or three large or hollow iron cylindric bellows, worked by a water wheel, to smelt with great ease, and to extract double the quantity of metal hitherto extracted from a like quantity of the same material .... for the term of 14 years pursuant to the statute.'

Note that Sheffield is only about five miles from Masbrough, a district of Rotherham, and close enough to be his place of work. Then on 21 December 1778 there was a further grant:

'unto Matthew Sanderson, of his new discovered process for the extracting of a mineral sulpher from pyrites, copper, and lead ores, separating its acid, and rendering it useful for every medicinal purpose ... for the term of 14 years pursuant to the statute' (Woodcroft 1854: 197, 221).

Whatever the merits of Sanderson's inventions, they appear not to have been a commercial success. The *London Gazette* of 14 December 1782 gave notice that a Commission of Bankrupt [*sic*] had been issued against Matthew Sanderson of Masbrough, Chymist and Refiner and that he was to attend for examination in Rotherham and to disclose his estate and effects on 30 and 31 December and 28 January. He appears to have done so because the Gazette published a further notice on 15 February that the Commissioners had certified to the Lord Chancellor 'that the said Matthew Sanderson hath in all Things conformed himself according to the Directions of the several Acts of Parliament made concerning Bankrupts' and that a Certificate would be allowed discharging him from bankruptcy unless cause were shown to the contrary before 11 March.

It was possible for creditors to object, for example if the Commissioners' haste to issue their Certificate effectively excluded them from participating, but this course of action was only possible if four-fifths of the creditors had already given their approval.

So, although it took the Assignees of his assets until 16 August 1786 to call a final meeting of creditors to declare a dividend and share out the proceeds of the bankruptcy, it is likely that Sanderson was freed from further liability for his previous debts by March 1783.

He then turned up in Manchester, when on 21 July 1783 Matthew Sanderson, 'chymist', enrolled his son Thomas at Manchester Grammar School. A Thomas Sanderson, son of

Matthew, was baptised in Rotherham on 13 May 1772 which is consistent with the presumed family history and makes him the right age for admission (Smith J.F. 1868: 124).

In September 1783 Matthew Sanderson, 'Chymist, Colour-maker and Perfumer' advertised in the *Manchester Mercury* his new shop at 53 King Street selling 'all Sorts of superfine Colours in their native or manufactured State' and various other artists' materials, also 'all Kinds of Perfumery Goods ... at as low a Rate as any other Shop in England ... with sundry other Articles in the Cosmetic Art' (*Manchester Mercury*, 23 and 30 September 1783). In July 1784 he advertised that he had moved his business to the White Horse, Hanging Ditch, Manchester 'where Gentlemen, Ladies, and Others, may be accommodated with all Kinds of the choicest and best Perfumes' and where he also continued to sell oil and water colours and 'other Articles made use of in the Art of Painting' (*ibid*. 13 July 1784).

What was Sanderson doing in Lumsdale?

We noted above that Sanderson started advertising the sale of the mill in October and November of 1783. Altogether there were five advertisements and the next three tell us more about this mill. When in July 1784 Sanderson, now (as we know) at Hanging Ditch, tried again to sell the mill he added 'heretofore used as a Smelting Mill' - so it had ceased operating as a smelter between November 1783 and July 1784 - and said that it was in a very populous Neighbourhood.

'It will be sold separate or together, with two excellent Iron Cylindrical Bellows, a Set of Stampers, and other Materials thereunto belonging, all for the purpose of Dressing and Smelting of Lead Slag, but powerful enough to Smelt Iron or other metalic Matters, being all in excellent Condition for the Purpose ...N.B. This will be no more advertised' (*Derby Mercury* 1 July 1784).

It was advertised again in November and December with even more attractive benefits:

'Water Mill called Offspring Mill or Lumbs Mill, lately used as a Slugg Mill, on a new Principle, capable of turning out upwards of six Times the Quantity of Lead Slagg or Lead Ore, in the same Space of Time of any other at present made Use of, and to much more Profit and less Waste than any other made [*sic* - mode?] of Smelting whatsoever, secured by Patent; but to accommodate the Purchaser, a Privilege will be granted on very easy Terms. Together with the Mill will be sold, the Cylinders, Stampers, and other Machinery and Appurtenances to the same belonging, a powerful Water Wheel, almost new, and situated on a strong Stream of Water, never deficient in the dryest Seasons. There is Room enough for any other Addition, either for a Cotton Mill or other Purposes, and Stone and Lime on the Premises' (*Derby Mercury*, 2 December 1784).

If we assume, and the evidence does seem to confirm, that it is the same Matthew Sanderson throughout this story, what can we infer? We have a man who was an enthusiastic inventor and entrepreneur, though not a very successful one. He could fail and re-invent himself. He acquired, perhaps around 1780, a slag mill in Lumsdale where he intended to create a smelting mill operating his patented process. It had, or he installed, a new water wheel. Then he changed his mind and the slag mill ceased operation. Maybe his process did not work as well as he had hoped or it was too late to take advantage of the opportunities for smelting in Lumsdale. Maybe his interest was really in his perfumery business in Manchester. He tried to dispose of the mill over a period of more than 12 months and perhaps never succeeded. He may be the Matthew Sanderson, a shopkeeper, who was buried in Warrington on 23 June 1786, aged 54.

Where was the mill?

Unfortunately, Sanderson's landlord is never identified and he is not mentioned as a tenant in occupation of any land sold. The terms of the lease are not consistent with the leases of the Bone Mill or the former corn mill site acquired by Watts, Lowe in 1783. As we have said in Chapter 1, maps and plans of the area above the waterfall between 1780 and 1848 show a building close to the Bentley Brook about where the outfall from the Lower Pond is now and that could have been his mill. There may well have been a spring near there: springs come and go in the Lumsdale hillsides. He could instead have been a tenant of Bonsall School near the top of the waterfall or possibly occupying land where the Upper Bleachworks now is. Could the contraption illustrated in the foreground of Nattes's drawing (Plate 11) be the last remains of his patented process? Unless more documentation comes to light or there is some serious archaeology in the right place, we may never know.

Red lead

We know that red lead was manufactured in Lumsdale because early writers of tourist guides said so. We noted above the comment of William Bray which continued, 'At this smelting house red lead is made by burning common lead a sufficient time, by which it is reduced in weight as much as 2 or 300 pound in a ton' (2nd ed 1783: 128). A little later William Mavor, largely re-printing Bray's *Sketch*, wrote: 'Red lead is made in considerable quantities' although there is no indication of exactly where this was in Bray's 'wild and dreary scene' of Lumsdale (Mavor 1798-1800: 229). Then, twenty years later Thomas Walford also noted that 'Between two and three miles from Matlock is the Lumbs smelting house where red lead is made' (Walford 1818: D).

So there is documentary evidence that red lead production was happening in Lumsdale between 1783 and 1818 but it may of course have been occurring for a longer period than that.

We do not know where the red lead smelting occurred except that Bray mentions the red lead smelter at the top of the waterfall in 1783. Crossley and Kiernan note that red lead mills 'were usually linked to smelting-mills which provided material for red-lead manufacture' (1992: 9) but that leaves several more contenders.

It is fortunate that *The Chemical Essays* of a Cambridge Professor (of Divinity!) are still readily accessible as they contain a wealth of information about red lead and its production in Derbyshire in 1785. This passage at the beginning of Essay VIII, headed 'Of the smelting of lead ore as practised in Derbyshire', suggests that (red) lead smelting required considerable skill:

'There is a certain standard of perfection in the exercise of every art, which is not always well understood; and after men do sufficiently comprehend it, many ages often pass away before they are fortunate or ingenious enough to attain it' (Watson 1785: 251).

Red lead is so called because it is often, but not always, red:

'The colour of the **red lead** admits some variety, which is occasioned by the different degrees of heat. If the heat is too small, instead of **red** it is yellow or orange coloured; if it is too great the **red** colour is changed into a dirty white … It has been asserted, that the reverberation of the flame and smoke upon the surface of the **lead,** is not a necessary circumstance in giving it a **red** colour' (ibid 1785: 341).

Watson describes a Derbyshire process which is clearly being done in a reverberatory furnace (cupola) where lead is calcined, such that the lead is changed into a yellowish-green powder which is then ground in a mill and becomes yellow after washing. After drying, the powder is put back in the furnace and after about 48 hours becomes red lead (ibid: 340-341).

So what is red lead? Historic England's stated reasons for listing the *Red lead mill, lead smelt mill, and corn mill to the east of Nether Loads Farm* (in Holymoorside and Walton parish, a few miles from Lumsdale) includes a helpful section:

'Red lead is an oxide of lead, which was used as a pigment (red lead mixed with oil formed the standard red paint until the 20th century), and as an ingredient in pottery glazes and in flint glass making. It was produced from metallic lead in a red lead oven (a furnace with fireplaces along both sides, a hearth in the centre, and a chimney over the loading door). The lead was first oxidised to form a litharge, then ground to a powder, then re-oxidised to form red lead. Red lead was known from the Roman period onwards, though documented red lead mills are of 16th to 20th century date. No remains of red lead ovens have yet been discovered. ... Red lead mills are important as the main source of raw materials for the paint industry, and are an unusual aspect of British metallurgy.' (https://historicengland.org.uk/listing/the-list/list- entry/1009708)

However, Storm in his book on eighteenth century paint materials says that red lead was not used very often as a red pigment.

'Its most important use in the finishing trades was as a priming material or as a ground for the more brilliant red colors. It was also used as a flux in the manufacture of glass and as an ingredient in lead crystal. The glassware industry created a great demand for red lead' (Storm 1982).

Roger Burt, focusing on the period 1700-1770, also states that the main consumers for white and red lead were the paint, glass and pottery industries but that the paint industry used only small – though increasing – quantity of red lead (1969: 261). Red lead was used in the glazes for earthenware and porcelain as well as in the production of 'flint glass', the better quality glass used for wine glasses, lenses etc. (ibid: 262-3). The demand for all these products increased in the eighteenth century so the market was buoyant (ibid) for investors.

The decline of the lead smelting industry

Consumer-led demand

Before focusing on the decline of lead smelting in Derbyshire and whether the end of the Lumsdale smelters was in line with trends elsewhere, it might be helpful first to know why lead mining and smelting became so very important to Derbyshire. Wood explains the reasons in some detail:

'Like its smaller British competitors in the Mendips, Yorkshire, North Wales, Lancashire, Staffordshire and County Durham, the Derbyshire lead industry of the mid-sixteenth century had served a primarily regional market. By a century later the scale of that market had expanded, as had the productive capacity of the industry. Demand came from a series of connected sectors. Internally, the rising wealth of early modern England's "middling sort" expressed itself in increased demand for pewter tableware. The growth of urban centres, in particular of London, required lead for roofing and piping. The same was true of the "great rebuilding" of the houses of the rural "middling sort", the gentry and, of course, the nobility' (Wood 1999: 72).

He goes on to say that the production of glass and paint also needed lead, as did the large European standing armies, so continental markets also expanded. The result was that, from the mid-sixteenth century to the last decade of the eighteenth century, 'thanks to the geological accident of the richness and size of its lead deposits, the Derbyshire industry was the pre-eminent international supplier of lead' (ibid; see also Kiernan 1989; Burt 1969).

When demand was high and the Derbyshire lead mines were producing the highest quality of lead, the smelting industry was profitable. However, the peak for lead production was in the 1760s and then other factors came into play.

The falling financial return from smelting

The lead industry in Derbyshire went through a crisis between 1796 and 1835 (Willies 1986: 271). 'Demand was not the cause, since this remained at a high level ... but rather it was the rise of foreign competition' (ibid): indeed the Napoleonic Wars increased demand. However, before 1801 ore prices failed to keep up with inflation and mines had gone into decline, notably at Winster and Ashover, which were nearby sources for the Lumsdale mills (Willies 1986: 276). The reason was that the lead vein was now poor or not accessible without investing in expensive machinery for pumping. At the same time the cotton industry with its new and improving technology was attractive as an alternative investment.

So the main factors that led to the end of the smelting industry in Lumsdale were that lead mining was itself in difficulties, that smelting required both more advanced equipment and economies of scale, and that investors were finding more lucrative means of making money. Consequently, 'the 1780s saw the end of the use of the small-scale smelting-mill, so that some hundreds of such mills had been finally replaced by a dozen or so more efficient cupolas' (Willies 1980: 459).

How important were the Lumsdale cupolas?

In relation to the much-contested definition of the (first) Industrial Revolution Ronald Tylecote argues as follows:

'In the case of iron there is no such difficulty; the Industrial Revolution began in Britain with the transition from charcoal to coke as the principal fuel. This transition brought about the release of ironmaking from the inhibition caused by the effective shortage of charcoal as a fuel' (Tylecote 2010: 122).

If we rely on Tylecote's argument, then the industrial revolution started in Lumsdale in 1749 when cupolas were introduced to use coal. We argue that the situation was more complex. In any case we do not know whether acquiring enough charcoal had been a problem in Lumsdale. Access to coal would not have been a problem but we have no evidence of coke making and we do know that not all cupola furnaces used coke (Brewer 1981: 42-43).

We have seen that Lumsdale was ahead of the game with three or four cupolas in operation for many years. However, we know that the cupolas on the site of Pond Cottages stopped operating in about 1790 but cannot be sure when the smelting mills lower down the valley stopped using a cupola. Farey's 1811 list of cupolas has twenty cupolas in it including 'Lumsdale in Matlock (formerly)' (1811: 366).

His list is more extensive than Glover's list of ten sites which suggests that a number in the area ceased operating between 1811 and 1829. Only seven cupola smelters were still operating in this area in 1829:

- *'Meer Brook,* or Devil's Bowling Alley, in Alderswasley Richard Hurt, esq.

- Lea, near Cromford (and slag mills) John Alsop & Co. Middleton Dale, in Stoney Middleton (and slag mill) John Barker, esq.
- Stone-edge in Ashover (and slag mill) William and Charles Milnes.
- Via Gellia in Bonsal Dale.
- Bonsal (and slag mill) John Alsop and Co.
- Stoney Middleton (and slag mill) Duke of Devonshire, Custom work for poor miners' (Glover 1829: 81).

Why the Lumsdale cupolas stopped operating earlier than some others in the area is not clear but we know that it was part of a Derbyshire-wide trend. Further, if investors believed that another use of the water power would be more profitable, then the nature of the production output changed. This is probably what happened in Lumsdale with its change to cotton mills and other industries. We will deal with cotton spinning in Chapter 6 but, first we need to back-track a few years to focus on other early industries in the valley, notably corn grinding and wool fulling.

5

CORN AND FULLING MILLS

Introduction

Lumsdale in the seventeenth century was almost undeveloped. At the top of the valley there was one mill race supporting some lead smelting (see Chapter 3) and there may have been some more smelting near the top of the waterfall. It is unlikely that anyone lived close to the smelting hearths and we have seen no evidence of any dwellings there at that time. At the foot of the waterfall there was activity of a different kind: it included corn milling and fulling of woollen cloth. We know something of that from the Wolley Manuscripts which included deeds relating to the Bown or Bowne family who owned part of Lumsdale. Those deeds refer to both corn and fulling mills but we should tell you now that we will not be able to say with any certainty where they were. There is also evidence that there was a corn mill above the waterfall and that is a little clearer. First we will deal with the history of the mills below the top of the waterfall.

The Bown(e)s and the fulling mill(s)

Adam Wolley, antiquarian

Adam Wolley (1758-1827) 'the Younger' was descended from the Wolley family established in Riber from around 1500 although his branch settled at Allen Hill on Matlock Bank and he lived in Matlock Bath (Bryan 1903: opp.250). His father, another Adam Wolley (1728-1801), 'the Elder' had married Elizabeth Hodgkinson, daughter of Joseph Hodgkinson, and both were very much involved in local affairs and business ventures, including those in Lumsdale as we shall see.

Among the documents collected by Adam the Younger is an abstract of the title of William White to land in Matlock (Wolley Mss. 6694 f.41). Such an abstract is a condensed history of someone's entitlement to a particular piece of land, and it showed that the land had much earlier been owned by the Bown family.

The Hurst

In the seventeenth century, the Bown family owned the Hurst, which is much of the area now known as the Hurst Farm estate in Matlock, north-west of the Alfreton Road. We know more about that family because Thomas Norris Ince, a solicitor from nearby Wirksworth, over the period 1824-1860, collected pedigrees and details of about 20,000 people. According to Ince, referring to Exchequer Bills, the Bown family had been on the Hurst since at least the time of Henry VII, the first Tudor king of England. In 1499 one Roger Bown of Matlock took a grant of a house and 6 acres of land at Hurst in Matlock from Thomas Babington Esq. 'and others' (Ince *Pedigrees* 042c). This is probably the Thomas Babington, born in Dethick, who was Sheriff of Derbyshire and Nottingham in 1498 and died in 1518 in Ashover where the magnificent tomb to Thomas and his wife Edith (formerly Fitz-Herbert) is in All Saints' Church. We do not know who the 'others' were who owned this land at the end of the fifteenth century.

It is the references to the mills the Bown family owned that confirm their estate extended as far as the Bentley Brook which flowed through Lumsdale to Matlock Green although it is difficult to be sure precisely which plot of land is involved in any transaction. The devolution of the legal title is very complicated and involves a number of medieval processes no longer familiar even to property lawyers but its very complexity has a certain fascination. The tale also reveals how useful it is to historians that families fall out and resort to the law to resolve their differences. You will also see that the various documents frequently refer to both fulling and corn mills although the documents do not tell us how long they had been there so we can only know what was there in and after 1682.

Many of the documents identify the land to which they relate as 'being now in the occupation of x and formerly of y' and that was all right because, at that time, everybody knew and remembered. However, we have in the Bowne family documents some from the seventeenth and eighteenth centuries which are precise in naming fields, closes, crofts, flats and pingles (all meaning much the same) so there can be no doubt. Unfortunately there is no corresponding map until 1849 and then, although every plot of land is named, the names have changed and it is usually impossible to link one with the other. A draftsman in 1774 anticipated the difficulty when he referred to 'the parcels of land ... called the Upper Orchard the Barn Croft the Upper Ox Close the Nether Ox Close the Fare Ox Close Nether Flates and the Upper Flates or by whatsoever names the said Closes have been called or Described' but that doesn't help.

The 1682 entail

The complicated story of land ownership on the Hurst and in adjacent Lumsdale - and therefore who owned and was operating the fulling or corn mills - begins when, in 1682, Anthony Bowne's son William married Ann Knowles. Ann's father paid a 'jointure' of £80 to provide for her (in lieu of dower) in the event of William's death, dower normally being a payment by the husband's family in case the wife became a widow. At the same time Anthony transferred his home and the rest of his Derbyshire estate to trustees for the benefit of the family. Anthony kept for himself for his lifetime, within the trust, a fulling mill and two Hurst closes and the benefit of the eastern half of his home but most of the rest of his estate was to be held in trust for his son William, then for any sons of the marriage 'in tail male' and then, in default of male descendants, for any daughters of the marriage (Wolley Mss: 6694 f.41).

'In tail male' means there was an 'entail' and we will come across a number of 'entails'. This one limited the succession of ownership to male descendants. Others were differently defined but all had the intention of preventing property being transferred outside the family. The house referred to above was known as Lynn Tree and was close to what is now the junction of Lime Tree Road and Hurst Rise in Matlock. There is now a memorial there to John Bowne of the same large family who emigrated to America in 1658 and was instrumental in establishing the right to freedom of religion there (see http://www.matlockcivicassociation.btck.co.uk/Projects/JohnBowne).

So Anthony Bowne, living in one half of the Lynn Tree house, was effectively the owner of one fulling mill in 1682.

Two fulling mills

William confirmed as owner

Very shortly after the entail was set up, in 1682 or 1683, however, by a quasi-litigious process of 'Fine' the trustees relinquished their interest in the fulling mill, meadow land and other pasture 'for all manner of cattle', and legal ownership reverted to Anthony Bowne (Wolley Mss: 6694 f.42). A few years later, in 1686, Anthony by 'feoffment with livery of seisin' (a sort of conveyance originally involving a ceremony with a spade on the land in question) transferred to his son William the Over Hurst close, presumably one of the two Hurst closes he had kept in 1682, and part of his meadow land, with a right of way over Nether Hurst close (ibid). In 1689 William bought by process of Lease & Release adjoining land, called Steers Pingle, from Anthony Flint (ibid). We have to infer that Anthony Bowne died around the turn of the century and that William inherited as his oldest son.

Another fulling mill

Moving on 18 years, we know from deeds in the possession of the Arkwright Society that in 1707 William Bowne, described as a 'Sherman', bought another walk or fulling mill from John Wilcockson together with an acre of land known as Lumms Fould. Bailey's Dictionary of 1742 defines a shearman as a shearer of cloth (Bailey, 1742: 762 and see below) - one who cut off excess nap and fibres from woollen cloth - and, presumably, that is what William was. With the land came a collection of rights over 'ways waters waste commons comon of pasture and turbary conveniencys priviledges emoluemts Banks ponds floodgates wears damms streams and apptnces whatsoever' [as written]. Clearly there was already in hand a significant amount of management of the Bentley Brook.

In 1721 William Bowne transferred that walk mill and Lumms Fould to his son Isaac, both then described as dyers (dyeing being a part of the process for producing woollen cloth), but in 1729 he took them back in consideration of a payment of £90. The description of the property, is expanded to include the following: 'all houses outhouses structures barnes Stables ffould Yarde Baksides gardens Orchards Woods underwoods ways waters wasts Comons Comon of Pasture & Turbary Convenenseys previlidges Emoliments Banks Ponds Floodgattes shuttles weares dames streames Wheels Stocks and Appurtinances whatsoever unto ye sd premises or any part or parsell thereof belonging' (Indenture 28 August 1729 in AS archive).

As you can see, these early legal documents were short on punctuation. More importantly the references to wheels and stocks confirm the processes being used in the walk mill because fulling stocks are the beaters operated by water-driven cams to felt woollen fabric (see below). It also confirms that this fulling mill was still operating in 1729.

The deaths of William and John

In 1729 William Bowne sold a half share of all this to his son-in-law Timothy Spencer. He died two years later, however, leaving two daughters, Anne who was married to Timothy Spencer and Mary married to Thomas White, and a son John. John inherited under the 1682 settlement as he was in the direct male line. Another son, Isaac, predeceased William leaving five daughters.

John made a Will giving nearly all his land to his sisters Anne and Mary, subject to some legacies and other benefits for his wife, mother (who had use of the east end of the house for life) and nieces, and left the majority of his personal effects to the two sons-in-law, Timothy Spencer and Thomas White. He gave one pingle (another name for a small piece of land), to his cousin Anthony. Problems arose when John died only two months after his father in 1731 (Ince: 042c; Wolley Mss. 6694 f.43).

A family disagreement: the Spencers and Whites

The Spencers and the Whites could not agree the division of the lands and other rights left to Anne and Mary and went to arbitration. The award was made in 1742. It is interesting because it now includes reference to a corn mill in the properties given to the Spencers. By the award, they received the east end of the house 'Lynn Tree' with a calender house (explained below), barns and stables, a house already in their possession near Lumbes Mill with the Corn Mill belonging to it, a dye house, kiln, other buildings, several named parcels of land including the Tenter Croft and the Wheatpiece with its Dyehouse, seats in the parish church and a share in the proceeds of the Manor of Matlock (Wolley Mss. 6694 f.43-44).

The Whites had the west end of the house, the Ox Closes etc.

referred to above, Walk Mill and Dyers Crofts with their walk mill and dyeing house, other buildings, seats in the church and a share of the Manor (ibid). It is possible to identify the site of the Whites' walk mill and dyeing house because in 1869 E.H. Garton purchased from the estate of Joseph Paxton some land including a close formerly known as Walk Mill Croft but now as Dyehouse Croft and two closes, divided from it by the brook, known as Upper Butts and Nether Butts and Yard. The plan attached to the deed and the 1848 Tithe Map both identify the land as the fields between Bailey's Mill and the Alfreton Road on Matlock Cliff. The same deed refers to a flax mill built by a John Bown, a corn mill and a former corn mill at Matlock Green - all powered by the Bentley Brook but outside the scope of this book (DRO D856/T/17). In other words, the Whites' fulling mill was lower down Lumsdale.

The 1742 settlement was implemented by a Lease & Release terminating the entailed interests (which had limited inheritance to the family) and transferring the estate to Timothy Spencer and Thomas White, including the pingle occupied by Anthony Bowne (Wolley Mss. 6694 f.44). In 1743, by another quasi-litigious process of Fine and Recovery further steps were taken by the Spencers and Whites to extinguish any entailed interests in their (wider) estates (ibid 6694 f.47).

In 1744 some of the daughters of Isaac (William Bowne's son who predeceased him) began proceedings in the Court of Exchequer calling on the Spencers and Whites to account for the legacy of £50 to be shared among them under John Bown's will and their claim was settled.

The fulling - now corn - mill property re-united

We noted above that in the 1742 award a corn mill was mentioned, awarded to the Spencers. In 1755 Timothy Spencer sold to his son-in-law John Smith the Elder, a dyer from Tansley, a half share in that mill, a former walk or fulling mill (see below), now still operating as a corn mill, and the kiln, stable and buildings belonging to it. He retained the other half share until his death in 1771.

The two half shares were brought together again in 1782 after the deaths of both owners. George Smith and other personal representatives of John Smith, and another Timothy Spencer, grandson of Timothy Spencer deceased, and other family members sold to Luke Wilson and Thomas Barton for £125 the following land and properties:

'All that Water Corn Mill known by the name of Lums Mill situate standing and being in Lumsdale in Matlock aforesaid together with the Kilne Stable and other Buildings to the same belonging And also all that piece or parcel of land in which the said Mill and Buildings are situate and standing containing by Estimation half an acre be the same more or less Together with all and singular Edifices Buildings Ways Waters Watercourses Streams Dams Weirs Goits Walls Hedges Ditches ffences Trees Commons Easments profits priviledges Commodities Advantages Emoluments Hereditaments and Appurtenances whatsoever to the said Mills Land and Premises belonging' (Indenture 20 November 1782 in AS archive).

This transaction and that of 1755 also refer to a 'kilne'. This would have been the kiln used to dry the corn before it was milled.

Fulling and corn grinding

Before we move to trying to locate the site of the corn and fulling mills it might be helpful to examine briefly what the processes used in each were.

Fulling

Fulling (or walking or tucking) is an ancient process which has provided common English surnames - Fuller, Walker and Tucker.

It had two aspects. First it involved cleansing woollen fabric, originally by hand (or rather trampling by foot) in stale urine.

Then it thickened, strengthened and helped to waterproof it by matting the fibres together or 'felting' them. From medieval times it became a mechanised process in fulling or walk mills.

As David Hey (2010) points out, 'Before the invention of scribbling and spinning mills in the late 18th century, fulling was the only mechanical process in the manufacture of cloth'. Scribbling is one of the processes to prepare fibres for spinning and entailed combing out cotton (or wool) fibres to straighten them. In a water-powered fulling mill wooden hammers called stocks or mallets, driven via a cam shaft linked to the water wheel, would pound the cloth. Fuller's earth was often part of the mix of water and additives used in this process. The soaking liquid, often urine, had to be collected and was stored in lants - there is a Lant Lane on Matlock Moor.

The fulling process 'was extremely noisy, and some towns banished fulling mills to their periphery' (Abingdon Area AHS: 2) which could explain the siting of such a mill in Lumsdale, away from people's homes in Matlock town.

Tenters

Although there is no direct evidence of bleaching as such in Lumsdale before about 1794 (see Chapter 8) the naming of a Tenter Croft on the Hurst strongly suggests that in the seventeenth century lengths of cloth were hung on tenter hooks and stretched out on tenter frames to dry and bleach in the open air and sunlight.

'After fulling, the cloth had to be stretched to regain some of the inevitable shrinkage, so fulling mills are normally associated with tentering grounds. It might finish at about three-quarters of the original length and breadth, but correspondingly thicker. It might be sold at this stage, but more often would be subjected to napping with teasels, shearing to remove the raised nap and produce a smoother finish, and dyeing' (Abingdon Area AHS: 2).

For a discussion of early bleaching in and around Lumsdale see Chapter 7.

Calendering

Calenders are heavy rollers used to press fabric or paper in order to give it a smooth surface finish. They complement the fulling, bleaching and dyeing process. We have seen reference to a calender house on the Hurst from 1742.

Grinding corn

On the Peakscan website at (www.peakscan.freeuk.com) Stephen N. Wood writes that gritstone has been worked into tools to grind grain for at least 2,000 years, the earliest evidence being querns, but that the millstones 'attract the attention of the visitor most often'.

'There are probably 1,500 of these scattered throughout the Peak, although approx 80% are within 2 kilometres of a line drawn from Moscar to Fox House and on to Dobb Edge in the grounds of Chatsworth. A few more are on Stanton Moor, scattered around Ashover and in the quarries between Little Eaton and Belper. In the early 20th century a significant number of stones were quarried at Darley Dale then exported for use in paper mills, but few are left today'.

He notes, however, that it is important to distinguish between millstones, which were 'used in pairs to shear grains fed into a narrow gap between their faces', grindstones, 'used to sharpen metal cutting tools etc. pushed against their edges' and edge runners which were 'cylindrical stones mounted on an axle and used to crush a variety of materials and even foodstuffs as they rolled around a pivot'. He goes on: 'Gritstone millstones quarried for milling flour were termed "Peaks" by millers. Up to the 18th century, millers in England used millstones quarried from a single grit block. These were "Peaks", but finer grained stones were also imported from the Cologne (Koln) area in Germany, and these were termed "Cullen" stones' (see also, for more detail, Watts and Watts 2016).

He then talks about the so called French stones about which there has been debate:

'In the 18th century, composite stones, made up from blocks of chert in a cement matrix, were often used to grind the increasingly popular white flour. Composites needed re-cutting less often and were less prone to discolour the flour; they were termed "French" stones, although they were manufactured in England (there are records of the chert blocks being offered for sale in Derby), as well as France. Many popular books claim that "French" stones replaced Derbyshire "Greys" because they were cheaper; in fact chert composites were much more expensive, but produced whiter flour, lasted longer and needed less maintenance.'

There are examples of both types in Lumsdale, notably the gritstone millstone in the south-east corner of the Upper Bleach Works and the 'French' burr stone near the Saw Mill (Plate 3). For more about the latter see Chapter 7.

The site(s) of the Corn and Fulling Mills

What can we learn from all this of the history of Lumsdale and, in particular, its corn milling and early textile industries? We know from the deeds that Anthony Bowne had a fulling mill in 1682 and, as we explain below, the references to the Tenter Croft, the Dye House and the Calender House all suggest bleaching, dyeing and finishing cloth on the Hurst estate. The history of bleaching in Lumsdale, so far as we know it, is in Chapter 7 but we have to try to locate both fulling cloth and grinding corn in the valley.

The local fulling mills

We have seen that Anthony Bowne had a fulling mill and that his son William bought another one in 1702. One of them was lower down the Bentley Brook towards Matlock. The other appears to have been somewhere in the Arkwright Society estate, but where?

In 1742 Timothy and Ann Spencer were awarded 'the Dwelling House near the Lumbes Mill with the Corn Mill thereunto belonging'. In 1755 Timothy Spencer sold to John Smith the following property:

'one undivided moyety or half part of all that water corn Mill ... in Matlock now in the occupation of the said Timothy Spencer which was heretofore a Walk Mill or fulling Mill and as such was formerly conveyed by William Bowne unto the said Timothy Spencer'.

So by 1742 that mill had changed from fulling to grinding corn and in 1782 Spencer and Smith sold their shares in the 'water corn mill' to Wilson and Barton. Chapter 6 describes what happened next to the site but we look in more detail below at the 1782 and other transactions.

The mystery half-acre

On 15 April 1772 John Smith and James Spencer, oldest son of Timothy, sold for £20 to Richard Walker, a miner from Matlock:

'All that piece or parcel of Land lying in a piece of ground adjoining to the Lums Mills in the said parish of Matlock ... as the same was then measured marked or Staked out and Bordered on the South Side by a Brook called the Lums Mills Brook and on the North side by the East Moor and on the East side adjoining to the said Lums Smilting Mills and on the West side to Land the property of the said John Smith and James Spencer belonging to the Lums Corn Mill containing about half an acre (be the same more or less) Together with all waters watercourses [etc] ... to the same belonging'.

The plot of land must have been upstream of the existing corn mill because Walker agreed, in order to protect the amenity of the corn mill, that he would not compete in running a corn mill and would not affect the flow or quality of the water. Specifically, he would not:

'Erect or build any Mill or Mills upon the said piece of Ground ... to be employed in grinding any sort of Corn or grain whatsoever or by any ways or means whatsoever turn molest avert Stop or alter the usual course of the water or brook running through the said piece or parcel of land ... whereby the Mill called the Lums Corn Mill standing below upon the said Brook belonging to the said John Smith and James Spencer shall be damaged hindered annoyed or Injured but that he ... shall at all times prevent the same by keeping the Stream or watercourse in good repair and Condition ... [and that he would not] buddle any lead ore or Slags or throw in any vestry or rubbish or by any ways or means whatsoever discolour the water whereby the same shall detriment or Injure as aforesaid any other work or Mill belonging to the said John Smith and James Spencer in the Trade of a Dyer or in grinding corn or other things' (Indenture in AS archive).

Almost straight away Walker transferred the land on to Adam Simpson on similar terms, the deed reciting that it was actually Simpson who had funded the purchase and was always the intended transferee (Indenture 9 May 1772 in AS archive).

The references to John Smith and James Spencer trading as dyers and grinding corn or other things is intriguing. It is understandable that they did not want Richard Walker or his successors competing with them as corn grinders or interfering with the water required for their own businesses. Their corn mill was, as we shall see, on the site of the Bleach Works but it is not clear where there was a dye works. Could it be the mill a little lower down Lumsdale which was sold as a bleach works in 1812?

Smith and Spencer were also concerned about pollution from lead processing in the valley above their mills. Lead ore was washed in buddles before smelting but the term is now used in relation to the earlier processes involving the bole. Maybe the term was still in use in 1782 in relation to washing ore for cupola smelting or secondary slag milling.

On 20 November 1782 the half-acre of land was sold again for £80 by the executors of Adam Simpson including Richard Arkwright, junior, his son-in-law. It included now *'all that new erected Building* [italics added] lately erected and built by the said Adam Simpson deceased situate standing and being in a piece of Ground adjoining to the Lumbs Mills' so it appears Simpson had complied with his undertaking and built something other than a mill, though what he built is not stated (Indenture in AS archive).

The geography of this half-acre is hard, if not impossible, to work out. If, as one would expect, it is in the area of what became the Lower and Upper Bleach Works and Lumsdale House, how could the brook form the southern boundary? Did the Bentley Brook at that time vere to the west a little further north than the spot where it now goes under the road? Bray, early in 1783, describes a little mill at the bottom of the water falls turned by a small branch of the stream which was conducted by a channel made for the purpose. East Moor was quite a long way to the north and included the waste and manorial land at the top of the valley which belonged to other people.

The Nattes drawing - again

The land on which the new building has been erected is said to adjoin a smelting mill on the east side but there is no other evidence of a smelting mill below the waterfall. Can the drawing by Jean Claude Nattes help? (Plate 11.) It shows, in 1798, a succession of buildings on the high west bank of the brook. Were they, or did they include, the 'new building' of Adam Simpson? They look more like domestic buildings than mills of any kind. What is the equipment in the foreground? There is a launder bringing water from much higher up and what appears to be a water wheel with no clear purpose. In front of that could be a pair of fulling stocks but they are not connected to a cam and would have to be decades old.

John Boucher interprets the equipment as including a water balance pump:

'This pump uses a constant inflow of water into a timber bucket on one end - as it fills up it overbalances the pump rods at the other end and makes a stroke - then being emptied at the bottom of the stroke. The capstan winch and pulley in the timber frame are typical of a shaft pumping installation, and would have no place in a fulling mill' (personal communication).

There is however no obvious purpose for a pump. There is no limestone here to be mined with a shaft and the coal outcrop is not near. Perhaps the answer is simply that artistic licence led Mr Nattes to include a feature of interest in the foreground and that it is a collection of redundant machinery that may or may not have been used in that location.

Another question, however: what was the function of the water wheel in the Upper Bleach Works on the edge of the stable yard? It was fed by water from the wooden launder along the side of the valley as late as 1905, perhaps even continuously from 1798. Is it that old? It did not appear to have a function in the drying processes carried on in that part of the nineteenth century bleach works. It has been suggested that it provided power to the tramway between the Lower and Upper Bleachworks but in 1905 there was a windlass for that purpose. An Arkwright Society booklet has said that the wheel pit contained the remains of a wooden water wheel and there is some ironwork visible today but there are many unanswered questions.

We can only say that the corn mill, formerly a walk or fulling mill, was on part of the acre of land bought by Wilson and Barton from Spencer and Smith, now superseded by the Upper and Lower Bleach Works. The gritstone wheel in the Upper Bleach Works, for which there is no obvious use in a bleaching process, could well be a survivor from an early corn mill on this site.

Wilson and Barton

The buyers of the half acre on 20 November 1782 were Luke Wilson, a miller, and Thomas Barton, a miner. On the same day they bought the Lumsdale corn mill - formerly the fulling mill - from George Smith for £125 (see above). They were brothers-in-law, having both married into the Fox family of Starkholmes in 1772 and 1777 respectively. They appear to have been investors in a wide field of enterprises. By an agreement with Richard Arkwright junior and his wife Mary, processed through the High Court in 1784 and 1785, the original of which is in the Arkwright Society archive, they bought from the Arkwrights a quarter-share in nine messuages (that is dwelling houses and their outbuildings), eight barns, gardens, stables and orchards, 150 acres of land, 50 acres of meadow, 100 acres of pasture and shares in ten lead mines and paid a sum of £1,100 for them.

They were now, in 1782, putting together an estate in lower Lumsdale.

Fairly quickly after their purchase, however, on 1 January 1783, Wilson and Barton sold on the combined property to a consortium of prospective cotton spinners by way of a lease for 1000 years at a sale price of £240 and a peppercorn rent. The property was the following:

'All that Water Corn Mill known by the name of the Lums Mill situate standing and being in Lumsdale in the Parish of Matlock aforesaid And Also all that piece of parcel of inclosed Ground in which the said Mill is situate and standing containing by estimation one Acre or thereabouts be the same more or less with all and singular other the buildings thereupon erected

And also all other the Mills Buildings pieces or parcels of Ground Hereditaments and premises which were heretofore purchased by them the said Luke Wilson and Thomas Barton of and from George Smith of Tansley in the said County of Derby Dyer and Timothy Spencer of Tansley aforesaid yeoman and of and from the Executors named and appointed in and by the last Will and Testament of Adam Simpson late of Bonsall in the said County of Derby Gentleman deceased or any of them

Together with all Ways Waters Watercourses Streams Dams Weirs Goits Walls ffences Easements priviledges Rights Members and Appurtenences whatsoever to the said Water Corn Mill piece or parcel of inclosed ground belonging or in any wise appertaining and the Reversion and Reversions Remainder and Remainders Rents Issues and Profits of all and singular the said premises hereby demised'.

The purchasers of the lease began trading as cotton spinners under the name of Watts, Lowe & Co. and their story is told in the next Chapter.

The other corn mill

The corn mill at the bottom of the ravine had stopped milling by 1783 but there was another corn mill at the top of the waterfall which was still in use forty-five years later. When

John Garton bought land from the trustees of Bonsall School in 1828 the purchase included 'All that Messuage dwellinghouse or tenement heretofore used as a Smelting Mill And also all the other mill heretofore used as a Smelting Mill but now used as a Corn mill situate lying and being in the parish of Matlock'. For the reasons explained in Chapter 3 we cannot be certain but it seems likely that this was the Grinding Mill or its predecessor. The presence of remnants of 'French' millstones in its vicinity is consistent although, as we say in Chapter 7, they could have been for grinding barytes. John Garton never claimed to be trading as a corn merchant however, though he may have had a tenant who did, and it seems likely that the mill was given over to barytes in any event.

The end of the 'old' industries

This chapter has tried to establish when and where there were other early industries in Lumsdale, notably fulling of woollen cloth and grinding of corn. Both needed water power - for the fulling stocks and the grinding stones respectively - and many of the old water powered mills along the River Derwent were at one time or another corn or fulling mills in the past. Caudwell's Mill at Rowsley is an example, as are the early mills on the Darley Abbey site near Belper. Both types of mills would have been important producers of essential consumer goods.

Wool - the textile on which fulling mills worked - was the staple cloth produced in, and exported by, Britain. The mechanisation of the production of silk (first at Thomas Lombe's silk mill built at Derby in 1721) and cotton (first at Richard Arkwright's cotton mill in Cromford built in 1771) inevitably led to cheaper clothing products. Cotton in particular was much more suitable for underwear. It is, therefore, not surprising that wool fulling and its associated dyeing and calendering processes declined as an industry along the Bentley Brook as well as elsewhere.

Woollen cloth, was of course, still needed but to compete the producers needed to invest in new technology and higher quality products. An example can be found in the nearby John Smedley Mill at Lea Mills near Matlock. Originally founded as a cotton spinning and muslin producing mill in 1784, by Peter Nightingale (who features in the Lumsdale story) and John Smedley, a decade or so later it extended its activities to include knitting and hosiery products. The company modernised its processes and premises and used high quality materials (see Wrigley 2011: 29-30; www.johnsmedley.com). In other words it succeeded by focusing on selling to the growing more affluent middle class market. Instead, in Lumsdale fulling mills had become corn mills.

One of the Lumsdale corn mills became the site of the new three storey cotton mill - a very different mill to the lead smelting, fulling and corn mills which preceded it. The scale and the extent of the mechanisation required to compete in the context of the developing industrial revolution meant that all future ventures needed to be on a similar scale. The corn mill lower down the valley which became Bailey's Flour Mill did survive, at least partly because the other Lumsdale corn mills did not and because it diversified: 'It was probably lack of competition and the relative isolation of the mill which led to the expansion of the complex in the eighteenth century to house a Malthouse' (Morris 2011: 15).

In the next chapter we focus on the mill which became the first mechanised factory in Lumsdale.

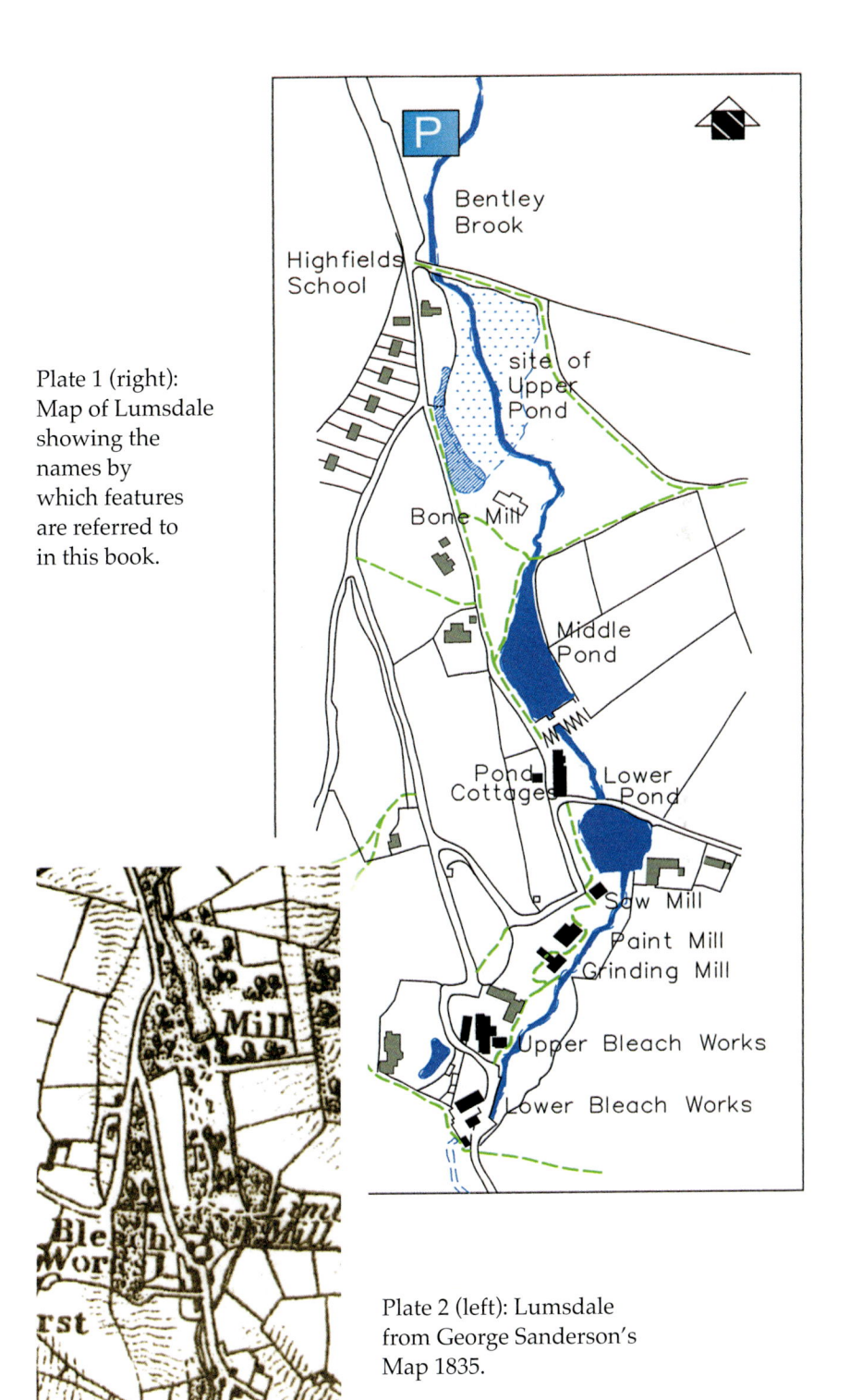

Plate 1 (right): Map of Lumsdale showing the names by which features are referred to in this book.

Plate 2 (left): Lumsdale from George Sanderson's Map 1835.

Plate 3: French burr stone near the Saw Mill 2016.

Plate 4: Postcard view of the Upper Pond, undated but probably c.1900, showing the dam wall, pond, the roofline of Ivy Cottage and cottages on the Chesterfield Road in the distance.

Plate 5: Postcard view of the Upper Pond, southern corner, with the sluice, the Bone Mill and the gable of the Bone Mill cottage c.1909.

Plate 6: Postcard view of the clapper bridge over the Bentley Brook at the point now known as the 'stepping stones' showing the wagon way to the quarries.

Plate 7: Pond Cottages, 2017.

Plate 8: Smelting House in Middleton Dale drawn by F.L. Chantrey, ARA, 1824.

Plate 9: The Paint Mill, 2017.

Plate 10: The oldest part of the Grinding Mill (right) with the Paint Mill beyond, 2017.

Plate 11: Lumsdale Mill near Matlock Derbyshire, drawn by J.C. Nattes, 17th September 1798.

Plate 12: Postcard view of Matlock Bank (near) View in Lumsdale 1906 showing the Grinding Mill, launder carrying water to the Upper Bleach Works and a pipe carrying spring water across the brook to the Lower Bleach Works.

Plate 13: Upper Bleach Works, 2017.

Plate 14: Postcard view of Garton's and other mills, Lumsdale, Matlock c.1900.

Plate 15: Lumsdale from the Wishing Stone Matlock c.1900.

Plate 16: Garton's Mill in a derelict state mid-20th century.

Plate 17: The last original Arkwright water frame
at Helmshore Mills Textile Museum.

6

COTTON SPINNING

'The rapid rise of the cotton manufacture in this country is a subject of astonishment to other nations'.

— (Glover 1830: XVI)

What has Arkwright got to do with Lumsdale?

In 1771 Richard Arkwright and three partners began building the first water-powered cotton mill at Cromford. In December they were advertising for skilled workmen to build the machinery and, although the building was not finished, it was in operation by March 1772 (Strange 2008: 2). It was originally a four storey building of 11 bays, 100ft (30.8m) long by 26ft (8m) wide. In 1785 it was extended by 38.5ft (11.7m) and another four bays. What you see today at the west end of the Cromford Mill yard is the extended building but a clear vertical line in the stonework marks the end of the original mill. The building included at its southern end an entrance lobby, a large office ('Mr. Arkwright's office'), both with hearths for warmth, and a staircase compartment. The main mill room measured internally about 74ft (22.5m) long by 26ft (8m) wide.

It was powered by water from the Bonsall Brook and the Cromford Sough turning a water wheel outside the building about mid-way along its length. The gearing from the wheel occupied the central section of the main room and reduced the space available for the water frames.

Nevertheless there was room for sixteen spinning frames, arranged in pairs along the length of the room, each with forty-eight spindles (Strange 2008: Appendix C). In 1776/1777 Arkwright built a second mill on the site, larger than the original mill at 124ft by 31ft (37.9m by 9.45m) and seven storeys high. The first mill was severely damaged by fire in 1929 but survives (at least to the height of three storeys) and the second mill was almost completely destroyed by fire in 1890. Production of cotton ceased in about 1840 however when Richard Arkwright, junior, lost the rights to the essential water supply.

Arkwright's ground-breaking factory system depended upon a suite of machines, all in the same building and with an organised work-force, to process raw cotton into spun thread. Edward Baines, writing in 1835, reviewed the different processes through which cotton went in its conversion into thread:

'The cotton is brought to the mill in bags, just as it is received from America, Egypt or India; ... It is passed though the *willow*, the *scutching-machine*, and the *spreading-machine*, in order to be opened, cleaned, and evenly spread. By the *carding-engine* the fibres are combed out and laid parallel to each other, and the fleece is compressed into a sliver. The sliver is repeatedly drawn and doubled in the *drawing-frame,* more perfectly to straighten the fibres, and to equalize the grist. The *roving-frame*, by rollers and spindles, produces a coarse and loose thread; which the *mule* or *throstle* spins into yarn' (Baines 1835: 242, italics in the original).

Arkwright's pre-eminence stemmed in large part from the fact that he gained patents for machinery to cover crucial stages of the raw cotton to thread process. Richard Arkwright's spinning machine, when powered by a water wheel, came to be known as the water frame. Plate 17 shows the last surviving original Arkwright water frame in the Helmshore Mills Textile Museum. (Samuel Crompton's mule - used in the last stage of the process outlined above - was a later development of it.) On 3 July 1769 Arkwright obtained a patent, giving him exclusive rights for fourteen years, for his spinning machine and on 6 December

1775 he obtained a further patent, again for fourteen years, for an improved carding, drawing and roving machine. Registration of the patent was intended to put the details and designs of inventions in the public domain but to give their inventor exclusive rights to them for the duration of the patent. Arkwright was thus able to charge substantial royalties for the use of his inventions. Lancashire spinners complained in 1780 that the rate was £7,000 for every 1000 spindles. In 1785 Robert Peel, grandfather of the Prime Minister, reported that the rate was somewhat less at £2 per spindle (Fitton, 2012: 93).

The high cost of buying licences to use Arkwright's technology encouraged many to take a chance by using his inventions without permission. Arkwright took steps to stop them, including legal action. In 1781 he began actions against nine alleged infringers of his carding patent and chose to proceed first against a Colonel Mordaunt who, he thought, would be an easy conquest. Mordaunt won, not because he could prove that Arkwright's patent had no merit but because a jury accepted that Arkwright had failed to describe it openly and adequately in his specification or, as Mordaunt's counsel submitted, 'had absolutely contrived to hide it' (Fitton 2012: 97).

In 1782 therefore, competitors of Richard Arkwright were anticipating the expiry of the spinning patent in July 1783 and considered themselves safe from prosecution under the carding patent as a result of the failed action. As Thomas Walsham put it in a letter to Jedediah Strutt, 'as from the loss of the Roving Patent in 1781 all the country became Spinners as soon as ever they cou'd get machinery' (Fitton & Wadsworth, 2012: 94). So it was that a group of men got together to exploit the power of the Bentley Brook to process and spin cotton in their own little factory and they called themselves Watts, Lowe & Co.

Watts, Lowe & Co, Lumsdale

Little was recorded about Watts, Lowe & Co in the Lumsdale

tour guide materials except that the firm opened a cotton spinning mill in the 1780s in competition with Richard Arkwright using his water frame technology, possibly in breach of his patents, operated it for about 30 years and were then bankrupt. That is broadly (but not wholly) correct but much more information is now available.

In tracing the members of the firm one must bear in mind that this is the period before national registration of births, deaths and marriages was introduced in 1837 and parish registers do not necessarily distinguish between two people of the same name. The information which follows has a consistency which is compelling but which, therefore, cannot be guaranteed.

The purchasers

Fortunately we have in the Arkwright Society archive the deed dated 1 January 1783 by which the Watts, Lowe consortium acquired from Luke Wilson and Thomas Barton a water corn mill called Lums Mill with an acre of ground and other mills and buildings together with rights over watercourses and other easements. That deed is reproduced in part towards the end of the last chapter. There were fifteen purchasers named in the deed with their home towns and occupations. Several had other interests in the textile industry. We do not know how they contributed capital or shared in the running or the profits of the partnership but we can infer that some contributed capital, some know-how and, in the case of others, it was maybe who they knew rather than what they knew. To put it more kindly, the partners had the right connections at the right time.

They were described in the deed as follows:

- Job Watts of the City of Bristol, Hosier
- Wintour Harris of the same place, Gentleman
- William Watts of the same place, Hosier
- William Green of the same place, Linen Draper
- George Ewbank of the City of London, Silkman
- Thomas Green of Newbury in the County of Berks, Plumber

- Samuel Statham of Nottingham, Hosier
- Thomas Martin of Nottingham, Hosier
- Thomas Else of Sutton in Ashfield in the County of Nottingham, Hosier
- William Milnes of Ashover in the County of Derby, Grocer
- John Milnes of Ashover, Grocer
- Thomas Lowe of Matlock, Cotton Manufacturer
- Adam Wolley the younger of Matlock, Gentleman
- Jeremiah Cooper of Matlock, Engineer and
- Benjamin Latham of Matlock, Cotton Manufacturer

We will tell you what we know about these people in the same order as they are named in the deed.

Job Watts

It was Job Watts who, with his brother and Thomas Lowe, gave his name to the firm. He was married in Bristol in 1763 to Mary Green so may have been related by marriage to William and Thomas Green. He had one Henry Green as his apprentice in 1777 (*Register of Duties Paid*: 77). He is recorded as a hosier in Bristol directories and poll books from 1774 to 1784. In 1775 Job Watts had been a subscriber to the Committee for the Relief of Persons Confined for Small Debts. He died in Bristol in 1792 (*Bath Chronicle* 15 March 1792).

He was interested in politics and in 1780 wrote to Edmund Burke, MP for Bristol, advising him that certain rumours and 'religious prejudices' were likely to affect his popularity in the run- up to an election. Burke had supported a Bill for the relief of persons in custody for debt and was criticised that 'he had used his earnest endeavours to effect the ruin of the credit, the trade and the fortune of his constituents'. He had also supported concessions to Ireland and a Bill for the relief of Roman Catholics. On 10 August 1780 Burke replied to Watts at length, thanked him 'as on former occasions I have been obliged to you for your hearty and effectual services' and assured him:

'I never thought it wise, my dear Mr. Watts, to force men into enmity with the State by ill-treatment, upon any pretence, either of civil or religious party; and if I never thought it wise in any circumstances, still less do I think it wise when we have lost one half of our empire by one idle quarrel, to distract and perhaps to lose too, the other half by another quarrel, not less judicious and absurd' (Weare 1894: 150).

We will return to him later.

Wintour Harris

Wintour Harris was a solicitor and attorney, probably baptised (as Winter Harris) at St. Mary Redcliffe in 1749. He held office in the Bristol City Corporation and was Deputy Chamberlain at the time of the Bristol Bridge riots in 1793, becoming involved in the extension of leases of the bridge tolls alleged to be in excess of the City's statutory powers (Jones 1980: 74). Later he became Chamberlain but on his death in 1818 it was found that his accounts showed a deficit of some £3,600. Sureties were called in but his estate was insolvent (Latimer 1887: 80; Latimer was the editor of the *Bristol Mercury* 1858-83).

William Watts

William Watts was also a Bristol hosier. When he advertised his business in High Street for sale in 1815 he claimed that he had been trading there for upwards of 53 years, that is from about 1762. It was bought by a Mr Edwards who was pleased to announce his succession to Mr Watts and to offer 'a most excellent assortment of Hats and Hosiery of every description' (*Bristol Mirror* 30 December 1815 and 24 August 1816). William had however been made bankrupt in January 1809 but he appears to have co-operated with his Commissioners in Bankruptcy and disclosed and handed over his assets such that in September they were able to give notice of intention to issue a Certificate, in other words to discharge him (*Bristol Mirror* 4 February 1809; *London Gazette* 12 September 1809).

The realisation and distribution of his assets dragged on for years however and the sale of his interest in the Watts, Lowe properties in 1813 was transacted and signed on his behalf by (in effect) his trustees in bankruptcy. In January 1816, shortly after he advertised his business for sale, he was made bankrupt again (*London Gazette* 6 January 1816) so it appears that his business was more popular than profitable. We will also come back to his earlier connections.

William Green, George Ewbank, Thomas Green

William Green was in partnership with another linen draper, William Tagart, in Bristol until 1796 (*London Gazette* 27 February 1796) but we know nothing more about him or about George Ewbank or Thomas Green.

Samuel Statham and Thomas Martin

Samuel Statham and Thomas Martin were in another partnership in Nottingham until 1787 (*London Gazette* 9 January 1787). Samuel was also in partnership with Edwyn Statham and Henry Garton as hosiers and chapmen until they were all formally bankrupted in 1806 (*London Gazette* 14 June 1808).

Thomas Else

Thomas Else was a hosier in the Nottinghamshire town of Sutton-in-Ashfield, home of the Unwin family who may well have employed him. George Bonser writes:
'The remarkable energy and business perspicacity of the founders of the family succeeded in establishing an enormous connection which at one time bid fair to rival the Strutts and Arkwrights, and the quality of the Sutton Ginghams and Nankeens was famous all over the country. (Note: Gingham was a cotton cloth dyed before it was woven, and was extensively used for Bed Curtains, while Nankeen was a cloth of firm texture made from a cotton of a yellow dye, and was of extreme durability. These, with

Hosiery, were the staple of the Firm). The first warehouse is said to have been built at the top of Mount Street, but was soon found to be too small, the works near Eastfield Side were commenced and the Mill Dam made c. 1740. ... To provide for further extensions Mills were built at Tansley near Matlock, the water there being of such excellent quality for bleaching purposes and a large traffic between the two works was carried on by waggons' (Bonser, 1948; chapter 19).

The Mills Index on the Derbyshire Heritage website attributes to Samuel Unwin not only the Tansley Top Mill and Spinning Mill but also Bailey's Mill on the Bentley Brook towards Matlock Green (http://www.derbyshireheritage.co.uk/Menu/Archaeology/Mills.php accessed 15.2.2019).

William and John Milnes

William and John Milnes of Ashover, described here as grocers but elsewhere as lead merchants, came from a family of considerable wealth with many interests in other mills and lead-working activities and connections to Ashover and Bonsall. Dorothy, daughter of a John Twigg married a William Milnes in 1752 and they had sons William and John (Ince *Pedigrees* 008d) who acquired and brought into the partnership much of the land at the northern end of Lumsdale. Ince notes 'This John Twigge gave most of his property to his cousins Milns of Ashover'. This appears to be the same John Twigg who was a lessee of land in Lumsdale in 1749.

William Milnes, senior, died on 14 August 1781 aged 60. William, junior, lived until 1814 and John was still living in 1829. Their sister Mary married Barker Bosley or Bossley, mentioned again below (Glover 1833: 57).

Thomas Lowe

Thomas Lowe has long been recognised as a Watts, Lowe partner local to Matlock, although the closeness of his involvement with other characters in the Lumsdale story has not been appreciated until now. He is not the Thomas Lowe who was Richard Arkwright's millwright. Describing himself as a cotton manufacturer, he must have had some previous experience and it does appear that he was the principal manager of the business. He died in 1803.

Adam Wolley

Adam Wolley, born in Matlock in 1758, came from another Derbyshire dynasty with homes on Riber and at Allen Hill. He was the attorney and antiquarian whom we mentioned in the last chapter as the man who collected and left to the British Museum a vast collection of documents, the Wolley Manuscripts, which are of great value to Derbyshire historians. He was involved in many transactions and, if he was not a party to them, he was often witness to the signatures. He died in 1827 leaving no sons.

Jeremiah Cooper and Benjamin Latham

Jeremiah Cooper may be the man of that name who died in Matlock in 1795. Benjamin Latham does not appear in the Matlock Parish Registers of the time but may be a member of the Wirksworth family of that name (Ince *Pedigrees* 101b)

The consortium

So how did this diverse collection of people come together and how did four of them come to be in Bristol? Six of them had connections in or near Matlock and the Greens may have been related to the Watts family but is there another family connection?

If you skip forward a generation you find that the first wife of John Garton, later the Lumsdale bleacher but then a farmer at Heaton Norris (now part of Stockport), was Lydia Allsop a widow from Matlock whom he married in Manchester Cathedral on 29 September 1814. One of the witnesses was a Joseph Watts. Lydia's first husband was John Allsop whom she married in Matlock in 1805. Her maiden name was Lowe.

Lydia Lowe, baptised in Matlock in 1781, was the daughter of Thomas Lowe and Hannah Watts, married in Matlock in 1768. Hannah's brothers included Job, baptised in 1738, and William, baptised in 1748.

Were these the Job and William Watts who were in Bristol from about 1762 or 1763? A Job Watts hosted a meeting on 19 November 1760 to consider enclosing the Matlock commons (*Derby Mercury* 17 October 1760). This could have been our Job or his father, another Job, who died in Matlock in 1764 and, as there is no Job or William Watts in the Parish Records after that date, it seems very likely that they moved to Bristol in the early 1760s.

So we have a very strong combination of men with knowledge and experience of hosiery and other fabric manufacturing, even cotton spinning, and other useful trades and connections, both locally and in Bristol, to wealth and a desire to invest in new technology when opportunity arose.

The Cotton Mill and Arkwright's patent

The mill which the new partnership constructed was similar to many other cotton mills built around that time. It was built of gritstone with walls 2ft thick. Its orientation was south-west/north-east with the Bentley Brook to the east and hillside to the west.

The external dimensions were about 61ft (18.5m) by 29ft 6in (9m), internally about 56ft 9in (17.3m) by 27ft 6in (8.4m). The width was just a few inches more than Arkwright's first mill at Cromford and fits into a pattern analysed by Stanley Chapman. He found that out of sixty-six cotton mills built between 1771 and 1799 half were built between 28ft and 30ft wide and, of thirty-three in which he was able to identify the number of frames, the largest number, seven, accommodated in the region of 1000 spindles (Chapman 1981, cited in Strange 2008: Appendix C). The length of the available floor space in Watts, Lowe's mill was somewhat less than the first mill at Cromford, however, and it is consistent with the number of fourteen frames which were eventually disposed of with some 800 spindles.

The archaeological review undertaken by Salford University in 2017 describes it like this:

'The early mill was placed at an approximate 45° angle to Bentley Brook, but parallel to its course slightly further to the north, suggesting that the original headrace for the mill was taken from the bend in the water course. It survives to a height of two storeys, which probably represents the original maximum extent, typical of early Arkwright-type mills, and was of eight-bays length. A small projecting tower at the western end of the south wall almost certainly represents a privy tower, a distinctive feature of the early Arkwright-type mills and with a stair tower projecting from the north-western corner. The waterwheel was placed externally against the western gable, within what appears to have been an open wheel pit, unlike those enclosed within wheel houses to the north. A large central aperture in the gable wall has a dressed semi-circular arch, and would have transferred power from the wheel into the mill. A slightly projecting aperture with stone surround high in the gable wall at the northern end of the wheel pit probably represents the course of the original headrace, with a timber chute probably projecting the water directly onto a backshot wheel' (Wild 2017: 63).

In fact the mill was originally of three storeys with an attic as is shown by photographs taken around 1900 before it fell into disrepair (Plate 14) and later in a state of dereliction (Plate 16). The stair gave access to and from a driveway off what is now Lumsdale Road at third floor level, convenient for delivering raw cotton to the upper levels of the mill for cleaning and carding before they went downstairs for spinning. The comment about the original headrace accords with a contemporary account. William Bray published the second edition of his *Sketch of a Tour into Derbyshire* in 1783 and, having included 'much new matter (derived from a repetition of visits to the principal scene of description)', referred to the Lumsdale waterfall and 'at the bottom is a little mill, turned by a small branch of the stream, which is conducted by a channel made for that purpose' (Bray 1783: 128). The preface to his book is, however, dated February 1783, very shortly after Watts, Lowe acquired the site so Bray may have seen the water supply to the preceding corn mill, or indeed both mills.

Watts, Lowe's business of cotton spinning was certainly active by the beginning of 1785 and was using the water frame invented or improved by Richard Arkwright. Arkwright was not content to see his patents fail however. He made a number of unsuccessful attempts to persuade Parliament to extend their life by statute. In 1783 he acted against a number of spinners for breach of his spinning patent before it expired and succeeded (Fitton 2012: 101). Then he launched an action against Peter Nightingale of Lea to try to recover the validity of his carding patent. At the trial on 17 February 1785 witnesses for Arkwright said they had been able to construct the machine from the drawings and specifications of the patent and the jury found in his favour without retiring. Just eleven days later on 28 February his lawyer, George Goodwin of Winster, arrived in Lumsdale 'to give Notice to the Proprietors of the Cotton Mills there not to work' (Fitton 2012: 105-113).

In response a number of cotton spinners trading in the Manchester market combined to take further action against Arkwright to have the Nightingale verdict annulled in an action by way of a writ of *scire facias* brought in the name of the Crown. *Scire facias*, literally 'to make known', was an ancient form of action which, in the case of patents, called upon the defendant to show cause why his patent should not be annulled. Among them, contributing towards the costs one shilling for each spindle employed by them, was Watts, Lowe & Co. (Wheeler 1836: 521).

The case was heard in Westminster Hall on 25 June 1785 and the evidence called was more wide-ranging than in previous cases. The judge asked the jury to consider three questions. Is the invention new? If so, was it invented by Mr Arkwright? And in any event, was it adequately described in the patent? The jury found for the Crown and against Arkwright. He sought leave to appeal but was refused and the patent was cancelled (Fitton 2012: Chapter 5).

We do not know whether Watts, Lowe & Co. complied with Arkwright's request to cease trading in February 1785. By June they were free to do so in any event and we have the occasional snapshot of their continued trading.

The history of the business

A complaint to the cotton supplier

On 11 August 1788 the firm wrote to Samuel Oldknow of Stockport, a major supplier of both cotton goods and raw cotton to the spinning industry and, from 1784 until 1828 a debtor to the Arkwrights, father and son, to whom he eventually owed nearly £206,000 (Fitton 2012: 239). The letter, which is the only original Watts, Lowe document we have discovered, survives in the Oldknow Papers at the John Rylands Library (SO/1/335, transcribed by courtesy of the University of Manchester).

Lumsdale Mills
11 Aug. 1788

Sir
Yours of the 8th Inst. We duly rec'd along with the Invoice of 20 Bags of Cotton Wool. We ordered of Mr. Parker only 10 Bags, which we were to have with the Merchts allowance. The tare allowed is considerable less than we have from London or Bristol so much as to make a penny [in the] pound differance – We are not satisfied with the tare by any means & and unless we can have the Merchts customary allowance we wish to have nothing to do with it. At any rate we will have only 10 Bags. We will get Mr. Milnes to write to Mr.Parker upon the subject, & in the interim we remain

Sir, your most h[um]ble servants
Watts, Lowe & Co.

It is interesting that they were dealing with one of the major players in the cotton industry, an associate of Richard Arkwright, and were prepared to challenge him. 'Tare' is the difference between the gross and net weight of a bag of cotton after taking into account the weight of the hessian sack or other packaging. The letter also shows that Watts, Lowe were also buying cotton from London and Bristol and that one of the Milnes brothers, William or John, was actively involved in the business.

The 1790s

In August 1790 Job Watts of the City of Bristol, Hosier, and Thomas Low [sic] of Matlock, Cotton Manufacturer, insured their cotton mill at Matlock ('brick, stone and tiled - First Class') with the Sun Fire Office for £300 and its utensils and stock, including machinery, for another £1000. The annual premium was £3.3s.0d. (£3.15p) (Policy no.572862 at DRO D504/3/4/19).

In 1796 and 1798 Watts, Lowe & Co and Thomas Lowe, with W & J Milnes, Adam Wolley, Luke Wilson and others whose names appear in the Lumsdale story, subscribed to the local Association for the Prosecution of Felons. They agreed to pay a yearly subscription of three shillings (15p) and resolved to pay rewards on a sliding scale for information leading to a conviction: for burglary or any other capital offence, three guineas (£3.15); for stealing grain or livestock, two guineas (£2.10); for stealing rabbits or vegetables, causing damage or any other kind of 'petit larceny', half a guinea (52p) (Derby Mercury 29 December 1796 and 14 June 1798).

In the 1798 Land Tax Assessments they are shown as proprietors of land occupied by a number of tenants. The premises include five dwellinghouses, later identified, in the schedule to an 1886 mortgage, as what we now call Pond Cottages, 'formerly made out of two cupolas and other buildings by or at the expense of Watts, Lowe & Co.'.

Dissolution

On 7 August 1807 the six remaining partners of Watts, Lowe and Co dissolved their partnership. They were William Watts, Wintour Harris, Thomas Green, William Lowe (oldest son of Thomas, who had died), John Milnes and Adam Wolley (*London Gazette* 29 August 1807).

In the meantime William Watts, Wintour Harris, William and John Milnes, Thomas Lowe and Adam Wolley had been in partnership with others as Barker Bossley & Co. in another venture at Cressbrook Mill. One partner left in 1802 and what was left of that partnership was dissolved on 20 February 1809 (*London Gazette* 31 August 1802 and 28 March 1809).

Sale of the cotton mill

In the *Derby Mercury* of 28 March 1811 there appears the following advertisement.

Cotton Spinning Machinery &c. at Lumsdale Mill
TO BE SOLD BY AUCTION
By Mr. JACKSON
Upon the Premises at Lumsdale Mill, near Matlock, in the County of Derby, on Wednesday the 10th Day of April, 1811 and following Days
ALL the Cotton Spinning Machinery, and other articles of every description upon the Premises (without reserve,) consisting of 14 Spinning Frames containing about 800 Spindles, a part of which is nearly new and has been very little worked, 21 sets of Cards with Covering, Drawing and Roving Frames, and Cans, Doubling and Twisting Mills, and Ball Winding Machines, large quantity of Skips, Roving and Spinning Bobbins, Willow, or Cotton Picking Machine, and every other Article necessary for carrying on the Spinning Business; also Cast Iron Materials for a new Water Wheel of 27 feet diameter, with Oak Arms and Rolled Iron Buckets, an upright Metal Shaft and sundry Wheels, a quantity of Old Cast Metal, Iron, Brass and Lead, Blacksmith's Bellows. Iron Anvil, and other Implements; also Turning Lathes, Work Benches, Cutting Engine, and a very exsive [sic] Assortment of other Articles.

Descriptive Catalogues may be had at the Bell Inn, at Derby; Bell Inn, Ashbourne; Angel Inn, Chesterfield; George Inn, Alfreton: Rutland Arms, Bakewell; at the White Lion, Ashover; at the Inns at Matlock Bath; and of the Auctioneer at Wirksworth.

So it appears that someone continued to operate the business after the partnership was dissolved in 1807, and invested in new spinning equipment and the parts for a new water wheel. It may well have been William Lowe who continued to describe himself as a cotton spinner in Matlock Parish Records until 1829. He was in possession or occupation of one of the converted Pond Cottages when they were sold in 1813 (see below) but not in 1821.

The fact that the sale in 1811 was 'without reserve' meant that everything must go, at any price, and indicates that the then owner had been forced to close the business and sell up without even being able to put together the parts of his new water wheel. We do not know the outcome of the auction but, with no reserve, it would be unusual for there to be no bids and no sale. So it would be very unlikely if any business continued after that date.

Then on 24 December 1813 the cotton mill building – probably an empty shell – and the whole of the Watts, Lowe estate in Lumsdale were sold for £1,500 to Gamaliel Jones a newcomer to Lumsdale. He came from a long line of Presbyterian ministers in Cheshire (Brooks 1848: 472) but his father, John, was a banker and tea dealer in Manchester. His bank, Jones, Lloyd and Co., was later absorbed into the District Bank and ultimately NatWest (Nightingale 2003). As we shall see in Chapter 7, Gamaliel did not follow in the family business but he obviously enjoyed the benefit of some of the family wealth.

The sale deed refers to the cotton mill and the acre of land on which it stood, formerly in the possession of William Watts and his partners in Watts, Lowe & Co but now unoccupied, two newly erected messuages or dwelling houses nearby, a croft of land which had contained one old dwelling house, taken down soon after 1791 and replaced by two others by or at the expense of Watts, Lowe & Co., the 52 acres which had been allotted to Peter Nightingale (in the enclosures of 1780) with the (single) large pond or reservoir created by or at the expense of Watts, Lowe and all the waterworks and other appurtenances which went with them. Separately mentioned and included (because they were still held under the 999-year lease granted in 1749) were the land and cupolas which William Milnes had bought in 1789 and 1790 and the five dwelling houses into which they had been converted soon afterwards by or at the expense of Watts, Lowe and Company (Deed of Release 1813 in private hands).

Who signed the sale deed?

Who, from the original fifteen members of the Watts, Lowe consortium were still involved in 1813? The parties to the deed were Luke Wilson and Thomas Barton (who had bought the site in 1782 and still owned the freehold), William and John Milnes (in whose names parts of the estate had been previously acquired), Wintour Harris, Thomas Green, Adam Wolley and William Lowe, (as other surviving former partners), John Worthington and Jonathan Simmons, (who held as assignees or trustees the assets of the bankrupt William Watts), William Watts himself (to confirm his agreement) and Gamaliel Jones. The deed has twelve red wax seals but only eleven signatures. William Milnes had died after the date of the deed but without having executed it but his son later confirmed the transaction on his behalf.

The sale price of £1,500 would today be represented by a sum of over £150,000 so, although two of the former Watts, Lowe & Co. partners may not have been able to pay their current debts and been bankrupted as individuals, we have seen no evidence that (as has often been stated) the firm itself was insolvent. They had substantial assets in the form of their Lumsdale estate and the surviving partners would have benefited from the sale.

The other cotton mill

Thus came the end of the Watts, Lowe era in Lumsdale – but that is not the whole story of cotton spinning in Lumsdale. Fitton told us that in 1785 Richard Arkwright arranged 'to give Notice to the Proprietors of the Cotton Mills there not to work' (Fitton 2012: 113) so it appears that there was more than one mill then operating. Fortunately we have another newspaper advertisement which gives a clue.

The *Derby Mercury* on 29 November 1787 advertised:

> To be sold by private Contract
> A COTTON-MILL, situate in the Parish
> of MATLOCK, and County of Derby, called the
> Upper Lums Mill, containing 5 Setts of Carding Machines,
> 1 Drawing, 1 Roving, and 5 Spinning Frames, all in complete Repair, and now at Work. – The Water Wheel is 20
> Feet Diameter, and supplied by a plentiful and regular Stream.
> Also a small DWELLING-HOUSE, with a Stable and
> other suitable Out-Buildings, adjoining to the said Mill.
> The above Premises are held of the Lords of the Manor of
> Matlock, at the yearly rent of 6£ under a Lease, 15 years
> whereof are now unexpired.
> For further Particulars apply to Mr. ADAM WOLLEY
> Jun. at Matlock, who will give Tickets to view the Premises.

So sometime before 1787 another cotton mill was operating in Lumsdale and, by reference to the Landlords and terms of the lease, we can identify the mill as the Bone Mill.

As we have seen in Chapter 3, when fifty-two acres in Upper Lumsdale were enclosed in 1780 the Lords of the Manor retained the right to lease 'Lumb's Mill with all the buildings, weirs, goits and appurtenances' (Bryan, 1903: 92). The term and rent payable under the lease match exactly the lease dated 19 October 1778 from the Lords of the Manor to George White of 'the Lumbs Smelting Mills for 24 years commencing 5 April 1779 under the yearly Rent of 6£' (Wolley Mss. 6669 f.257d). White's Mill is shown on the first edition of the 1" Ordnance Survey map of 1840 and its location and physical description, including the size of the wheel pit, match what we now call the Bone Mill below the Upper Pond.

It appears that the mill was still smelting lead in 1779 so did it become a cotton mill at the same time as the three storey cotton mill lower down the valley - or earlier or later? By 1821 the building had become a bone mill (Bryan, 1903: 52) but we do not know how long it continued as a spinning mill.

The Lords of the Manor retained their rights as landlords and they demanded (and the Garton family paid) the £6 rent until they sold in 1907 to Ernest Richard Farnsworth (Particulars of sale DRO D504/131/4). In 1938 however the whole estate was sold freehold and the rent is paid no more.

The end of cotton spinning in Lumsdale

The exact date of the end of cotton spinning at both the cotton mills in Lumsdale is not known but it would appear that sometime in the 1810s the remaining Watts, Lowe & Co consortium and the lessees of the Bone Mill site decided that cotton spinning was no longer an attractive investment. This is perhaps not surprising for both personal and business reasons.

Members of the consortium might have wished to realise their assets in the cotton mill to provide for themselves in old age; after all some members had already died and two had been made bankrupt. However, the economic context is the crucial factor. Many mills had been built using Arkwright's technology but in the face of competition from the buoyant Lancashire cotton producing area - with its easier access to cotton via the port of Liverpool - only the bigger and more up-to-date mills could survive. The cotton mill at Holymoorside (between Matlock and Chesterfield) did survive, partly one imagines because the nearby Lumsdale ones did not and partly because in the 1840s new owners upgraded the technology (http://holymoorsidehistorysociety.com/page19.html). Clearly the Lumsdale cotton spinners decided the time was ripe to take their money and, if possible for them, invest elsewhere. It is worth stressing that, whilst the partnership was dissolved, there is no evidence that the business itself was insolvent.

However cotton firms that did continue, according to Chapman, found that the principal constraint on their growth 'taking the century 1760 - 1860 as a whole, was clearly the difficulties and cost of marketing' (Chapman 1979: 66).

'A small firm might grow within the connexions of an established concern, but to grow beyond this size meant breaking into the intensely competitive domestic market, or into the speculative overseas markets, and most lacked the means or connexions to do so' (ibid).

Maybe the owners and lessees of the Lumsdale cotton mills realised that the connections they had would not have been sufficient for the more complex industrial and financial landscape of the nineteenth century. By 1821, however, the cotton mill had been resurrected as a bleaching mill - an industry which survived for almost a century but which proved to be the last phase of industrialisation in Lumsdale.

7

BLEACH, BARYTES AND BONE: THE GARTONS

'Most bleacheries are overgrown with the moss of secrecy, prejudice and tradition, and harnessed to rule-of-thumb methods that have been evolved from primordial ancestral experience'

— (Mathews, 1921: V)

The bleaching process

Early bleaching

In the introduction to his *Experiments on Bleaching* in 1756 Francis Home wrote in Edinburgh of the history of bleaching cloth:

'It was, no doubt, soon discovered, that the sun and the dews, or frequent watering, were capable, in hot climates, of whitening cloth. This was certainly the most ancient practice; and is still used, as I have been told, in the *East Indies*. But colder and more variable climates were obliged to substitute somewhat in the place of the heat which they wanted. Hence the use of salts in bleaching. Chance no doubt made the first discovery; but when or where these were first used history is silent. Their use began probably in some of our most northern countries. The cloth would at first be boiled in a lixive of alkaline salts, and then exposed to the influence of the sun and dews. This method is still used in the bleaching of yarn, and coarse open cloths. But in this climate it is very tedious. I tried the experiment last summer with some coarse cloth; but after it had been boiled once in a lixive, laid out wet, and exposed for four months, it had not attained even to a tolerable degree of whiteness. The summer indeed was unfavourable for the experiment, as there was much rain and little warmth. But from what I saw, I should despair of ever drawing any advantage from this method' (Home 1756: 21).

Most of the bleaching in Europe was carried out in Holland and cloth was sent back and forth for treatment (Matthews 1921:10). Nevertheless Matthews, writing in America in 1921, includes an illustration titled 'Grassing of Linen in Old England' showing eight women at work in the open air. In the foreground is a cauldron surrounded by fire and a number of jugs. One woman appears to be working fabric in a shallow tub on a trestle table. Two are beating cloth with bats or flails. One is hanging strips of linen on tenters (tensioned on tenterhooks – hence the expression). A fifth, in fields on the other side of a steam, is overseeing long strips of linen laid out on grass. In the distance another is carrying a vessel or bundle on her head. The last two are folding a length of cloth (ibid 5).

It is possible that such a process was carried on in Lumsdale during the eighteenth century and the tour notes prepared by the Arkwright Society identify the large circular stone tub above the Paint Mill as a bleaching vat (Plate 9). It is explained that there would have been some kind of agitator to ensure the yarn was completely soaked and a lid to keep the bleach in. If there was primitive bleaching in this part of Lumsdale it would have been convenient to carry the fabric over the brook by a bridge to the fields on the other side for crofting. Fields to the east of the brook are however shown as 'Belland' on a map of Tansley in the 1840s. That suggests they were still contaminated by lead waste from the smelting that was going on in Lumsdale at about the same time in the early and mid-1700s. Would anyone have attempted to bleach fabric white when there was lead smelting going on nearby?

The earliest documentary reference we have seen to bleaching works is in a newspaper advertisement in 1812 (below) although in 1893 the Farnsworth bleach works were said to have been in existence for two hundred years and, when in 1936 the works were closed, since 1794 (*Derby Daily Telegraph* 5 May 1936). We have found no reference to bleach workers in the Matlock Parish Records before 1813 although, if they were women, their occupations as parent of a child being baptised or party to a marriage are unlikely to be stated. One has to question also whether there was a local demand for bleaching before Arkwright built his cotton mill at Cromford in 1771. Maybe archaeology will one day shed more light on the early bleaching in Lumsdale.

Eighteenth century progress

During the second half of the eighteenth century understanding of the bleaching process advanced rapidly. It was still however a long and painstaking business. In 1773 Robert Peel, the same one who campaigned against Richard Arkwright and his patents (see Chapter 6), set up a calico-printing factory in Bury and he expanded his business to include all the processes of cotton production, including bleaching. James Wheeler, writing in 1836, recounts:

'Bleaching was at that time a very delicate process, requiring much attention, and occupying a month or six weeks in its performance. By day and night Mr. Peel's mind was so completely wrapped up in his business, that it was quite usual with him to leave his bed at the most unseasonable hours, and in the most inclement weather, for the purpose of going to his 'bleach-crofts', to ascertain how the goods went on, or to call his men to remove them if the night were unfavourable' (Wheeler, 1836: 520).

So what was so delicate and time-consuming about the bleaching process?

Edward Baines, drawing heavily on an article in the Encyclopaedia Britannica, wrote in 1835 that 'The bleaching process, as performed in the middle of the last [i.e. eighteenth] century, occupied from six to eight months'. He then set out why.

'It consisted in steeping the cloth in alkaline leys for several days, washing it clean, and spreading it upon the grass for some weeks. Then steeping in alkaline leys, called *bucking*, and the bleaching on the grass, called *crofting*, were repeated alternately for five or six times. The cloth was then steeped for some days in sour milk, washed clean, and crofted. These processes were repeated, diminishing every time the strength of the alkaline ley, till the cotton had acquired the requisite whiteness' (Baines, 1835: 246).

'The first considerable improvement in bleaching in Great Britain, consisted in the substitution of a more powerful acid for sour milk. Dr. Home, of Edinburgh, about the middle of the last century, introduced the practice of employing water acidulated with sulphuric acid; by the quicker operation of this liquid, the souring of the cloth was effected within a few hours, whereas it formerly occupied days and weeks; and as the souring process had under both modes to be repeated, so much time was saved by the use of sulphuric acid as to reduce the whole operation of bleaching from eight months to four.

The grand improvement in bleaching, however, was in the application of *chlorine*, formerly called oxymuriatic acid, to the art' (ibid: 247).

Though by then 'only' taking four months the bleaching process was clearly a dangerous occupation with sulphuric or oxymuriatic acid involved. Abraham Rees, in his 1819 Cyclopædia or Universal Dictionary of Arts, Sciences, and Literature, devoting thirteen double-column pages to bleaching, revealed health and safety issues. For example, in relation to the souring process he stated:

'This process consists in immersing, for the space of twelve hours, or more, the yarn or cotton in a mixture of water and sulphuric acid (vitriolic acid), well incorporated; the proper strength of which mixture is about the acidity of lemon juice, and is *usually directed by the taste*. The sour kettle should be made of lead ... The construction of this apparatus is upon the same principle as the warm vats made use of by the blue dyers, the intent not being to make the liquor boil, but to keep it at a degree of heat which the hand can long and easily bear'.

Then, after discussing the new processes invented by Mr Scheele, involving 'oxygenated muriatic acid, procured by mixing manganese with marine (i.e. hydrochloric) acid', he discussed the invention of M. Berthollet, who sought, not entirely successfully, to absorb the resulting gas in water:

'One of the first [attempts to produce the effect by other means] practised by the bleachers of cotton-hose at Nottingham, was to receive the dephlogisticated muriatic gas into a small air-tight chamber, in the upper part of which the goods were suspended from a frame, while at some distance below was water, sometimes impregnated with ley of potash, and sometimes with lime water or water mixed with lime. The gas was introduced betwixt the fluid and the goods, amongst which it ascended and mixed at the same time, by occasionally immersing the goods in the fluid below, it was sought to modify the action of the acid. This was effected by means of a pole or long lever, connected with the frame on which the goods were suspended, the centre of which pole moved on a swivel fixed in a hole in the partition, occasionally stopped with clay, and enabled a person to let the goods down into the fluid, not always without inconvenience, which occasioned it the name of the *Bedlam Process*' or (as Rees added to very similar paragraph on cotton manufacture) 'as the workmen, if they inhale the gas, are stupefied' (Rees Vol.4: 576; Vol. 22:454).

Lumsdale in 1812

Whether or not there was bleaching in Lumsdale in the eighteenth century, by 1812 Lumsdale had certainly kept abreast of the new technology. We have an advertisement in the *Derby Mercury* which uses many of the technical terms we have heard.

It advertises the auction on 13 March 1812 of:

'ALL those very Valuable Freehold Premises,
and upwards of Three Acres of Land adjoining thereto, and Two Tenements standing thereon, situate in Lumsdale, near Matlock aforesaid.
The Situation is extremely desirable, and replete with every convenience for carrying on the Bleaching Business to advantage. In the Land is a spring of fine soft Water, with a regular and constant supply. In the Buildings is a Water Wheel, of 24 feet diamater, with three pair of Fallers, three Bedlams, a Retort for making the Oxygeniated Muriatic Acid, the Receiver of which holds 570 Gallons, nearly new, and worked by water; a Bucking Keer with Pump, worked by water; a Steam Boiler nearly new; a Boil-House, Dry-ing Stove, and Brimstone Stove, Warehouse Room, and Counting House: with every other Apparatus and Conveniency relative to the Business.
Immediate possession may be had'

(*Derby Mercury*, 5 March 1812).

The three pairs of fallers would be hammers for beating the fabric (like fulling stocks) raised by a cam and powered by the water wheel. It appears that this was the bleaching mill lower down Lumsdale then acquired by the Farnsworth family as a going concern. We will return to the Farnsworths in Chapter 8.

The industrial history of the Upper Lumsdale valley in the 19th century was dominated by another family - the Gartons - who made the valley a very important centre for the bleaching of cotton. So who were the Gartons?

John Garton, bleacher and landowner

His rise to eminence

John Garton arrived in Lumsdale in about 1820 and set about making his fortune. In May 1821 he was already in possession of Watts, Lowe's cotton mill and was carrying on a bleaching business there. He had been born in Basford, Nottingham in 1795, and was only 22 when in 1817 he married Lydia Allsop, née Lowe, 14 years older than he was. Lydia's first husband John Allsop was the first child of another John, a farmer and miller in Darley Dale. John Allsop senior made his will (and presumably died) in 1803, so John junior would have inherited and passed on his wealth to Lydia (Ince *Pedigrees* 16c). Anna Maria Garton, their only recorded child, was baptised in Matlock in 1822. Lydia died in Matlock in 1828 and John was apparently married again to a Mary Hall. We have not found a record of that second marriage but John referred to his wife Mary and the eldest child was baptised as Edward Hall Garton, named after her father when it was quite common for the mother's (or grandmother's) family name to be added as a Christian name.

John Garton's rise to eminence was rapid after his arrival in Lumsdale. By the time he remarried he had already become well known. In his Directory of 1829 Stephen Glover wrote:

'In a county which is rising so rapidly in manufacturing interest, the business of bleaching and that of dyeing become necessarily important. It appears indeed that Derbyshire was distinguished in very early times for its fullers and bleachers. There are bleaching-houses and grounds in about eighteen towns and villages. ... One of the most eminent in the county is that of Mr John Garton, at Lumsdale near Matlock' (Glover, 1829: xxix).

John was a subscriber to (so helping to fund) a number of Stephen Glover's books about Derbyshire and received favourable (but justified) mention. In his 1830 Peak Guide Glover referred to the extensive bleachworks, and bone mill in Lumsdale, the property of Mr. Garton and included Garton's house 'The Lums' in the chief residences in the area (1830: 104, 124).

So how did John Garton create an estate which covered much of the Lumsdale valley and surrounding farmland as well as land at Snitterton and Oker?

We know that between 1834 and 1844 John and Mary had seven children, all baptised in Matlock and that they spent the rest of their lives in Lumsdale. We also know that when the Garton estate was sold in 1906 the sale particulars recorded that the bulk of the property had been acquired by John Garton between 1821 and 1859 (DRO D504/131/4). Some of the original deeds of transfer survive in the Arkwright Society archive at Cromford Mills. Others are at the Derbyshire Record Office or in private hands and some information has to be inferred.

John Garton's first acquisition in Lumsdale was on 12 May 1821 when he took a conveyance of land summarised as 'Mills at Lumsdale, an Allotment of 52 acres made to Peter Nightingale of Lea and the Leasehold Hereditaments on Lums Hill formerly a Cupola' (from an abstract in private hands), the same property which had been conveyed to Gamaliel Jones by an indenture dated 24 December 1813 (original deed in private hands). This was the indenture referred to in Chapter 6 by which the survivors of the Watts, Lowe consortium sold their cotton mill and the rest of their Lumsdale estate to Jones. A solicitor's note on the abstract in 1907 confirms that the lease referred to was the 999 year lease dated 10 June 1749 of the Pond Cottages cupola site which was then handed to John William Wildgoose 'together with other documents carrying the leasehold title down to Milnes from whom they passed to Mr Gamaliel Jones and Mr John Garton'.

Gamaliel Jones - wealthy eccentric

What had Gamaliel Jones been doing (apart from collecting any rents) with the mill and other land in the seven years since he acquired them at the age of 64? One suspects very little as we do not learn much about his time in Matlock until after his death when his name appears in the High Court action *Pearson & wife v. Smedley* in 1838 (*The Jurist*, 8 September 1838: 758). Gamaliel Jones was 'an old bachelor of very eccentric habits and considerable wealth' (*Leicester Chronicle*, 2 February 1838 under the heading 'A Valuable Lodger'). He lodged for about the last 20 years of his life with James and Anne Pearson who were 'poor persons' living in Matlock and they looked after him well. On 15 January 1834 he set up a trust, retaining a life interest for himself but giving everything he owned to Anne absolutely on his death which occurred in July of that year when he was 85. The trustee was Anne's brother Peter Smedley. During his lifetime Jones transferred £6,000 into a bank account in Smedley's name where it remained. Jones's estate was estimated at £20,000 or £50,000, depending on which report you read.

After Jones died in July 1838 some £5,000 was transferred to the Pearsons but Smedley claimed £1,000 as a gratuity for his services as trustee. When the Pearsons refused he instructed the bank not to pay over the balance to them, alleging that Jones had not been of sound mind when he set up the trust. The Pearsons sued. The Vice-Chancellor was not impressed with evidence of Jones's alleged imbecility.

'Those persons who are most capable of giving an opinion are in favour of his being of sound mind. The contrary opinion is expressed by ignorant people, and those who feel themselves slighted in not being remembered by this gentleman.'

Having been content to act as trustee for many years Smedley could not now allege that his very appointment was tainted by incapacity. After some interesting discussion in court about whether Mrs Pearson as a woman was entitled to anything in her own right, she and her husband were awarded a judgment for the £1,000 *(Derbyshire Courier* 10 February 1838).

Expansion of the Garton estate

Returning to John Garton we find that on 25 December 1828 he bought from the trustees of Bonsall School for £400:

'All that Messuage dwellinghouse or tenement heretofore used as a Smelting Mill And also all the other Mill heretofore used as a Smelting Mill but now used as a Corn Mill situate lying and being in the Parish of Matlock in the said County of Derby at or near a place there called the Lums formerly in the tenure or occupation of [——] [sic] Whitfield since of Messrs William and John Milnes but now of the said John Garton his undertenants or assigns'.

These were, as we discussed in Chapter 3, in the area of the buildings we now call the Paint Mill and the Grinding Mill, located near the top of the waterfall in Lumsdale (Plate 10). Then Garton set about acquiring land to the west of Asker Lane. On 23 June 1829 he bought from Richard Hursthouse for £30:

'All that cottage or dwellinghouse with the garden thereto belonging situate at or near a place called the Hurst in the parish of Matlock aforesaid and now or late in the holding or occupation of the said Richard Hursthouse or his undertenant' (Indenture in AS archive).

The plot is identified as plot 306 on the 1848 Tithe Map and the dwelling house is now called Yew Tree Cottage in Asker Lane.

John Garton's estate continued to grow after 1833. In 1839 he bought for £950 the malthouse and stables, part of what later became Bailey's Mill, lower down the Bentley Brook towards Matlock Green and nearly six acres of land north of the Brook towards Smuse Lane (DRO D856/T/9). The following year he bought for £3,600 the water corn mill itself with a dwellinghouse and drying house and adjoining land on the Nottingham Road (DRO D856/T/11) and for another £1,400 eleven acres to the east between the Brook and Nottingham Road (DRO 856/T/10).

Censuses show that the mill was let for many years from the 1840s onwards to Joseph Blackwell and then his son Richard. They eventually vacated and in 1858 Garton offered it to let with the seven-bedroom house and thirty acres of meadow, arable and pasture land, also a malt kiln with another six acres (*Derbyshire Advertiser and Journal* 17 September 1858).

In the 1840s John was occupying a large swathe of land east of Lumsdale which he had rented from Bonsall School (Tansley Tithe Map 1846).

The creation of the Lower Pond was sometime during the ownership of John Garton. It is not shown on the Tithe Redemption Map of 1848 nor on the plan drawn on a deed of 1859 but its construction may have been related to the diversion of a public right of way from Tansley into Lumsdale advertised in the Derby

Mercury in October and November 1854 (*Derby Mercury* 11 October 1854, 1 November 1854).

By the 1859 deed John Garton acquired the eastern bank of the Bentley Brook opposite what had then become (and is still known as) Garton's Mill, or the Lower Bleach Works, by an exchange of land with the Bonsall School Trustees (DRO D858/T/17). He gave the School in return a plot of useful pasture south of Oakstage Lane and he then owned both banks of the brook and the rights that went with them. By his Will dated 19 April 1860 he referred also to his closes of land at Snitterton, his farm land and hereditaments at Okerside, and a freehold property at Mill Town, Ashover.

John Garton the businessman

Family connections

John Garton's development as a businessman of substance can be traced though his census returns. In 1841 his occupation was described as bleacher and his household included three female servants. Bagshaw's Directory of 1846 describes him as bleacher and manufacturer of sulphate of barytes (Bagshaw, 1846:382). By census day 1851 his business had diversified and he was described as a bleacher and paint grinder. White's Directory of 1857 lists him in Matlock as a bleacher, a barytes manufacturer and a paint and colour manufacturer, apart from his other interests, and in Tansley as 'bleacher and paint works' (White, 1857: 442, 259). In the 1861 census he was described as a bleacher, farmer of 103 acres and paint grinder employing 86 men, women and boys.

It cannot be a coincidence that John Garton's in-laws, the family of his wife Mary Hall, were also bleachers. They may have been related to the family of bleachers who lived at Basford Hall in Nottingham. Robert Hall (1756-1827) was one of the first to use chloride of lime in the bleaching process: 'A process which formerly took a month was now reduced to one day' (Fry 2016), with consequent increased profit. His eldest son, Samuel, developed a process for singeing off the floss on cotton (ibid). The Hall family sold Basford Hall in around 1840. Mary's brother Edward Hall, born in about 1801, moved from Nottingham to Fernilee at around that time. He was there at the time of the 1841 census with his wife and two children, aged two and one, only the second of them having been born in Derbyshire.

The Gartons may however have already had interests in Fernilee. An on-line catalogue of deeds offered for sale on eBay includes a lease of a cottage and some land at Fernilee, north-west of Buxton by one William Thomasson to John Garton and William Garton, both of Lumsdale, bleachers (Durtnall undated).

When Bagshaw wrote his *Gazetteer* in 1846 Edward Hall was living at Shallcross Hall (Bagshaw, 1846: 543) in nearby Shallcross, and he was still there in 1851 when the census notes him farming 160 acres and employing twenty-three women and sixty-eight men in his bleaching business at Botany (elsewhere Botney) Bleach Works at Horwich End on the River Goyt (ibid 548). Fernilee and Horwich End are now part of Whaley Bridge which by 1831 had been linked to Cromford when the Cromford and High Peak Railway created a route from the Whaley Bridge branch of the Peak Forest Canal to the Cromford Canal. Edward Hall's son and grandson, both called Edward, born in 1840 and 1872 continued the bleaching business at Botany Works.

By 1908 Edward Hall and Brother had become part of the Bleachers Association Ltd which in turn became a part of Whitecroft Industrial Holdings. In 1952 Bradbury Lees and Co Ltd was established by Robinsons as a holding company of Edward Hall and Bro. Ltd. The bleach works handled all cotton bleaching for Robinsons' Chesterfield works. The plant closed in 1999 (DRO D5395/10 Catalogue summary).

Technical development of the business

It is difficult to know how the Gartons developed their bleaching business during John Garton's time. He obviously did well and made money to buy land and build Lumsdale House. A plan of the bleachworks dated 22 March 1885, twenty-three years after John Garton died, shows the water wheel still in position at the south-west end of the former cotton mill and two large Lancashire boilers between it and the smithy yard (DRO D504/3/1/2-3 and Wild 2016:7). There is a large water tank to the west of the site below the Lumsdale House garden wall. Two more tanks have been created north of the mill and a stone tramway links the Lower Works to the Upper Works. It appears that the wet processes were carried out in the Lower Works and the bleached fabrics were carried on wagons to the drying rooms in the Upper area. The Upper Works also still have a water wheel fed by water brought from the Grinding Mill at the top of the waterfall by a wooden launder supported on stone piers along the side of the ravine.

We have found no reference to the building of the Chimney. It is not shown on the 1848 Tithe Map but is there on the 1879/80 1:2,500 Ordnance Survey map. The Salford survey notes the following:

'A recessed axle mount in the west retaining wall above the wheel pit has been remodelled, with a stone chamber, placed on cast-iron rails, which served a later flue, having being inserted. Cast-iron bearing boxes inserted into the opposite wall possibly hosed (*sic* - housed?) pipes from the later boiler, or may possibly suggest the replacement of the waterwheel with a steam engine during the latter phases of the bleach works' (Wild 2017: 66).

Within the old cotton mill the clearance of debris by the Arkwright Society in the 1980s revealed two large troughs made of slabs of stone bound with strips of iron. They are clearly made for soaking fabric but would not have been directly heated. There are other stone vessels around the site. There is evidence of channels beneath the floor which would have taken spent water from the wheel and the washing processes and drained it into the Bentley Brook which flows in a culvert under the smithy yard.

In 1854 a train was derailed in the shunting yard at Chesterfield. One of the trucks was heavily laden with hampers of vitriol, eighteen or nineteen of which burst through the roof of their truck and rolled down the embankment blackening the grass and soaking into the ground so that 'the boots of the men working on the spot were burnt on their feet, as they were compelled to stand on the ground which was thoroughly saturated with vitriol'. The report ends. 'Vitriol is very extensively used in the bleach works at the Lumsdale factories, Matlock' (*Derbyshire Times*, 1 July 1854).

So we know that sulphuric acid was being used but we have no evidence of the precise methods used and nor does any of the iron-made equipment survive.

The newspapers record the occasional incident at the Lumsdale bleachworks. In 1830 torrential rain caused widespread flooding and damaged several weirs and bridges in Lumsdale (*Nottingham Review,* 2 July 1830). Much later, in June 1856, a thunderstorm damaged the gable end of a large building, broke about fifty panes of glass and scattered tiles across the road. There was said to be about £3,000 of cotton on the premises but fortunately there was no fire (*Derbyshire Advertiser*, 6 June 1856).

Barytes

We have noted that during the 1840s John Garton was listed not only as a bleacher but also as a paint grinder or barytes manufacturer. That is a new industry in Lumsdale.

On his 'Summer Saunter through the Hills and Dales of Derbyshire' in 1868 James Croston found in Matlock Bath:

'Opposite the High Tor the river is spanned by a little wooden bridge that leads to the Crystallised Cavern, close to which is a mill for grinding barytes. This mineral, provincially termed 'cawke', is found in considerable quantities in the limestone districts of the Peak, it is generally associated with calcareous spar, and frequently forms the matrix of the richest lead veins; it is of a dingy white or dull yellow tint, and after being washed and ground, is manufactured into a pigment of fine white colour, known among painters as Dutch lead' (Croston 1868: 220).

In fact - as we noted in Chapter 2 - Derbyshire was by far the largest producer of barytes. In his Mineral Statistics for 1858 Hunt notes that out of 13,337 tons produced in the United Kingdom of Great Britain and Ireland, 8000 came from Derbyshire and in particular the Matlock area (Hunt 1860: 376). Specifically barytes was found in the area along the eastern edge of the limestone near Matlock.

In Lumsdale the Paint Mill was undoubtedly grinding barytes in the 19th century as limited excavations within the Mill found in 1970 and 1986/7. The 1970 excavation notes refer to a number of brick-lined troughs extending north-south containing a thick layer of barytes 4" to 6" deep and leading to flues in the north wall. There were found 'some pieces of iron lying beside each other in the form of a hoop or some segment of a circle pattern' (AS archive). Unfortunately no radius is mentioned but these could be straps from around the circumference of French burr grinding stones.

French Burr Stones

What were these French stones and how did they come to be in Lumsdale? D G Tucker writes that, as the Industrial Revolution developed in the 19th century, a rapid growth in population and a demand for finer flour led to a requirement for millstones which were superior to the local gritstone. Accordingly it became necessary to import French burr stones which had been used in England for centuries but on a very small scale. They came from the Marne valley near Paris, were made of very hard rock and were imported in small pieces so that 'a millstone has to be fabricated by the assembly of a number of pieces (e.g.25) rather like crazy paving, cemented together with plaster of Paris, the working face being dressed smooth and the back smoothed off with plaster, the whole being reinforced by iron hoops shrunk on to the circumference' (Tucker 1973: 7).

The Barytes Mills page on the Shropshire History website contains details of a number of mills which operated there from the 1830s until 1928. Hanwood Mill had twenty-four French burr stones and at Cothercott Mill ten pairs of French stones were used to produce 200 tons of barytes each week, sold for use in making barium meals. (For a fascinating discussion of French burr stones at George Washington's Grist Mill and how to dress them see www.vimeo.com/87811042).

In Lumsdale one complete French stone lies near the Saw Mill (Plate 3) and parts of others have appeared in the ground near the Paint Mill and Grinding Mill. If they were imported in the middle of the nineteenth century, then they are probably too late to be used in the corn mill which John Garton bought in 1828 and do relate to grinding barytes. The mounds of waste below the Saw Mill and the nearby French burr stone suggest that the Saw Mill was also grinding barytes at some stage.

The Gartons' barytes production was not on the scale of some of the Shropshire factories. The censuses of men living in Lumsdale who were engaged in barytes or paint production show none in 1841, two in 1851, none in 1861, only James Davis and his son as 'barytes manufacturers' in 1871, and none thereafter. Edward Hall Garton's entry in 1881 discloses that he was employing eight men in the paint trade and they must have had a longer walk to work. John Garton described himself as a barytes manufacturer and/or paint grinder in 1851 and 1861 and Edward did so in 1881 but not later. We can therefore infer that barytes manufacture in Lumsdale ended in the 1880s.

The other grinding industry in Lumsdale in which the Gartons had an interest was bone crushing.

Bone

The mill

As we noted above, Glover referred to Mr Garton's bone mill in Lumsdale (1830: 104) and we know that the Bone Mill was just below what is now the Upper Pond. What we do not know for certain is when it started grinding bones because, as the last chapter explained, we cannot be certain when it stopped being a cotton mill. 'Our' Bone Mill is not on Farey's list (1813: Vol II 449-450) but we are told that it was operating as a bone mill in 1821 (Bryan, 1903: 52). Perhaps John Garton decided that was a good use for the building and apparatus when he acquired it in that year.

It is also not clear when it stopped operating as a bone mill. The Lumsdale census returns make no mention of anyone working as a grinder of bones there: indeed we have found only one such reference in any of the local censuses and that is to a bone works labourer in Middleton in 1901. As we noted in Chapter 1 it is named as the Bone Mill on a map of 1880 and, when it was sold in 1906, the particulars said that is was 'formerly used as a Bone Mill'. That is all we can say.

The end product

We also cannot be certain as to why bones were being ground but the most likely end product was fertiliser, given that Derbyshire was still largely agricultural. We may now be aware that bone meal is sold at garden centres for use as a fertiliser but, in a book detailing the travels in the 1780s of an American (who corresponded with George Washington), there is this comment made about farmers in the area between Sheffield and Matlock Bath: 'Always curious for innovations in manufactures and in agriculture, Elkanah wrote down that local farmers used a fertilizer he hadn't heard of - bones and horns pulverized by grinding wheels' (Bangs 1946: 99). Elkanah records that John Bunting of Ashover found ground bone to be ineffective, however, except on turnips (ibid 451).

Bernard O'Connor (undated) explains why bones started to be used for fertiliser:

'As the science of analytical chemistry developed in the early 19th century the early chemists understood that it was calcium phosphate that the plant roots needed. When it was discovered that bones were rich in calcium they too were used on the fields. Burnt or crushed they were spread on the fields to increase crop yields'.

Bones are, however, slow to dissolve and release their minerals but from the 1830s sulphuric acid was added to help dissolve animal bones (ibid). Providing such an ingredient would have been no problem for John Garton, given that it was used in the bleaching process. It was also clear, as the nineteenth century progressed, that agriculture needed to be more productive given that the growth of towns entailed there being less land for growing food but more urban workers to feed.

However there was another use for bone in the nineteenth century - the making of 'bone' china. The early development is attributed to Josiah Spode though that is contested: 'The original basic formula of six parts bone ash, four parts china stone, and three and a half parts china clay remains the standard English body' (see www.thepotteries.org/types/bonechina.htm). Note that the recipe requires bone ash, that is bone that has been calcined - roasted to a high temperature - to make it easier to crush. Stoke-upon-Trent had kilns for such a purpose but calcining could be done after crushing (Ploszajski, 2015) so the Lumsdale Bone Mill might have sent crushed bone to the Potteries. Research on the Derby porcelain works showed that sourcing suitable bone was problematic in the 1790s (Anderson 2000: 139-141) and that may have continued into the nineteenth century. After the Cromford Canal was opened in 1794, linking it to the Trent-Mersey network, there would have been a better haulage link to the Potteries area.

Source

So where did the bones come from? Visitors to Lumsdale are sometimes told that the bones were stolen from London graveyards and this rumour has a long history:

'If Middlesex farmers may wonder to be told, that Coal-ashes [for fertiliser] are disregarded in Derbyshire, they can scarcely be less surprised to learn, that several Ship Loads of the Bones, collected in London (some from the Church yards as I have heard), find their way into the interior of Derbyshire annually, and are there ground by Mills, erected on purpose, into a most potent and valuable Manure' (Farey 1813 Vol II: 449).

Other evidence suggests more prosaic collection methods: for example, the Strutts at Belper paid their work people 1s 6d (7.5p) per cwt for old bones (Bangs 1946: 451).

Process

How the bones were crushed in also not clear. One would expect that grindstones would be used but Farey says of the two bone mills he describes that the bones were 'pounded' by forge hammers (Farey 1813 Vol II: 449-450). Archaeology might be able to tell us more but there is currently no evidence.

End of the John Garton era

Throughout his life John showed a degree of interest in matters of public welfare. For example, in 1829 he subscribed two guineas to the new Derby General Infirmary (*Derby Mercury*, 30 December 1829); in 1855 he gave £5 to the Patriotic Fund relating to the War in the Crimea - and his servants contributed another 10 shillings (*Derby Mercury*, 10 January 1855). In 1856 he joined the committee set up to build and endow a new Anglican church in Wessington (*Derby Mercury*, 3 June 1857). In 1858 he entered a two-year-old short-horned heifer in the Wirksworth Farmers' Show and won first prize (*Derbyshire* Advertiser, 29 October 1858). Further, in 1861 he was one of the ratepayers who petitioned the Churchwardens to convene a meeting with a view to creating Matlock as a local authority under the Local Government Act 1858 (*Derbyshire Courier*, 16 November 1861), a process which resulted in the division of the old Matlock parish into the separate districts of Matlock and Matlock Bath. Benjamin Bryan tells the story of how Matlock Bath jumped the gun in 1861 and obtained an order by wrongly proceeding without Matlock's consent and then took four years to sort out the muddle (Bryan 1903: 55).

Yet, when John Garton died on 26 June 1862 his passing was barely noted in the local press. He had, however, established himself as a major figure in the history of Lumsdale, owning the whole estate there and also the corn mill and malthouse later known as Bailey's Mill in lower Lumsdale, cottages at Snitterton, a farm at Okerside, Darley, a freehold at Milltown, Ashover and bequeathing other unspecified freehold and copyhold land and other property. He had also rebuilt Lumsdale House as a substantial family home.

Lumsdale House is built on what appears to have been the site of old cottages pulled down for the purpose. The present building is now described as a small villa in two storeys with a hipped roof and stone gables, tripartite sash windows and a Doric porch. It was extended twice in John Garton's time. The presence of a monkey-puzzle tree and other features in the landscaped garden have suggested the influence of (and maybe design by) Joseph Paxton of Chatsworth. Later the house had a large walled garden with a Gothic gardener's cottage above and a similarly detailed gardener's shed close to the bend in the road (Morris 2010). We have seen no evidence that the shed was ever a chapel, as is sometimes said.

In 1856 John's daughter Harriett married the Rev. Melville Holmes, who had been at Tansley since 1846 and became Rector when the Tansley Parish was formed in 1866. The following year they moved on and in due course they settled at Wadsley near Sheffield. She was the only one of his children who married. John, Elizabeth and Mary all died in infancy. Anna Maria, his daughter by Lydia, Edward and Lucy Ann stayed in Lumsdale.

It was Edward who further enhanced the estate and carried on the businesses.

Edward Hall Garton

On his father's death Edward Hall Garton became head of the family, living at Lumsdale House with his mother, half-sister Anna Maria and sisters Emma and Lucy. He continued the family bleaching business and in the 1871 census is described as bleacher, barytes manufacturer and farmer employing forty-seven men, twenty-two boys, three women and seventeen girls. In 1881, carrying on the same businesses he was employing six men as shepherds and labourers on his farm, fifty in the bleachworks and eight in the paint trade, besides two housemaids and a cook.

Edward further expanded the Garton estate in Matlock. In 1869 he bought for £2,947 the mill at Matlock Green with Huntsbridge

House and rights in the watercourse through the land on which the petrol station now stands (DRO D857/T/11) and leased it to his cousin-in-law Mary Bailey who in turn assigned the lease to her son Ernest Henry Bailey (DRO D857/E/1).

In 1875 Edward began to consolidate his ownership of the western edge of Lumsdale by purchasing for £750 some four acres of land on the hillside immediately behind and to the west of Lumsdale House (Indenture 1 December 1875 in AS archive). In 1883 he bought for £162 a cottage and garden land in Asker Lane, referred to as numbers 304 and 305 on the Tithe Map - the next plot to the south of Yew Tree Cottage, now its garden, and the house and gardens known as Corner Croft (Deed 4 July 1883 in private hands). He also acquired the piece numbered 411 then called Intake and now Lumsdale Terrace.

In 1877 he paid £1,600 for thirty-one acres in Cuckoostone Dale west of the Bentley Brook, now the fields to the north-west of the Chesterfield Road between the Fairway View (Cardinshaw Road) housing estate and Sandy Lane. When land on the other side of the Chesterfield Road was sold in 1880 for quarrying in the northern part of the gritstone edge above what is now Quarry Lane the advertisement said:

'Under a portion of this Lot are valuable Beds of the "Lums Hill Gritstone" which has gained such a notoriety throughout the kingdom for its quality, endurance and purity of colour. Ample evidence of this is exhibited in the property of E.H. Garton, Esq., adjoining this Lot, where quarries have been in existence for 30 years, but have now exhausted themselves in consequence of being worked up to the boundary of this Estate' (*Derby Mercury* 28 July 1880).

He also quickly began to make a name for himself, winning prizes for his cattle at the Bakewell Farmers' Club and the Midland Agricultural shows in 1862 and for many years ahead (see, for example, *Derby Mercury,* 8 October 1862 and 11 October 1865).

He liked to reward his workers with roast beef suppers. In March 1863 he contributed to the celebration of the marriage of the Prince of Wales by providing his workers in Lumsdale with a good dinner of roast beef and plum pudding (*Derby Mercury,* Wednesday 18 March 1863). Then in January 1867 there was another great feast when Edward entertained about fifty of his workmen to a roast beef and plum pudding supper and a similar number of their wives and children the following day. On each occasion he presided, his three sisters and Henry Ernest Bailey were among those present and Mrs Garton, his mother, also presented a helping of roast beef and plum pudding to every other resident of Lumsdale. The Rev Melville Holmes, Edward's brother-in-law, delivered 'an excellent speech on the good feeling that existed between Mr Garton and his workpeople' (*Derbyshire Advertiser,* 11 January 1867).

In 1870 the roast beef supper for the workmen and farm labourers, in a beautifully decorated large room at the works with singing and other amusements, had to be spread over two days and the women and children enjoyed tea on the third day. It was noted that Mr Garton was continuing the old family tradition of kindly paying all his workpeople their wages for Christmas Day and Good Friday (*Derbyshire Times and Chesterfield Herald,* 22 January 1870), the two 'common law' public holidays in England before the Bank Holidays Act of 1871 which added four paid holidays.

Edward Garton's fairness to his employees is demonstrated by a case before Matlock magistrates in September 1875. Charles Gratton was seen by a police officer on duty in Lumsdale at 2 o'clock in the morning leaving Garton's yard with three pieces of wood. He ran back into the yard, dropped the wood and initially denied leaving the premises. Then he decided to come clean, admitted the attempt and said he wished to go and see Mr. Garton and ask his forgiveness. Mr. Garton was unsympathetic (as one would be if woken up at 2 a.m.) and told the officer he must do his duty so

Gratton was duly charged with theft. In court Edward Garton gave evidence and said that Gratton had worked for him from a boy and he had never had cause to suspect him. He believed Gratton was taking the wood to make a greenhouse on his (Garton's) property and not to sell and that he did not wish to press the case. He had only brought it forward because he was a Member of the Society for the Prosecution of Felons and he would employ Gratton again.

Nevertheless the Justices convicted and sentenced Gratton to three weeks' imprisonment but without hard labour (*Derby Mercury* 29 September 1875).

The extent of his activities in public office is reflected in the numerous references to him in local papers. In 1871 Edward was appointed to the Board of Guardians in an election which drew pointed criticism from the *Derbyshire Times* both for the negligent way in which the electors of Matlock Bath had conducted the voting process and for the way in which the voters of Matlock Parish had appointed three of their own (*Derbyshire Times* 15 April 1871).

In 1878 Edward Garton led a campaign to increase the representation of Matlock on the Board of Guardians at Bakewell (*Derbyshire Advertiser*, 5 April 1878) which was partially successful and prompted 'A Dity in the Olden Style' about 'yon Lumsdale chap' by 'Owd Showby', a disgruntled loser in the subsequent elections:

> 'When I'd been a gyardian farty 'ear [*forty years*]
> Yon Lumsdale chap embarrased me
> By sending extra gyardian there
> Yon Cromford chap and *Harrased* me.'

and five verses later:

> 'But now the gyardian lection's oer,
> Yon Lums and Cromford rot um O!
> The voters stuck um up at top
> And Showby at the bottom O!'
> (*Derbyshire Times*, 16 April 1879).

In June 1880 Garton was one of those local Conservatives who set up in Matlock a Conservative Working Man's Club where they could play games, exchange ideas and read Conservative literature 'with less fear of such absurd stories finding credence as those with which the Radicals flooded the district during the late election'. He later served on the committee (*Sheffield Daily Telegraph*, 29 June 1880; *Derby Mercury*, 1 June 1887).

Edward Garton took the chair at a public meeting in November 1880 to propose the creation of a Matlock cattle market and at another meeting two years later when the fortnightly market appeared to be under threat from the new weekly market at Bakewell (*Derbyshire Times and Chesterfield Herald*, 27 November 1880, *Derbyshire Courier* 25 November 1882).

In 1881 he presided over the Matlock Bridge Local Board (*Sheffield Daily Telegraph*, 6 October 1881) and in 1897 he chaired the committee which organised the royal Diamond Jubilee celebrations for 700 people in Tansley (*Derbyshire Times*, 26 June 1897).

He had been less enthusiastic about celebrating the Golden Jubilee in 1887, at least when it came to contributing to the cost of a project in Kensington. At the meeting of the Bakewell Board of Guardians which he attended on 22 March:

'The Chairman read a circular respecting the proposed Imperial Institute: ... It's about the Queen's Jubilee. – Mr. Harrison: Is she going to send us something? (Laughter.) – The Chairman proceeded to re-read the circular, and when he came to the words "subscriptions will be received" Mr. Harrison observed "Oh dear, that's it." – Mr. Young: I think we have heard enough. I don't think we need trouble the Chairman to read any more. – Mr. J.R. Crossland said that the Queen having had the pleasure of reigning 50 years, Her Majesty ought to give something if anyone did. ... It was decided that the letter lie on the table. – Mr. Crossland: She ought to give a million. Where has she had her money from? Out of the taxpayers. (Laughter)' (*Derbyshire Times*, Saturday 26 March 1887).

He was a sidesman at All Saints' Church on Matlock Bank (*Derbyshire Courier*, 8 April 1899) and a director of the High Tor

Recreation Grounds Company Ltd. when plans were made to provide a new and graceful suspension bridge to afford access across the river from the main road (*Derbyshire Times*, 7 March 1903).

Two years later he presided over the Bakewell Rural Council when they referred the question of the preservation or removal of Winster Old Market Hall to the Highway Committee (*Sheffield Daily Telegraph* 14 March 1905) but that year, in June 1905, Edward withdrew from operating the bleachworks and leased it to the Farnsworths, George Henry and Ernest Richard, for a term of 21 years. He continued with his Council work, being re-elected to Bakewell Rural District Council and attending the first meeting of the new Council on 27 April 1906.

However, on 6 May 1906 he died suddenly from congestion of the lungs, aged 73. The brief obituaries noted that he had been a prominent Conservative and Churchman and for nearly 40 years a member, and often chairman, of the Bakewell Board of Guardians (*Sheffield Daily Telegraph*, 10 May 1906).

His estate was valued at £20,560.5s.1d gross. By his Will he left some small legacies, including 2s.6d. (12½p) per week for life to each of his old servants Joseph Hughes and William Knowles, and the residue of his estate to Lucy, his only surviving sister, for life and then to his cousin Edward Hall.

Lucy and Emma had continued to live with him at Lumsdale House. Emma died in 1900. Harriett returned there after her husband died in 1893 and she died in 1903. Lucy lived in Derby until 1935.

The sale of the Gartons' Lumsdale Estate

The Lumsdale Estate was offered for sale by auction on 29 August 1906. It included twenty-five acres of farm 'in good heart' and the bleaching works then leased to Messrs. Farnsworth with the valuable water power of the Bentley Brook. Lumsdale House was described as charming country residence, exquisitely situated in a sheltered position about 500 feet above sea level, having three entertaining rooms, seven bedrooms, laundry, dairy, kitchen etc.

There was also stabling for eight horses with two loose boxes, coach house and sheds (*Derbyshire Times*, 25 August 1906).

It was bought, with twenty-four acres of land, for £3,800 by the Farnsworth brothers. They also bought two acres of land in Matlock for £200 and Ivy Cottage for £200. Councillor John William Wildgoose bought five cottages and three acres of land in Asker Lane for £640, twenty-five acres in Lumsdale for £950, another cottage with a garden and four acres for £320 and eleven acres in Cuckoostone Dale for £410 (*Derbyshire Courier*, 1 September 1906). In the event George Henry Farnsworth dropped out of the purchase and the land was conveyed to his brother Ernest Richard on 25 February 1907. It was he, briefly, and Mr. Wildgoose who began another era in Lumsdale's history - but first we must look at the story of the Farnsworth family and their contribution to the history of Lumsdale.

8

BLEACHING IN THE FARNSWORTH ERA

Richard Farnsworth

The Lumsdale Bleaching Works of Mr Richard Farnsworth were featured in a guide to the Matlocks and Bakewell published in 1893. They were then said to have been in operation for 200 years (we think wrongly) and in the Farnsworth family for the last eighty. The accompanying photograph shows the works some 175 metres lower down Lumsdale than Garton's Lower Bleach Works, mainly on the site to the west of Lumsdale Road now occupied by Lumsdale Glass Studio but including a large chimney on the other side of the road in front of the cottages of Radford Row. These works are therefore outside the boundary of the area of Lumsdale owned by the Arkwright Society but the Farnsworths eventually took over Garton's bleach works and so the histories of the two businesses are intertwined.

The text of the 1893 guide describes in some detail the process for giving a snowy white appearance to cotton, mainly then being sent from Lancashire, and so we reproduce it below.

'As the cotton arrives it is taken to the sorting room, where it is got ready for the first operation viz: boiling in lime and soda, the next operation consisting of a good beating - a very proper operation, too, either for cotton, or little boys and girls even, who have dirty faces - which process is carried out by immense steam beaters worked by steam, which descend rapidly one after another into a revolving drum of soap and water, and in which is placed the cotton. After this preliminary cleansing process it is removed to the boiling kiers until deemed ready again to undergo a further washing and beating, after which it is again boiled and finally transferred to the Patent Bleaching Vacuum Kiers. For the thorough bleaching of cotton and other goods these kiers are essential, and the process consists of creating a vacuum by means of air pumps worked by steam, and allowing the bleaching liquid to penetrate every portion. When the cotton is bleached and washed it is partially dried by centrifugal apparatus, and is removed to the large drying rooms, upon immense carriages running upon tram lines' (compiler unknown 1893, reprinted by the Arkwright Society 1984).

This, however, was state-of-the-art bleaching in 1893. The arrival of the Farnsworths in Lumsdale eighty years earlier would coincide with, and appear to relate to, the advertised sale of the bleaching mill which was already a going concern there in 1812. We reproduced the wording of the advertisement in Chapter 7. The previous owners are unfortunately not identified but the offer was: 'All those very Valuable Freehold Premises, and upwards of Three Acres of Land adjoining thereto, and Two Tenements standing thereon, situate in Lumsdale' and the advertisement stated that 'The Situation is extremely desirable, and replete with every convenience for carrying on the Bleaching Business to advantage' (*Derby Mercury* Thursday 05 March 1812: 1). It mentioned the fallers, bedlams, muriatic acid retorts, bucking kier, brimstone (sulphur) stove and much else necessary for bleaching at the beginning of the nineteenth century.

There is little to see of the mill now but the headrace is shown on OS 1:2500 maps from 1879 until 1922. The 1846 Tithe Map and the 1879 OS map show relatively modest works sandwiched between Lumsdale Road and the Bentley Brook. By 1899 the buildings, still to the west of the road, are more substantial but the 1922 map shows the works almost doubled in size and spread across the road to the east where a variety of businesses are now based.

The first of five generations of Farnsworths to be bleaching in Lumsdale was Richard, born in Mansfield in 1776 and married there to Ann Hibbard in 1797. It would be Richard who acquired the above bleaching mill in 1812. Their son John, apparently their only child, was born in Mansfield in 1798. The next section looks at his career.

John Farnsworth

John married Hannah Lees at St. Giles', Matlock in 1829 and their ten children were baptised there between 1830 and 1849. John is described throughout as 'bleacher' and, until 1843, as resident in Lumsdale. In due course John was joined in the bleaching business by three of their ten children - Richard, born in 1830, Thomas and Henry.

In 1841 Richard senior, still employed in cotton at over sixty years of age, and Ann were living in Tansley Parish, which had been created only the previous year and included part of lower Lumsdale to the east of the Bentley Brook. John and Hannah were living next door with their first eight children. The Tansley Tithe Map shows the Farnsworth home at Lumsdale Villas overlooking the bleachworks. For a while, until it was dissolved in 1834, there was a partnership between John Farnsworth and William Garton, who would be John Garton's younger brother (*London Gazette* 10 January 1834: 65).

John Farnsworth was clearly active in civic life in Matlock. In 1848 he was honoured with the presentation of a silver cup for his long and valuable gratuitous services as honorary secretary of the Association for the Prosecution of Felons. He made a 'neat and feeling speech' and 'an evening of rational enjoyment was then p ssed [sic] by the numerous party assembled'. (The missing vowel is an unfortunate type-setter's error: *Derbyshire Courier* 29 April 1848). At the next AGM in February 1849 'after ample attention had been rendered to the well-being of the inner man' (again!) it was reported that there had been no prosecutions in the past year and the meeting agreed that a contribution of four shillings from each member would be enough to cover contingencies for the next twelve months (*Derbyshire Courier,* 10 February 1849).

John also evidently did well for himself. In 1846 he bought House Close (with an existing house, then or later called Bank House and Old Bank House) and Long Close, two plots of land to the south-east of Wellington Street on Matlock Bank. Having property on Matlock Bank was obviously seen as a move up the social scale and the 1851 census shows that he had moved there with Hannah, nine children and one domestic servant. The house was described, when it was later advertised for sale, as a delightfully situated and substantially built residence with outbuildings, yards, gardens, pleasure grounds and appurtenances and it was the family home for much of the next sixty-five years (see more below).

In 1851 Richard their grandfather, aged 74, was lodging in Lumsdale with William, a carter, and Mary Dunn who had no apparent family connection with him. They are next door to John Garton but Richard Farnsworth is clearly not living in wealthy retirement although he is still described as 'manager' and so presumably still engaged in the bleachworks. However, Richard died over the new year of 1860 and is buried in Tansley churchyard. In 1861 John was employing ten men and boys including, presumably, his sons Richard, Thomas and Henry, all bleachers, but John also died only two years later.

Richard Farnsworth junior

The name of Richard Farnsworth appears in the newspapers from time to time and, as there do not appear to be any other Richard Farnsworths around Matlock at the time, we must assume he is 'our' Richard, grandson of Richard Farnsworth senior. In 1857, then aged 27, he was summoned by George Smith who alleged Richard had knocked him down and given him a black eye.

Richard was ordered to pay 9s. 6d (47p) costs (*Derbyshire Advertiser* 20 February 1857). In 1859 he was fined 40 shillings (£2) for trespassing on farmland on Matlock moor in search of game (*Derbyshire Courier* 5 November 1859). In 1864 he was acquitted, for a change, of assaulting Samuel Haynes (*Derby Mercury* 13 July 1864).

Richard married Louisa Roper, the daughter of a Matlock innkeeper, in 1864 and it would seem that his anti-social behaviour then ceased. They had three children - George Henry (known as Harry) in 1865, Hannah Leeys who died in infancy in 1867 and Ernest Richard in 1868. For some time after his father died, Richard carried on the business (still bearing his grandfather's name) in partnership with his mother Hannah. The partnership was, however, dissolved in June 1871 (*Derbyshire Advertiser* 16 June 1871) and, as is shown in the 1871 census, Richard carried on in his own right with six men and six boys in his employ.

Old Bank House

Hannah stayed at Old Bank House until she died in June 1872. The house with the two plots of land below it were then placed on the market together with some land on Bent Lane (at the far end of Cavendish Road) (*Derbyshire Times* 21 August 1872). An interesting piece by David Baker about Hopewell House, further down Wellington Street, tells some of the story of that property and land on Matlock Bank.

The Hopewell House deeds show that a John Farnsworth purchased the land from Thomas Leys. (That will be John Farnsworth the grocer born in 1832, Richard junior's younger brother.) He was bankrupted and the Old Bank House was offered for sale by his trustees (*Derby Mercury* 27 August 1873). The family must have raised the money to buy it in or prevent a sale for in 1874, after Hannah's death, they transferred the house to Richard. In 1889 Richard sold the lower part of the estate to Lawrence Wildgoose to build Hopewell House (Palmer 2006). (The Bertie Farnsworth referred to by Baker came from the other large, unrelated, Matlock family of that name - see the footnote to this chapter.)

However, at the date of the 1891 census Jonas Brown, formerly manager of John Smedley's hydro, was occupying Old Bank House as a hydro with four visitors and he was still there in 1895 (*Kelly's Directory*) but died in 1897. The business of Old Bank House Hydropathic Establishment was then offered for sale as a going concern (*Derbyshire Advertiser* 25 September 1897). From the beginning of 1898, Old Bank House was offered as a let for over a year (*Derbyshire Advertiser* 15 January, 18 March 1899) and then became the Farnsworth family home again. (It is now a care home known as 'The Views'.)

A diversion to the Wragg saga

In 1881, however, when the census shows Richard living in Lumsdale with his wife Louisa and sons Harry and Ernest, both still scholars, his personal behaviour again came under scrutiny. He was then employing five men and nine lads. His neighbours were Edward (a cotton bleacher from a family of Lumsdale bleachworkers) and Ann Wragg, who were soon to figure in the Farnsworth story.

Edward Wragg and Ann were married in Derby in 1869. Between 1870 and 1875 they had four sons but the marriage broke down in 1881 when, according to Edward, Ann had an affair with Richard Farnsworth. In 1883 Edward began divorce proceedings, no.8887, in the Probate Divorce and Admiralty Division of the High Court ('Wills, Wives and Wrecks') (National Archives, J77: 299). He alleged that in July 1881 Farnsworth, then 50, had taken Ann, 30, to Blackpool and committed adultery with her there. Then between March 1882 and May 1883, after she had left Tansley and gone to live in Wollaton, Richard had visited her there and had committed adultery with her 'on divers occasions there and at divers other places'.

Edward Wragg also claimed £200 damages from Farnsworth for loss of consortium, that is the loss of Ann's company and wifely services. The action for damages for the loss of consortium of a wife under English common law survived until the Administration of Justice Act 1982.

Richard Farnsworth and Ann Wragg engaged the same London lawyers and both denied the affair, saying also that, if there was any adultery, Edward knew about it and had connived at it. Connivance on the part of the Petitioner was until 1969 a bar to a successful petition and this was a common belt-and-braces form of pleading. There were various interim applications to the court, no doubt within Richard's means but costing Edward a lot of money. Edward was ordered to answer some Interrogatories - formal questions intended to elicit details of the facts alleged in support of the claim. Neither the Interrogatories themselves nor any Answers are available and it may well be that Edward was not able provide more specific particulars. Eventually in January 1884 he was ordered to pay Ann's accrued costs amounting to £18.10.0 and to pay into court another £25 to cover her future costs. He seems to have been short of admissible evidence to prove his case and he must have run out of money. The suit did not proceed and the court file was closed. We will never know whether the court would have found the case proved.

On census day 1891 Louisa Farnsworth was at home in Lumsdale but Richard was not there and we have not found him recorded elsewhere. Ann Wragg was back in Tansley Knoll by 1891 looking after three of the boys and Florrie, an illegitimate daughter born in 1890, and stayed there until her death in 1915. Edward left and in 1911 was an inmate in the workhouse at Belper. He died in 1920. They were never divorced.

It is extraordinary that Edward ever began the proceedings. He could have expected them to cost him between £40 and £50 even if they were not defended. We do not know what he was earning but in 1881 average annual full-time earnings were £48.20, general labourers £34, agricultural labourers £39.60, clothing workers (men) £53.40, and linen and hosiery workers £36.30 (Feinstein 1991 cited by Boyer 2004 vol 2: 286; see also Feinstein 1990).

At that time he would also have had to pay his wife's costs in any event. It was very rare for a labourer to petition for divorce, especially if he lived away from London (personal communication: Professor Rebecca Probert). He might have been excited by the prospect of receiving damages but how did he raise the money in the first place? Did someone with a grudge against Richard help him and then drop out?

When Richard made his Will in February 1897 however he gave all his personal estate (that is everything except land) to his sons Harry and Ernest Richard subject to providing for 'their Mother' during her life and subject to the payment of an annuity to Ann Wragg. Then he gave to his executors as trustees 'all that Cottage at the Knowl in Tansley … in the occupation of Mrs. Ann Wragg' and seven cottages and five acres of land on trust to pay the net income to the said Ann Wragg. He directed that his sons pay the annuity of £10 per annum and his executors the rents to Ann Wragg until her daughter Florence attained the age of 21 years, then to divide it equally between them. When one of them died the survivor was to have the whole amount. On Florence's death leaving children, they were to receive their mother's share. However, 'I direct that if the said Ann Wragg lives or cohabits with any man then her interest under this my Will shall cease'. Then by a Codicil dated 22 December 1898 he added another £25 per annum to the annuity on the same terms (DRO D504/131/4).

Richard's wife Louisa had died in November 1897. We can infer from his failure to mention her by name in his Will or to make any specific bequest in her favour that all was not well between them. We can also infer that Edward Wragg was right.

If there were still any doubt, Florence knew enough to name 'Richard Farnsworth (deceased) Bleacher' as her father when she was married in Tansley in November 1910. The *Derbyshire Courier* reported that 'Tansley was greatly interested in the wedding' with 100 guests, a fully choral service and a long list of presents 'both numerous and costly' - and that the happy couple departed on honeymoon to, of course, Blackpool (19 November 1910).

We have called this section 'a diversion' because it appears to be a purely personal matter which played out in Lumsdale and is of no relevance to the industrial history there. Yet the fact that Edward Wragg began the divorce proceedings, in the High Court in London, is so very unusual that we wonder whether there were problems in the business - or 'rival' groups in the area - such that Edward was used, encouraged, and perhaps at the beginning financed, by others with another agenda. We may never know.

Acquiring the Garton business: George (Harry) and Ernest Richard

The business, nevertheless, appeared to be thriving at the end of the nineteenth century - the 'state-of-the-art' bleaching process was described at the beginning of this chapter. When Richard died in 1900 the business, still in Lower Lumsdale, was carried on by the fourth generation - Harry and Ernest Richard.

In 1902 a very laudatory piece appeared in the *Derbyshire Times* by the 'Gleanings in the Peak' columnist:

'A stroll through Lumsdale a day or two ago, where the banks of the pretty stream will later be covered with rhododendrons, brought me to the bleaching works carried on by Messrs Farnsworth Bros., and I was courteously shown over the place and had the very interesting processes explained to me. The pure whiteness of the skeins of thread and cotton after they had been subjected to the orthodox treatment, was wonderful--I saw the tanks of chemicals for bleaching and then the machinery where pure water takes away all trace of the chemicals and leaves the material soft and snow-white in appearance. Mr E. R. Farnsworth, I believe, is something of an inventor and one or two parts of the machinery used in his works he has patented. The firm have just completed a Government contract' (26 April 1902).

Ernest Richard Farnsworth had indeed been granted a patent no. GB189719393A in 1897 for an Improved Method of and Apparatus for Milling and Finishing Yarns, Tapes and the like. The abstract reads:

'Yarns and threads, finishing and dressing. Yarns, tapes, and the like are milled and fulled, coloured or dyed, and sized &c by apparatus such as that shown in the Figures. The material is fed through troughs, and is operated upon by fulling fallers which are raised and allowed to fall by wipers. Between or under the troughs are tanks of which, in the apparatus [shown], the tanks contain water … a soap solution or a colouring-liquor, … a washing- solution, and … a sizing-solution [for dipping yarn to strengthen it]. Through these tanks the material is led …The rollers serve as feeding and squeezing rollers, and the [other] rollers as guide- rollers. When hanks are treated, they are connected together by twine &c. as shown [etc.]' (accessed at https:/ / patents.google.com/ patent/GB2017776B/de).

However, the accounts of the partnership between Harry and Ernest for the half year to 31 December 1900 show a mixed picture. The turnover was £2,308. Bleaching materials cost £239, wages £342, coal and slack (very small pieces of coal) £112, carriage including horse expenses £236 and 'discounts' £231. After other expenses there was a profit of £980 which was carried to the partners' capital accounts yet they had drawn, between them, only £137 during the half-year. They had debts owing to them of £1,537 (two-thirds of their turnover for the period), an overdraft of £191 and £293 cash in hand (DRO D504/80/3). This is a very large proportion of, presumably, unpaid bills and the partners appeared to be ploughing most of their profits back into the business.

Yet in 1905 the Farnsworth bleachers took a decision to extend their business. On 14 June 1905 Edward Hall Garton granted a lease of his own bleachworks to Harry and Ernest for a term of 21 years at an annual rent of £100. The lease sheds some light on the nature of the works as they were at that time. It included both water wheels, those in the Upper and Lower Bleachworks, and access to the water power they needed.

Also included was the use of the spring, underground tank and reservoir under the garden in front of Lumsdale House. A new feature is the use of water from another spring on the eastern side of the Bentley Brook together with the use of the pipe carrying the latter across at high level across the Bentley Brook.

This pipe is clearly shown in a photograph of the lower valley on a postcard (Plate 12) published by Raphael Tuck, copies of which posted between 1906 and 1910 still exist. The description printed on the back says, 'Matlock. Lumsdale. This is a charming view of part of Matlock, situated steeply upon the right bank of the river which here has flung itself into a waterfall. The opposite bank is a limestone mass out of which yew and fir and ivy grow almost at the water's edge'.

The description is reminiscent of Bray's reference to the point 'from which the water falls a great height' to which we referred in Chapter 4 but there is no limestone in the Lumsdale valley. Has the copy-writer confused the Bentley Brook and the Derwent? One of these cards posted in Matlock on 5 May 1910 to an address in Paris has found its way back to a private collection in Lumsdale. The sender wrote, 'Lumsdale is a charming little hamlet, high in the hills.'

By the 1905 lease referred to above Garton also granted to the Farnsworths the right to use 'the large flue (and any branch flues) carrying smoke to the chimney above the works and also the tramway (with windlass chain and appurtenances) which connects the lower part of the works with the upper part' (lease in private hands). One of the many outstanding questions is whether there were any flues leading to the chimney apart from the one which is visible in the ground and at the base of the chimney. What a pity the lease left that open to speculation!

Garton also granted a right of way without payment over his road, the stretch of Lower Lumsdale from the Tansley to Matlock road to the lower end of Mr E. H. Bailey's corn mill dam. He reserved to himself rights to use the mills and the water of the Bentley Brook and from the reservoirs higher up the valley and Lumsdale House with its stables, coach houses and gardens. He also kept rights to the timber and the fish.

The purchase of 'Lumsdale' by Ernest Richard Farnsworth 1907

Following Edward Garton's death in May 1906 the extensive Garton estate in Lumsdale was sold. On 25 February 1907 Ernest Richard Farnsworth took, in consideration of £5,028, a conveyance of almost the whole of the Lumsdale valley from the northern end of the Top Pond to below the Lower Bleachworks. The purchase included Lumsdale House and grounds with its stables, coach house and coachman's house, all the bleachworks, saw mill, ruins of the paint mill and the three ponds. Excluded were Pond Cottages and the plot of ground to the west of them bought, together with cottages and other plots of land to the west of Asker Lane and fields on the hillside to the east of the valley, by John William Wildgoose.

On the same date Ernest Farnsworth and J.W. Wildgoose executed a deed defining certain rights where their interests coincided. Wildgoose was to own the roadway past Pond Cottages, the start of the lane from there towards Tansley and the bridge at the head of the Lower Pond, subject to Ernest having rights of way. Ernest had the other bridge at the southern end of the Middle Pond subject to Wildgoose having a right of way for all purposes except to carry stone by means of stone drugs (carts, often horse-drawn, for transporting stone).

Wildgoose obviously had plans to develop the quarries overlooking the valley, so he also had rights of way across the land between the Upper and Middle Ponds to the wagon way leading up from the (then) bridge. Wildgoose was also granted the rights to improve utility services to his properties within the estate and, pending new sewers etc. to discharge waste on to some of Ernest's land. Wildgoose, the builder of much of Matlock, thereby made investments which his family company has realised, at least in part, over 100 years and several generations later (authors' title deeds).

Ernest, meanwhile, had married Fanny Evans in 1901 and they had set up home in Old Bank House. Their only child Helena Louisa was born in 1906 and Ernest died in 1909 aged only 40. Fanny inherited his estate.

In December 1909 Lumsdale House was leased for seven years to Joseph Thomas Cusworth, a retired grocer from Louth and in 1911 the eleven rooms were occupied by him with his wife, daughter and one servant. At this time the walled garden is reputed to have become known as Cusworth's Garden (Drabble 1997). After that the tenants were Mary Hoysted and her brother Charles William Hoysted, a retired clergyman, until their deaths in 1913 and

1916 respectively. From 1922 until his death in 1928 it was the home of Col. Edward Ellis Jackson, former chief engineer at Lea Mills (*Derby Times* 16 June 1928).

The Farnsworth era in Lumsdale came to an end in the 1920s at least in part as a result of the frailty of the fourth and fifth generations. The story of those failings is told in detail in two sequences of newspaper reports.

George Henry (Harry) Farnsworth

The last years of the Farnsworth business

After Ernest Richard's death in 1909 Harry had carried on the business but from about 1914 he had been addicted to drink. The business was effectively run by his wife and older son James. She died in January 1916 and when James came of age, also in 1916, he was given Power of Attorney to take charge.

In 1920 the family business was in a bad way. For three or four years it had been receiving writs and Harry had often been asking his solicitor to deal with them. James claimed (though it was denied) that in about April 1920 Harry took him into partnership with a one-third interest but James had problems of his own, as we shall see later.

In June 1920 the company was 'heavily fined' £14 for failing to notify an accident and to comply with regulations about employing children (*Derbyshire Times* 19 June 1920). In 1922 the Matlock Gas Company had to sue for unpaid charges of £8.5s.4d. (£8.27) (*Derby Daily Telegraph* 24 May 1922).

In June 1927 the contents of Harry's comfortable Lumsdale home were removed and sold in auction. It is not clear how much of the catalogue was his but it included 'Antique Mirror, Mahogany Dining Table, Player Piano in dark Rosewood case, in perfect condition, and other Effects, removed from Lumsdale, Matlock, re G.H.Farnsworth' (*Derby Daily Telegraph* 4 June 1927).

In 1928 a report of proceedings against the company demonstrates both its inability to pay its debts and the confused arrangements for its management. Robert Hollingsworth of Shirland sued Richard Farnsworth & Sons for £33.6s. (£33.30) the price for twenty-four tons of outcrop coal supplied to the company during the 1926 mines stoppage. The coal order had been given by James who was the paid manager until March 1927. Yet it was said that the company had been in receivership since 1924 and that the receiver, Mr J W Best, had been unable to find any record of the transaction. Nevertheless, judgment was given for the full amount claimed (*Derby Daily Telegraph* 8 March 1928).

1929 action

The story of the final collapse of the company is told in newspaper reports of a five day trial in the High Court in London in January 1929. George Henry Farnsworth sued, represented formally by his daughter Louisa as his 'next friend' although they had been estranged for years. He had been certified insane in 1925 and was certainly by then incapable of representing himself. The defendants were his son James, his former friend George Smith Marple, the company Richard Farnsworth Ltd. (see below), accountant John William Best, solicitor Frederick William Gill and Barclays Bank (widely reported including by the *Derby Daily Telegraph, Nottingham Evening Post, Sheffield Daily Telegraph, Sheffield Independent, Yorkshire Post* 17 - 26 Jan 1929).

By 1920 Harry's behaviour had become, to say the least, eccentric. His doctor gave evidence that by then he was already a chronic alcoholic. It was said that he stuffed his pockets with rubbish, slept by the furnace at the bleach works and sometimes out in the open as a tramp or on a rug at the top of his house. He was 'just a human derelict who did not know that his wife had died'.

At that time James met George Marple, a Sheffield iron and steel merchant who said he had known Harry for 30 years. Marple was also a cricketer who made one appearance for Derbyshire. They agreed that Marple would try to help the company out of its difficulties and would manage it in James's absence - about which more later. There was a difference of opinion as to whether his motives were philanthropic or whether it was an attempt to recover costs and loans for which James was liable and for which he counterclaimed in the action. Marple engaged an accountant, Best, to carry out an inspection of the books and on 28 October there was a meeting at which it was decided that it would be prudent for Harry Farnsworth to sell the business to a new limited company for some £17,710 which could be used to discharge his personal debts. Marple raised £8,500. A report at the time said:

'Mr G.S.Marple of Messrs. Marple and Gillott, of Sheffield, has acquired a financial interest in the firm of Messrs. R. Farnsworth and Co., bleachers, of The Lumsdale, Matlock. It is stated that the business is to be modernised by the introduction of up-to-date plant and electrical lighting' (*Derbyshire Times* 25 September 1920).

Richard Farnsworth Ltd. was incorporated on 6 May 1921 (DRO D504/85/14/3). George Henry Farnsworth and his daughter Kate were the subscribers and the first directors were Herbert Mountney (his brother-in-law), F.W. Gill the family solicitor and Mr Marple, for whose benefit and protection, no doubt, some 7½% cumulative preference shares were created (*Derbyshire Advertiser* 13 May 1921).

In the same month the sale of the business to the new company had been completed and it was this transaction that the family now sought to set aside on the grounds that Harry was mentally incapable of understanding in 1920 what he had been induced to agree.

The trial began on Wednesday 16 January 1929 with opening speeches which continued into Thursday and then evidence from Kate about her father's mental state.

On Friday another daughter and James gave evidence that, by reason of excessive drinking, their father had lost all self-control. Before adjourning for the weekend the Judge offered advice to all parties that they should seek an agreement. Otherwise any outcome could result in 'hopeless confusion' - possibly returning the company to a man incapable of running it and with awkward issues over liabilities which were personal to James and not the company's.

On the Monday morning the judge was indisposed and the court reconvened on Wednesday without a settlement between the parties. James gave further testimony and James Burton, a Matlock tailor who had known Harry for 40 years, claimed that Harry had not been fit to do business since 1916.

Mr Gill gave first evidence for the defendants. He had acted for Harry for 30 years and had held Power of Attorney for him. He had been involved in the discussions, which Harry fully understood, and, at Harry's request, had reluctantly agreed to be a director of the new company. He and Harry's brother-in-law held shares as trustees for Harry. He was aware that James opposed the transfer to the company and, on Harry's instructions, had done his best to avoid informing James. He was asked by Counsel the question which was crucial to the outcome of the trial:

Counsel: 'Apart from the time when [Harry] was drunk, did he show any signs of insanity?' Witness: 'So far as I know, certainly not. He was weak-willed but not weak-minded'.

Mr Marple was too ill to attend the trial but his evidence had already been taken 'on commission' and was read to the court. He said that during many discussions with Harry about rescuing the business and transferring it into the company he had never had the remotest idea or any suspicion that Harry was insane. He was aware that James claimed a one-third interest but had not timed the creation of the company to coincide with James's involuntary absence, explained later in this chapter.

Judgment was given, after five expensive days of evidence and argument, for the defendants. The judge said that he was not satisfied that the plaintiff was at the material date incompetent to enter into the contract and he was perfectly satisfied that Mr Gill and Mr Best - but only reasonably satisfied that Mr Marple - all believed the plaintiff was competent. The action was therefore dismissed with costs - another drain on their resources.

The auctions for sale of the bleaching business and estate 1929

Shortly afterwards, on Thursday 6 June 1929 two separate auctions were arranged at the Horseshoe Hotel, Matlock Green.

At 3 o'clock on the direction of the Receiver for the Debenture Holders of the company there were offered for sale the Farnsworth bleaching business (said to have been founded in 1794) as a going concern. The sale included the freehold mills lower down Lumsdale, machinery, a commodious house, gardens, cottages and over four acres of land (*Sheffield Daily Telegraph* 1 June 1929). On the day of the auction James intervened and claimed that it should not proceed because he was a one-third partner in the business and did not consent. The auctioneer had come prepared with a copy of the High Court judgment and over-ruled him. James then walked out, 'accompanied by some Army officers'. (Why they were looking after him then is not clear but please read on.) Then bidding, for the whole estate as a single lot, only reached £6,100 and the lot was withdrawn (*Derby Daily Telegraph* 7 June 1929).

It appears that what remained of the bleaching business was soon afterwards bought by Derwent Mills, then based at the former Victoria Hall on Matlock Bank. They extended the buildings lower down Lumsdale and in 1931 sold out to Paton & Baldwin (*Derby Daily Telegraph* 6 March 1931).

Then at 4 o'clock the second auction took place. The late Ernest Richard Farnsworth's Lumsdale estate was offered for sale by the executors of his Will.

After four cottages and some land at Matlock Green had been sold the Lumsdale estate was offered, first (unsuccessfully) as a whole and then in seventeen lots. Lumsdale House, for which bidding reached £800, the Lower and Upper Bleachworks, the Stable yard and the Ravine all failed to reach the reserve and did not sell. The Donkey Field to the west of the Lower Pond (with the chimney, which strangely was not mentioned), the Ponds and the Bottle Tip, let for £20 p.a. to Matlock U.D.C., also did not sell. Ivy Cottage was sold to its tenants for £230. Beech House, then two cottages, was sold to Mrs Kate Saunders, one of the tenants, for £300. Oak Cottage and plots of building land were also sold (*Derby Daily Telegraph* 7 June 1929).

As a result of the failed bids, the core of the Lumsdale valley, for over 150 years the home of industry, remained unsold in the Farnsworth estate and then entered a period of neglect.

The fifth generation of Farnsworths

So what was it that had caused James Richard Farnsworth such difficulty and embarrassment around 1920? A generation later the story would have made good material for Ealing Studios.

His military 'career'

James was used to a comfortable life but he seems to have had scant regard for rules. As early as 1914 he was caught driving a motor car through Matlock Bath with no rear light and fined 20s. (£1) with 7s. (35p) costs (*Derby Daily Telegraph* 10 September 1914). He persistently failed to comply with registration and licensing requirements so that by June 1917, when he failed to register his 'racer', he had already collected ten convictions and was fined £10.5s.6d (£10.27) (*Belper News* 8 June 1917).

In 1915 he had volunteered for military service and was placed on the Reserve. He fancied joining the Royal Naval Air Service or Royal Flying Corps, thought that had been agreed and was so disgruntled when he was called up in May 1917 and assigned to the Sherwood Foresters that he did not comply. He was arrested as an absentee on 19 February 1918, taken before the West London Magistrate and escorted back to Matlock.

On 20 February he was posted to the Irish Guards and ordered to proceed to Caterham but never arrived and was at large until 26 October. Five days after his arrest and while under confinement at Caterham he disappeared again for three weeks.

After another week back at Caterham he left again on 2 December 1918, climbing over a wall following a visit to the ablution room and running off. The sergeant in charge of him lost his rank and two years' seniority for letting him go. This time he was at large until he was picked up in Matlock on 25 April 1920. On 18 May while under confinement again at Caterham he mysteriously escaped again (this time in handcuffs) and was apprehended in Blackpool on 6 October. Appearing in court the following day he was granted bail on his own surety of £500 and £500 from George Marple, the same man who had bailed out the company. It was very rare for as much as £1,000 to be offered and that in itself made headlines. All the money was paid into court, apparently by Marple (*Lancashire Evening Post* 7 October 1920).

The 'Blackpool Bail Case' was next called on 26 October and James failed to appear. His solicitor thought he was in the confines of the court because he had travelled with him from Sheffield the previous day and stayed in the same hotel. The Chief Constable reported however that a few minutes previously the defendant had been seen heading for the railway station. He did not return and the magistrates forfeited the £1,000 bail money.

It transpired that, on his way to court with Mr Marple, James had recognised someone and shouted 'you _____ have let me down', struck Marple in the face and bolted. The defendant had driven in a taxi towards Preston and, although two police officers had given chase in a motor cycle and side car, they had failed to catch him (*Derbyshire Times* 30 October 1920). Not surprisingly the Marple family aided the police in their renewed search for the culprit and led police to a hotel in Sheffield where he was arrested. Notwithstanding their co-operation the magistrates declined to relieve George Marple of his penalty (*Lancashire Evening Post* 13 November 1920).

Back in Blackpool again on 4 November James's solicitor did not stint on sarcasm. He commented that in 1915 'people were being sworn in in shoals, when they were converting police officers into lieutenant colonels one day and chief constables into privates another'. (The Chief Constable present only partially agreed.) 'Two years after the war, when peace is signed and the League of Nations is an accomplished fact, this august department, the War Office, the home of lethargy and red tape turns up two years afterwards and tries to get this man into the Army.' The Justices felt they had no option but to hand James over to military escort and the Chief Constable had the last word: 'Take him downstairs and keep on his heels'.

James finally stood trial at a Court Martial held in the Tower of London on 8 December 1920. He faced four charges of desertion, escaping from military custody (all from Caterham) and negligently losing his kit. He pleaded not guilty. He told a complicated story of his protracted efforts to negotiate with the Army over where he should serve, including an attempt by him to sue the Army for defamation, and alleged that the Army's actions against him were motivated by personal spite after he had unwisely got into an argument with a major in a hotel in Derby. He said that when he was before the West London Magistrate in February 1918 a deal had been done whereby, if he dropped his libel action, the charges would be dropped and he could join a corps of his choice.

Counsel for James conceded that his client was 'a hot-headed impulsive fool who, when he thought he was in the right, acted in a manner in which no sane man would act.' By escaping, he argued, James was able to save his business and family from ruin. If he had not done so it would have been sold for a mere song (*Dundee Evening Telegraph, Lancashire Evening Post* 9 December 1920).

The cases were found proved and the *Hartlepool Northern Daily Mail*, for example, quoting the *London Daily Mail* under the headline 'One day in the Army instead of 1013', reported that James had been sentenced to two years' hard labour (14 December 1920).

In fact the sentence was subject to review by the General Officer Commanding the London District and he remitted six months so James served 18 months.

Daily Mail in contempt

There was however a sequel. On the same day that the sentence was confirmed it was reported that Counsel for James had moved the Divisional Court of the King's Bench to 'attach' or detain the editor of the *Daily Mail* for contempt of court for reporting the outcome of the Court Martial prematurely and publishing information, not to the credit of the defendant, which had not actually been given in evidence (*Sheffield Independent* 22 December 1920).

Before the Divisional Court on 19 January, Sir Edward Carson Q.C, no less, represented the editor of the *Daily Mail*. After some legal argument on the novel point of whether the civil court could adjudicate on matters arising in a Court Martial, he explained the nature of the complaint, firstly that the *Daily Mail* had prejudiced the outcome of the trial by reporting the two year sentence before it had been reviewed and mitigated. Then James had complained that the paper reported things that had not been said at the trial at all as if they were evidence - for example his 'Dash for Liberty' at Blackpool. In relation to that incident Mr Justice Coleridge commented 'Struck his surety? That was the unkindest cut of all.' 'No', said Carson. 'There was something more unkind than that because the surety had to pay a thousand pounds.'

What had really upset James though was the assertion that while he was on the run he had 'remained in London and become well known to the police through his association with women of ill-repute' (*Pall Mall Gazette* 19 January 1921).

Giving judgment on the following day Coleridge J. held that the court did have power to deal with the matter and that publishing the report could have influenced the reviewing officer and was a serious contempt. The editor should have known that those attending the proceedings were subject to an obligation of secrecy and that the outcome should not have been reported. The editor escaped jail but was fined £200 (*Nottingham Evening Post* 20 January 1921).

James's later 'career'

It has to be said that the authorities did not try very hard to track James down and keep him in their care, at least not until April 1920 when the case attracted widespread press coverage. There does seem to have been a good deal of confusion resulting from James's attempts to join the flying services both before and during the time when he was already technically in the Army and it was in September and October 1920 that steps were being taken to transfer the business into the limited company. Nevertheless, James did seem to get involved in somewhat dubious arrangements. In 1926 James attempted to take from John Maskery of Wirksworth the lease of an empty mill. Maskery claimed any agreement had been made by his wife without his knowledge or consent and the court action was withdrawn (*Derbyshire Advertiser* 14 May 1926).

In 1930, after the family company had folded, he found himself in court again described by police as a shifty customer who for some considerable time past had done no regular work and appeared to have been living on his wits. He had just been convicted of obtaining by deception food to the value of £1.10s (£1.50) from a Derby lodging house keeper when he had failed to pay for a night's food and lodging and made a number of excuses which the Magistrates did not believe. He said that during the eight years when 'on and off' he had been manager of the Lumsdale mills he had acquired chemical knowledge. He had been living in a house in Derby with a chemical works at the back and had invented 'Quadralene' which was used by laundries for washing and bleaching and had worked for Derby Chemicals. Another of his inventions, Cargloss, was used for cleaning motor cars. Certainly Derby Chemicals had applied to register Quadralene as a trade mark (*Chemist and Druggist* 13 October 1928: 463) but the police disputed much of what he claimed. He was convicted and sentenced to two months' hard labour (*Derbyshire Times* 21 June 1930).

Reasons for failure

By then the High Court action had failed and the business had closed down. Was that entirely due to the inadequacy of James and his father? Not really.

We saw in the last chapter that the Hall family - related to the Gartons - carried on bleaching at the mill Edward Hall had set up in 1830, the Botany Bleach Works near Whaley Bridge. While that firm over the years became part of ever bigger companies the plant itself did not close down until 1999.

However, that firm was on the Lancashire side of Pennines and so it was easier to access cotton for bleaching from the Lancashire mills. The successful bleaching firms also realised that expansion and modernisation were essential. Factories no longer needed to use water power - many used steam power. As Hills and Pacey (1972: 25) have argued, 'the growth of the cotton industry and the development of the steam engine came to be closely connected'. So the reasons for the end of bleaching at 'Garton's Mill' did lie in part with the Farnsworths for their seeming inability to understand the need for drastic changes. Yet if they had done so, they would also have realised that Lumsdale by the 1920s had more disadvantages than advantages as a place of production.

Post script:

When the authors were married in Matlock in 1970 Ernest Richard Farnsworth's daughter saw the announcement in the newspaper and wrote to the bride's father, Fred Farnsworth: 'Dear Cousin, I think I can call you that … I figure out that my Uncle Harry at Lumsdale must have been your Grandfather.' He replied, correctly, that there was no connection between the two families but that his father had known her father and mother very well. 'Your father used to be a good cricketer and he watched him play many times … I can understand, with me living in Lumsdale and your father's family living there and owning one of the mills, you thought I was one of them'.

9

A FRAGILE VALLEY

What happened next?

The Bleachworks

After the failure of the Farnsworths' legal action what was left of their business was acquired by Derwent Mills Ltd. on 29th December 1929 *(Derbyshire Times* 21 June 1930).

Their main operation was on Smedley Street in Matlock and was known for spinning yarns from the fur of Angora rabbits. It appears that Derwent Mills intended to make some improvements - Matlock Council approved their plans for a transformer house at Lumsdale House *(Derbyshire Times* 20 December 1930) - but in March 1931 the whole company was bought by Paton & Baldwin *(Derby Daily Telegraph* 6 March 1931) later known as Patons & Baldwins.

Although R. Farnsworth Ltd. had nominally been in occupation of the Upper and Lower Bleachworks site at the time of the 1929 auction, the 1905 lease from Edward Garton to the company had expired and the freehold remained in the estate of Ernest Richard Farnsworth. We have no reason to think that Paton

& Baldwin ever took possession of the bleaching works but they did continue to operate the Farnsworths' main factory lower down and to the east of Lumsdale Road. In 1936 however they closed down the cotton bleaching, dyeing and mercerising departments there, affecting sixty or seventy workmen (*Nottingham Evening Post* 5 May). They carried on processing wool and the Tansley mills also continued to operate. The Chairman of the Matlock and District Publicity Association complained in 1937 that 'they had mill chimneys in the Lumsdale which were spreading clouds of black smoke over the countryside for 24 hours a day' (*Derbyshire Times* 30 April).

So, without any businesses operating, the estate put together by John Garton gradually deteriorated, roofs collapsed and walls fell down. The cottage in his old stable yard was declared unfit for habitation in 1936 (DRO D 504/131/4). From 1922 an area of land to the east of the Bone Mill had been let to Matlock Urban District Council as a waste tip and that was perhaps the most active part of the estate. In February 1932 it was on fire.

'The smell was vile and the residents of Lumsdale and Matlock Moor had had enough of it. Rats had been driven from the tip and had entered houses and they would soon want the Pied Piper of Hamblin [sic] to collect them' (*Derbyshire Times* 20 February 1932).

The Council met and resolved to send in the Fire Brigade. In September 1933 the Council's rat catcher reported that he had caught 500 rats there in the last ten weeks. However the tip was again on fire and the vermin had scattered, adding to the misery of the local residents (*Derbyshire Times* 23 September, *Belper News* 22 September).

In the absence of industry the valley continued to attract visitors but they were now more interested in leisure activities, especially fishing in the several ponds, and rambling along the footpath links between Lumsdale, Tansley, Matlock and further afield.

Angling

Angling had in fact been popular in Lumsdale before the turn of the twentieth century and continued to be popular as long as the ponds were maintained and stocked.

During the 1890s the newspapers frequently carried reports of the excellent fishing in Mr. Garton's ponds, which were 'within an easy walk of Matlock Bridge and may be fished in any legitimate manner for [?2s.*illegible*]6d. a day or 1s.6d if fishing is not commenced until one o'clock' (*Derby Daily Telegraph* 2 August 1894). There was of course the occasional illegitimate catch. Two Tansley boys admitted poaching trout in 1888 and were fined one shilling each and costs. 'Smith said "We're caught fairly this time", showing plainly that they had been at the game before' (*Derbyshire Advertiser* 28 December).

Fishing in the Lumsdale ponds made national news in 1903 when four men from Sheffield were prosecuted for fishing for trout without a licence. A water bailiff working for Trent Fishery Board found them with their rods and lines. One of them when challenged gave a false name and address and claimed, falsely, that he had a licence at home. Two made off and were caught hiding behind a hedge two fields away. The defending solicitor, citing previous authority, argued that the ponds were artificial constructions and not part of a river and so the Fishery Board had no jurisdiction to demand a licence or to prosecute. The Board resisted that argument, saying that 'if every pond - every mill dam - was held not to be a tributary, half the waters of the kingdom would be exempt'. The Bench, who on the same occasion were very sympathetic towards other unlicensed fishermen who pleaded ignorance, accepted the defence case and dismissed the summonses.

The Fishery Board was not content to leave the matter there, believing that it raised an important matter of principle, and took the case on a point of law to the Divisional Court. There the Lord Chief Justice presided. The Fishery Board contended that the defendant was fishing in waters that found their way in a natural course eventually into the rivers Derwent and Trent. The defence argued again that the ponds were artificial reservoirs and so no licence was needed.

Giving judgment the Lord Chief Justice found that, as the water ran down continuously until it joined the Trent without being diverted or turned into another course, it did not cease to be a tributary of the river and so the appeal succeeded. Thus did Lumsdale contribute to the law of the land (*Derbyshire Times* 21 June 1902 and 4 April 1903).

From 1911 until at least 1929 the exclusive rights to fish in all three ponds were let to the Sheffield Trout Anglers Association at a rent of £12.50 p.a. (DRO D504/131/4) (*Sheffield Independent* - 21 February 1929). As late as 1990 the warden appointed by the Arkwright Society was still selling day licences.

In winter the ponds were also excellent skating rinks (see for example, the *Sheffield Daily Telegraph* 28 December 1904).

Rambling

A turn-of-the-century postcard (Plate 15) shows a smart couple walking past the Smithy on what, in the absence of any sign of workmen, must have been a Sunday stroll. Bryan notes, from personal observation at about the same time, that Mr. Garton kindly made no objection to the visits of 'wishers' who were 'registering an inward wish for gratification of some desire' to see the Wishing Stone at the top of the bank behind his house (1903: 119). Many of those, no doubt, will have walked from one of the Matlock hydros.

In the 1920s rambling became more organised. For example, the *Derby Daily Telegraph* on 1st August 1924 recommended a route from Matlock Station to Stretton via Bentley Bridge. Then, during the 1930s, around the time of the Mass Trespass on Kinder Scout, the Ramblers' Association was formed and on 31 July 1936 a correspondent to the *Derbyshire Times* complained that, rather than promoting games in the pleasure gardens, the Council should indicate the nice walks to places like Lumsdale, Riber and Farley. Staveley Rambling Club needed no encouragement. They walked to Chesterfield, then to Ashover for lunch, around Lumsdale in the afternoon and back home (*Derbyshire Times* 16 October

1936). During 1937 the same newspaper reported several other serious excursions by Chesterfield Spire Rambling Club and also Williamthorpe Cycling Club calling at Lumsdale.

None of these activities helped to preserve the industrial heritage of the Lumsdale Valley, however. Deterioration of the buildings continued apace and even local people began to forget the important history of the valley. Without the marriage of Mr and Mrs Mills, just after World War II broke out, what we now see could have been lost.

Mrs Mills's Legacy

'As the buildings in the upper section of the valley fell out of use, they were abandoned and became derelict. The valley, which once had been known for the stark beauty of its rocky outcrops, well-maintained ponds and its waterfall - as well as its noisy, dirty and busy industrialization - became thickly wooded, dark and forgotten'.

Deterioration

This extract from the tour notes for leaders of Arkwright Society guided walks down the valley points up the rapid deterioration which had taken place. The fortunes of the valley took a turn for the better in 1938, however, when Arthur Neville Mills, known as Neville, a Bakewell accountant, bought John Garton's house (Lumsdale House), and all the Lumsdale Valley which had not sold in the 1929 auction, for £275. The house was derelict and, among other things, needed a new roof. In 1940 he married Marjorie Bowler and it was her passion for the Lumsdale Valley that ensured its survival as a place of historic beauty and made possible its conservation for generations to come. She was also very attached to the Norfolk Broads where she was photographed on holiday (Page vii).

In 1970 and 1972 the Paint Mill was investigated and partly excavated during the course of an Industrial Archaeology Summer

School. It was found that the within the western cell of the main building there was a drying floor dating from its time as a barytes mill. This had channels lined with brick somewhat in the manner of a Roman hypocaust (O'Meadhra 1970). The hearth and flues were examined again in 1972 but left uncovered and destroyed by vandals (Drabble 1978).

Many of the buildings were in ruins. See for example Plate 16, a photograph of Garton's Mill taken before 1976 when part of the gable end shown there became unstable and was taken down. In 1977 part of the Saw Mill collapsed (Drabble 1986).

Mrs Mills accordingly offered the Arkwright Society the opportunity to take over responsibility for the historic industrial parts of the valley, first on lease but with an understanding that she would bequeath the freehold on her death. So she gave the Arkwright Society a lease for fifty years from 1977 at a rent of £5 a year. She reserved to herself the right to use the land as a bird sanctuary and to go on to the land to watch birds and collect firewood. The Arkwright Society agreed:

'to use the demised property for the purpose of preserving and restoring the early industrial buildings thereon and furthering the interest of the Arkwright Society and the public generally in Industrial Archaeology and the setting up of works contemporaneous with the buildings and more generally to preserve the historic character of the demised property with the right to set up a museum on the demised property with the power to charge for admission'.

Lumsdale Project

In June 2013 the Arkwright Society published a Lumsdale Project Master Plan with a vision of 'conserving Lumsdale's unique environment of ruined mills, ponds and waterfalls and developing interpretation and public access to this much visited valley while preserving its atmosphere of romantic decay'. The introduction records:

'Despite many offers for the stone for building, she [Mrs Mills] refused to permit demolition of the mill structures. She preferred to keep them in their picturesque decay, surrounded by trees and undergrowth, offering a home to a wide variety of wildlife ... In 1976 she'd recognised that she could not protect and manage her property single-handedly - the buildings near the road were in danger of falling on to the highway and the dams which once retained the mill ponds had either to be repaired or pulled down. Alongside these difficulties an increasing awareness was growing of the archaeological significance of the site' (Arkwright Society 2013: 7).

The Project Master Plan also relates:

'In 1979, a committee of Lumsdale residents and Arkwright Society members was formed and a plan for the area devised. At the heart of the Arkwright Society's strategy for the valley, there were three guiding principles:

- the mills and other buildings would not for the most part be restored but preserved in their ruined state,
- the public was to be offered access to as much of the site as could be made safe by means of paths, stiles and fencing,
- the charm of the wooded areas was to be retained wherever the trees were not endangering structures or public safety' (ibid)

During the lifetime of Mrs Mills the Arkwright Society carried out a lot of work in accordance with these guidelines.

The 1980s

Between 1981 and 1983 work was focused on clearing the Lower Pond and Mrs Mills transferred her freehold interest to the Society to assist with the funding applications.

In 1982 work began on the Smithy and by December 1983 it had been restored and re-roofed. Also in the summer of 1983 the viewing platform was erected in the Grinding Mill, serving the additional function of tying the eastern wall more securely to the rest of the building. The Arkwright Society also created the footpath through the mills, down new steps, along the side of the ravine (following the line of the former wooden launder) and down again to the road beside the Upper Bleach Works.

In 1984 and 1985 the Society turned its attention to Garton's Mill. The floor was cleared of a thick layer of rubble revealing the stone bleaching troughs which are still *in situ*. The north wall was crumbling and the stone from the upper part was used to restore accurately the ground and first floor elevation of the south wall. The boundary wall along the northern edge of the site was also rebuilt. In the same year there was a lot of vandalism around the Paint and Grinding Mills with walls pushed down and safety railings uprooted (Drabble 1986).

Some work to buttress the south-east and north-west corners of the Paint Mill in December 1986 disturbed more of the brick flues beneath rubble and the South Peak Archaeological Survey was called in to supervise the removal of debris. A report by Richard Hill with photographs is in the AS archive. It contains information about the brick flues in the disturbed areas and also a flagstone floor which extended south outside the building towards the Grinding Mill. Close to a fireplace in the south-east corner, though not necessarily connected with it, were twenty-nine pieces of Derbyshire marble which looked as if they could have formed at least part of a fire surround.

A Conservation Area and a Scheduled Monument

Mrs Mills died in 1996. The estate then passed under the terms of her Will to the Arkwright Society which has since continued to care for the Lumsdale Valley as far as its resources as a charity allow. It continues to permit public access and it strives to improve the valley's woodland and wetland habitats which now form part of a conservation area.

The original designation of Lumsdale Conservation Area was in April 1980 but the boundary of the area was amended in

November 1995. A *Lumsdale Conservation Area Character Appraisal* was completed in early 2010, followed by public consultation. The Council proposed to exclude the fields and quarry tips overlooking the upper valley but, after representations from Lumsdale Project members, they relented and agreed no changes affecting Lumsdale (Morris 2010). The continuing protection soon helped with resistance to development spreading south from Bentley Bridge.

In May 2014 part of the Conservation Area owned by the Arkwright Society was listed (Number: 1417570) by English Heritage as a scheduled monument. It was listed for the following principal reasons which are reflected in this book.

- **Survival**: for the exceptional standing remains and buried deposits which depict the continuity and change in the form and function of the industrial landscape within this section of the Lumsdale Valley;
- **Potential**: for the stratified archaeological deposits which retain considerable potential to increase our understanding of the buildings and their associated industries ...
- **Group value and Diversity**: for the range, complexity and number of industries represented here but also for the diversity and extent of archaeological features which link the industries not only to each other but also to the water source offered by the Bentley Brook;
- **Historical importance**: for the historic association with Richard Arkwright and Watts, Lowe and Co. who spread Arkwright's revolution to the valleys with water power; Lumsdale was caught up in the 'gold rush' which followed Arkwright's loss of patent on his machinery and was part of the first wave of expansion of the Arkwright factory system in 1783-84.

(See https://historicengland.org.uk/listing/the-list/list-entry/1417570 - the page also includes a map).

The Smithy was also listed Grade II in February 2016 as an

historic building in its own right as a good example of a small early-to-mid nineteenth century smithy which clearly reflects the industrial process for which it was built, with the fixtures and fittings required for metal working, an important reminder of the role of smithies in the industrial process in general, and within the context of the Lumsdale valley in particular.

Picturesque decay

To honour and fulfil Mrs Mills's wish that the valley would be preserved in its 'picturesque decay' is, however, a very difficult undertaking. The *Lumsdale Conservation Area Character Appraisal* sums this up as follows:

'[T]he simple action of trying to prevent further decay does require extensive intervention, consolidating & re-pointing ruins and active involvement in selectively felling trees, as well as cutting down undergrowth & removing seedlings, trees and ivy from the masonry. Progress is slow and structures are deteriorating slowly. Steps are often dished and worn. The complex at Lumsdale is very extensive and difficult to manage & monitor. There is a delicate balance between preserving the special "green and peaceful ambience" of the valley, the natural beauty & drama of the upper Lumsdale valley & the prevention of accelerated decay to structures' (Morris 2010: 54).

The rest of this chapter will, therefore, consider the reasons why this is no longer 'a secret valley' and the steps being taken to conserve and consolidate the ruined mills, as well as to protect the wildlife, trees and vegetation.

No longer secret

In Chapter 1 we quoted part of Moore's *Picturesque Excursions from Derby to Matlock Bath* (1818) which gave a view of the valley that is very different from what we see today. He referred to the 'dusky sterility' which 'seems to hold an everlasting reign' and said that 'not a tree, nor a patch of green is seen, to cheer the gloom of the savage waste, yet several dwellings are there'. For him the 'gloom' of the place was only mitigated by the fact that men were making money in the valley. Even so 'the want of verdure and trees renders the colouring monotonous' (1818: 60-61).

Postcards from around 1900 show relatively few trees in the open parts of the valley apart from some Scots pines above the Middle Pond. Now there are many trees which have self-set and grown in the intervening years. The Upper Pond has silver birches, the tree cover makes a rich area for woodland birds, standing dead wood and rocks encourage bats and invertebrates whilst badgers and foxes also visit. The valley is home to many common birds, including varieties of tits and finches, and nuthatches, goldcrests, dippers, tree creepers and woodpeckers are also often seen - even, though rarely, a kingfisher. Buzzards mew overhead and herons land in treetops.

However, there is in many places a 'want of verdure' because of the increased footfall which is not always on the paths to which the Arkwright Society directs visitors. On a sunny holiday weekend counts done by local volunteers suggest there may be more than a thousand visitors.

The great increase in visitors is relatively recent and can probably be traced back to a particular publication. In June 2014 Derbyshire County Council distributed free to all residents - without notification to the Arkwright Society - a publication entitled 'Your Derbyshire' with a photograph of the Lumsdale waterfall on the cover and a piece about 'Our secret county'- '5 hidden gems', the first of which was the Lumsdale Valley:

'Take an atmospheric walk through the hidden Lumsdale Valley, just outside the centre of Matlock. Lumsdale is one of the best examples of a water-powered industrial archaeological site in the county and offers lush greenery, imposing ruined mills, spectacular waterfalls and a peaceful escape from the crowds' (*Your Derbyshire* Issue 4).

The residents of Derbyshire quickly came in their hundreds to see the spectacular waterfalls and spread the news using the internet. Hundreds of photographs have been posted and more shared using smart phones. Many visitors walk with their smart phones in hand following directions to the waterfall. On a fine weekend the valley is neither peaceful nor an escape from the crowds.

The conjunction of this publication and the increased use of the internet and mobile phones for instant pictures to disseminate to friends and family means that now the 'spectacular waterfalls' are a magnet for photographers who vie to post on-line the 'best' photographs.

This attraction is also the result of Google Maps and other on-line sites referring only to the 'Falls' in Lumsdale. Most visitors - often on a day trip from, for example, London or the Home Counties - have come only because they know of the waterfall. They do not know that the valley is a precious historic industrial site or, indeed, that it is owned by a charity and kept clean and tidy by volunteers. For this reason, and to help guide visitors through the valley, free leaflets are normally available at the top of the valley and there are four interpretation boards to explain the mills and the importance of the site.

However, the majority of visitors are responsible and are very appreciative of the natural beauty. Others come to see the evidence of industry - or to learn it from the boards - and are as fascinated by the history as we are. The next two sections will tell you a little about what has been involved in looking after this valley.

Woodland management – flora and fauna

For some years members of the Lumsdale Project Group aspired to re-water the Middle Pond and took active steps after 2010 to achieve that objective. In 2011 the Arkwright Society commissioned an ecological survey from Aquascience. They found that predominant habitats within the site included stream watercourse, a modest area of successive wet woodland or carr, some semi- natural broadleaved woodland, scrub, stonewalls and marshy rough pasture. The central area of the former pond (called Zone 2, with Zone 3 on the bank to the east) was covered by various willow species more than 5m tall, some alder and elder. 'The semi-natural woodland area in Zone 2-3, which was to be impacted by the proposed middle mill pond re-instatement, showed little woodland botanical interest. In fact the proposed application area within Zone 2-3 showed the least botanical conservation value of all the vegetation zones surveyed across the wider footprint of the area shown in Map 2. The relatively young age structure and nature of the trees present in the application area Zone2-3 also left few ecological features or little diversity for protected species such as bats or nesting birds. Furthermore, this area of carr showed all signs of an ecological succession to dry land if left to nature' (Aquascience 2011).

In due course the proposal was approved and the trees were felled. With financial support from the County and District Councils, Toyota Charitable Trust and the Co-operative an impressive Master Plan was developed and a successful application made to the Heritage Lottery Fund. The grant paid for the Middle Pond to be excavated and the Lower Pond to be de-silted. Spoil from the Middle Pond was carted up the slope and spread on a friendly farmer's field. Silt from the Lower Pond was either moved to make up the banks or pumped up the hill and stored in porous bags until it had dried out and could be spread. Three weeks after the start of the work the water had cleared and the ponds returned to nature.

Ancillary to the main works the Project included creating a silt trap or sump (a modern lum) at the top end of the Middle Pond, building dipping platforms for use by local school children, and designing and installing interpretation boards at four points in the valley. It also included plans to safeguard the conservation of the habitat, flora and fauna of the valley for future generations.

In 2015, after a group of Lumsdale Project volunteers attended a training course, a Woodland Management Group was formed and carried out a detailed examination of the valley. They divided the Lumsdale estate into seven sectors or compartments, each with different needs and attributes, and set out management prescriptions for each. So, for example, the Upper Pond area was to be protected as a rare example of wetland and left untouched.

Volunteers could keep the Bone Mill and paths clear of

undergrowth but an outbreak of Japanese Knotweed would need professional attention. At the Middle Pond the silt trap would need emptying periodically, old trees would need monitoring and perhaps removal. Some dead-hedging and new planting by volunteers would enhance and limit access where necessary. In the gorge there would a long-term project to remove invasive rhododendron and re-open the traditional views towards of the waterfall from the lower valley. Throughout the valley footpaths and steps were to be kept clear and overhanging branches removed. Trees causing damage to buildings would be removed or reduced and ivy trimmed. Where necessary to prevent access, fences would be maintained and eventually replaced with hedges of hawthorn and hazel.

The initial survey has been developed into a ten-year plan but all these tasks take volunteer time - and money for expert help - and so each year the Woodland Management Team sets priorities. The volunteer working parties each month, with the occasional help of other conservation volunteer organisations and groups from local industries, have lists of target jobs for each session. The amount of work which is done in any year is amazing and is making a difference.

The fruits of their labours will in the long term help to define areas of public access, protect the valley from erosion and the buildings from degradation, keep open the watercourses and restore native and appropriate ground cover and foliage for the benefit of all fauna, human and otherwise.

Conserving the industrial heritage

When listing the valley as a Scheduled Monument Historic England recognised the potential of the archaeological remains to increase our understanding of the buildings and their associated industries:

'Such deposits can not only identify the sequential development of the individual industries but can also reveal the intricate network of water management features which physically linked, and were integral to, the functioning of all the industrial processes.

In all its guises, the archaeological evidence has the potential to aid the understanding of the significance of the valley in the social and economic structure of the communities within the wider landscape' (https://historicengland.org.uk/listing/the-list/list- entry/1417570).

Very little archaeological work has ever been done in Lumsdale. In 1970 and 1972 some excavation was done in the Paint Mill during WEA summer schools (see above). There is a brief narrative report of the 1970 work by Cearbhall O'Meadhra in the Arkwright Society archive together with on-site drawings but, so far as we know, the excavations have never been written up and published. Then members of the South Peak Archaeological Survey (Hill and Shackleton-Hill 1988) were asked to 'undertake controlled removal of the remaining rubble' and report after personnel removing debris from the Paint Mill had disturbed more of the brick flues. The Arkwright Society has a diary of the work, undertaken in difficult conditions over the New Year, and a set of photographs but it does not claim to be a formal excavation report. Crossley and Kiernan did some field work, noting for example the distribution of lead smelting slag, in preparation for their article (1992) and there may have been some excavation of the Bone Mill but we cannot trace any report.

SPAB

The 2014 scheme to rehabilitate the ponds drew attention to the fragile state of some of the ruined buildings and the upstanding remains in Lumsdale have now received more attention. In 2017 Lumsdale was very fortunate to be chosen for the summer working party of the Society for the Protection of Ancient Buildings (SPAB). Further Heritage Lottery funding was secured to pay the expenses of the SPAB exercise and Historic England funded a major operation to consolidate and make safe some of the buildings in the Upper and Lower Bleach Works.

Before work could commence a detailed survey was carried out by Terra Measurement Ltd. of Ambergate. They mapped all the structures from the Lower Bleach Works up to the Bone Mill and used a combination of photography and laser scanning to record in minute detail the elevations of the walls. Using their laser scans from many different locations and millions of pinpoints they compiled a 'fly-through' of the valley up to the Lower Pond wall moving (virtually) through apertures where even a drone would fail. A structural survey by Capstone Consulting Engineers (Ruddy 2017) highlighted the most vulnerable structures and contractors for Historic England consolidated the curtain wall of the Lower Bleach Works, an unsupported wall in the Upper Bleach Works, the Saw Mill and walls beside the stream.

Each year SPAB chooses a location for a week's summer camp. They bring experts in the kinds of work required and offer experience in conservation to a large group of willing volunteers, some already working in areas of conservation and others who are students in training. So in July 2017 Lumsdale Project volunteers hosted over 100 SPAB experts and volunteers (some camping nearby) and provided them with cooked breakfast and refreshments during the day.

SPAB focused on the Lower Bleach Works. They completely restored the small stone building which had been burnt out some years previously, with a new roof and new door and window frames. They cleared the outside of the north wall of Garton's Mill and restored the original window frames with caulk. They made their own lime mortar and spent many hours repointing walls within and outside the Works. They cut turf, added sedum plants and 'soft-capped' exposed walls to provide protection against the ingress of water. Others with a penchant for abseiling scaled the Chimney and began the re-pointing of the stonework. That work was completed in 2019.

Volunteer work

And so the work continues. The Woodland Management team and volunteers are also concerned to conserve the industrial heritage and the work scheduled for 2019 includes a survey of the underground watercourses and tunnels, cleaning the viewing platform in the Grinding Mill, clearing rubbish from wheel pits and mill races where accessible, removing or reducing trees and saplings which pose a risk to structures, reducing ivy growing on walls, defining pathways and maintaining a photographic record to identify erosion and other changes over time.

All this is to be done alongside the requirement that, as the whole site is a Scheduled Monument, 'Archaeological remains [are] to be untouched: advice required on how to protect it' (from the Activity plan finalised after the Woodland Management Meeting on the 7th January 2019).

The authors are Lumsdale volunteers and writing this book has been part of that 'work'. In the next chapter we will briefly summarise our understanding of the valley's industrialization but we also wish to acknowledge there the contribution of the workers who made the industries possible.

10

CONCLUDING THOUGHTS

Introduction

This book is entitled 'Lumsdale: the Industrial Revolution in a Derbyshire Valley'. In Chapter 2 we reviewed all those reasons why Derbyshire itself was so important in the industrial revolution. We have also tried to point out, on the basis of the evidence we have collected, those factors and developments that appear to account for the early establishment of many important industries in this small valley. Before we summarise our thinking on that, however, we wish to pay tribute to those who did the work as smelters, grinders, fullers, spinners in the cotton factory, bleachers and all the associated trades such as blacksmiths, millwrights, stone masons, and joiners.

The workers

Nowhere have we found evidence that it was difficult to attract a workforce to the various industries in Lumsdale over three centuries. Agriculture and lead mining had been the only choices for many of the working class for many years.

Lead smelting and later, briefly, cotton spinning were options.

During all these earlier stages it is difficult to find evidence of who lived or worked in Lumsdale.

The homes

The Lumsdale deeds held by the Arkwright Society at Cromford provide the names of a number of people who owned or were in possession of homes in the valley from the early eighteenth century. However, 'possession' in law did not necessarily imply that they personally occupied the land although occasionally the person in actual occupation is named in order to help to identify the property concerned. So we know that in 1721 Henry Knowles was in possession of a dwelling on Lumbs Fould. Sometimes a house is named in sale particulars as when Adam Simpson advertised for sale his smelting mill and said 'There are two small Houses close to the Works fit for Workmen' (*Derby Mercury* 2 September 1784).

Until then, however, Lumsdale must have been an unattractive place to live with lead smelting going on in at least three locations in the upper part of the valley so it is very likely that there were few residents until the last decade or so of the eighteenth century. When John Garton bought the land at the top of the waterfall from Bonsall School Trustees in 1828, however, it was described as 'all that Messuage dwellinghouse or tenement' but it is unlikely that any of those named in any of these documents actually lived there as they were all substantial landowners. So, to find evidence of who was living and working in Lumsdale we have to look elsewhere.

The Parish Registers

The Matlock Parish Registers contain information about the baptisms, marriages and burials of about twenty-five families living in Lumsdale in the first half of the nineteenth century and they include working class families.

The Registers can then give us glimpse of the people who lived and probably worked in Lumsdale but normally it is only the husband or father whose occupation is stated. The wife or mother in the family may have been working but that is not disclosed so we know nothing about, for example, any female or child workers in Watts, Lowe's cotton mill between 1783 and 1807 or later.

We mention a few of the families below: they all provide links with material in previous chapters, but mainly in relation to bleaching. For example, several were former miners, presumably lead miners who needed another industry, and several generations became bleachers. We mentioned the family of Obadiah Allen in Chapter 2. Another former miner was Robert Bunting and he and his wife Isabella appear in the registers when their children were born between 1824 and 1839. In 1824 and 1826 Robert was a miner but he is later shown as a labourer and in 1839 as a bleacher.

There were also three couples called Allwood who lived in Lumsdale: Richard, there in 1816, was a cotton spinner, in 1825 Job was a framework knitter but in 1845 Thomas was a bleacher. Job's son, another Job, who married Harriett Allen in 1845, was another bleacher. James Toplis, husband of Elizabeth, was shown as a bleacher at the baptisms of their nine children from 1817 until 1836 with one exception (as a weaver) in 1819. When their sons Marcus and Joseph had children around 1850 they were both shown living in Lumsdale and were a labourer and a bleacher respectively. There are workmen bleachers in four other Lumsdale families mentioned in the parish records but most of the other working men are shown simply as labourers. There are however a miller, a cotton spinner, two gardeners, a joiner, a waggoner, a shoemaker, a mechanic and a book-keeper.

The censuses

Much fuller information is contained in the censuses available for the period from 1841 to 1911. From 1801 censuses have been conducted in the United Kingdom every ten years but in the early years, in general, only numerical summaries were kept and we have names, ages, addresses and occupations only from 1841. The enumerators who visited every house and institution in the land always visited on a Sunday. The 100 year closure rule, introduced after the 1911 census, means that we shall not see the 1921 census in detail until 1 January 2022.

When looking for local information we have examined the census entries identified as "Lumsdale". They are listed in two different enumeration districts, the homes to the west of the Bentley Brook being in Matlock Parish and those to the east being in Tansley Parish which had become independent of the Parish of Crich in 1840. We have taken Ivy Cottage as the northernmost and Tansley Wood House as the southern limit, partly because it was consistently the home of the Radford family and readily identifiable. In 1841 the Tansley part of Lumsdale is not specifically named and we have assumed which entries relate by analogy with later years.

The 1841 census lists sixteen households on the Matlock side of the Bentley Brook and the enumerator appears to be working up from Lumsdale House, then occupied by John Garton with his wife and sisters and three servants. His sister-in-law Helen Bailey is living close by with a young female servant and her son, Henry Edwin Bailey, then two years old and later to give his name to Bailey's Mill. The other fourteen homes included one in the Lumsdale House stable yard, Beech House, Pond Cottages, the Bone Mill cottage and Ivy Cottage, also possibly Oak Cottage and perhaps two more on the site of what is now Moorland View. Fifteen adult bleachers are noted but the millwright, blacksmith, labourer and gardener may well also have been employed by the Gartons or Farnsworths.

The number of residents employed in bleaching is little changed in the 1851 census. Apart from John Garton there are, in Matlock Parish, seven heads of families employed in the bleachworks with six other adult family members. John Garton describes himself as a bleacher and paint grinder and two other men are shown employed in the barytes works. Other occupations include two agricultural labourers, cooper, waggoners, carters, coachman and gardeners.

Children

We know that the cotton mill - if, as we assume, it was based on the system copied from Sir Richard Arkwright's mill at Cromford - must have employed women and children. Yet we have no evidence for this, presumably because of the lack of potential sources for such information.

It is the 1851 census in which for the first time we have details of children in employment. There are five, aged between 9 and 13, in the bleachworks. Two others, aged 12 and 13, are working in a cotton factory and a third is a cooper (maker of wooden casks or tubs). There are fourteen children in eight families described as scholars. None of the wives is shown as having an occupation.

In 1861 there are eight heads of twenty-two families shown simply as labourers and only Garton and three others shown specifically as bleachers. Among other family members there are however fourteen employed in bleachworks plus six children aged between 9 and 12. Across the Matlock and Tansley parishes there are twenty-three children shown as scholars. John Garton is noted as employing eighty-six men, women and boys whilst John Farnsworth, living on Matlock Bank, was employing ten men and boys in his bleachworks including, presumably, three of his sons.

Changing occupations

The 1871 census is more specific about the nature of men's labour. Out of twenty-three Matlock parish families there are thirteen adult bleachers and again three children employed in the bleachworks, one of them a girl. Edward Hall Garton is employing forty-seven men, twenty-two boys, three women and seventeen girls. Richard Farnsworth has six men and six boys in his bleaching business lower down Lumsdale. In the 1881 and 1891 censuses there is only one child worker, with eighteen scholars in 1881 and nineteen in 1891 as you might expect. The 1870 Education Act had set up 'Board' schools (for example what is now Castle View School in Matlock) although elementary education was not always free until 1891.

From 1881 the number of Lumsdale residents specifically identified as employed in bleaching diminishes with only two of the heads of Lumsdale families in Matlock parish named as such, apart from Edward Garton, with Richard Farnsworth and two others in Tansley. The eight general labourers, night watchman and two carters may have worked in the businesses and the gardeners and coachman may have worked for the Gartons and Farnsworths in a personal capacity. However, Edward Garton is noted as farming ninety acres and employing six men, shepherds and agricultural workers, bleachers fifty men and women and in the paint trade eight men. The majority of those must have walked to work from elsewhere.

If we move to the last census data available we find that by 1911 there are still about a dozen local men engaged in bleaching but the range of workers has again become more diverse with two men working in Matlock's hydros as laundryman and stationary engine driver, house painters, heath cutter and motor driver.

So the occupations of those working or living in Lumsdale show a move towards the servicing of leisure pursuits: working at the hydropathic hotels for rich visitors, driving them by train or car and painting the houses of the better off. Both Lumsdale and its workers are moving out of industry.

The first industrial revolution

'The term "Industrial revolution" has long been criticised, not least because the changes were not quick in bringing about a major or an irreversible transformation of the UK economy' (Wrigley 2015: 9). Indeed, Nicholas Crafts has argued that 'growth was considerably slower between 1780 and 1821-30' than had previously been thought (Crafts 1985 quoted in Wrigley 2017: 9; see also Crafts 2017) and Knick Harley that 'Expansion of the industry led to dramatic declines in the prices of cotton goods as early as the 1780s. There is no evidence of super-normal profits thereafter' (Harley 2012: 516).

Nevertheless, the period 1750-1820/1830 is generally viewed as the early or first industrial revolution, 'characterized by a flurry of invention and innovation' (Tann 2015: 94).

Others have asked what specific factors 'pushed' the 'revolution' into being. One argument is that whilst inventions and innovations are important they needed to be workable with no production 'bottlenecks'. So 'Arkwright's key innovation was the effective introduction of an integrated flow production system' (Tann 2015: 106) and, whilst that had not perhaps been fully possible in the relatively small cotton spinning mill at Lumsdale, the early Garton's Mill had certainly used a flow of processes to take the cotton through the full bleaching process.

It has also been argued, notably by Allen (2009), that the Industrial Revolution occurred as a product of a high wage economy but Jane Humphries and Benjamin Schneider argue that their new empirical evidence 'offers little support for the high wage economy interpretation of the spinning innovations of the industrial revolution' (2019: 153). What we have realised throughout the book, however, is that new inventions and new or transformed mills needed financing and the documents showed us that Lumsdale could attract a network of people - often connected by kinship, marriage, or geography - who had money to invest. Some in those networks were people with 'old' money, others were speculators willing to take a chance and not all succeeded as the personal bankruptcies revealed.

It has always been accepted that the proximity of natural resources and water were vital to the industrialisation process but the issue of available water has been rethought by Terje Tved. In an article entitled 'Why England and not China and India?' he reviews the historical use of water and the cultural values arising from it, concluding that in Britain 'habits of thought were geared not towards river control and flood defence but toward mills and locks, and had been so for centuries' (Tved 2010: 50).

'The rapid economic development of the latter part of the eighteenth century had been in the making for generations, as thousands upon thousands of millers, engineers, and boatmen had experimented with and improved technologies and machinery, exploiting countless small, silt-free, benign brooks and year-round streams in this part of Europe' (ibid).

During the times of the Bowns, the Whitfields, and the Milneses Lumsdale had been harnessing and developing the power of water - through its lead smelting, fulling and corn grinding. Watts, Lowe & Co., the Gartons and the Farnsworths built on that for their spinning and bleaching. Sadly, those benefits also led to its decline as an industrial leader:

> 'Finally, it needs to be recalled that the water system of England eventually proved to be an obstacle and a barrier as development continued during the nineteenth century, in terms of both transport and power'
>
> — (Tved 2010: 49)

So we end the book where we started – with the Bentley Brook.

LIST OF PLATES

Cover: Drawing by Sarah Burgess of the Upper Bleach Works in 1999. © Sarah Burgess

Page vii: Photograph of Marjorie Mills on holiday in the Norfolk Broads. © Mrs Sally Goodall

Plate 1: Map of Lumsdale by Julian Burgess showing the names by which features are referred to in this book. © Julian Burgess

Plate 2: Lumsdale in an extract from George Sanderson's Map of the Country 20 Miles Round Mansfield 1835

Plate 3: French burr stone near the Saw Mill in Lumsdale, 25 June 2016. © Alan Piper 2019

Plate 4: Postcard view of the Upper Pond, undated but probably c.1900, showing the dam wall, pond, the roofline of Ivy Cottage and cottages on the Chesterfield Road in the distance. Author unknown; accessed on Facebook Old Matlock Pics Public Group.

Plate 5: Postcard view of the Upper Pond, southern corner, with the sluice, the Bone Mill and the gable of the Bone Mill cottage c.1909 ©picturethepast.org.uk

Plate 6: Postcard view of the clapper bridge over the Bentley Brook at the point now known as the 'stepping stones' showing the wagon way to the quarries. Date early 20th century. Author unknown.

Plate 7: Photograph of Pond Cottages, 4 July 2017. © Alan Piper 2019

Plate 8: Smelting House in Middleton Dale drawn by F.L. Chantrey, ARA, engraved by W.B.Cooke from the illustrated edition of E. Rhodes Peak Scenery; or, Excursions in Derbyshire, 1824.

Plate 9: Photograph of the Paint Mill, 8 April 2017. © Alan Piper 2019

Plate 10: Photograph of the oldest part of the Grinding Mill (right) with the Paint Mill beyond, 20 January 2017. © Alan Piper 2019

Plate 11: Drawing by J.C.Nattes of Lumsdale Mill near Matlock Derbyshire, 17th September 1798. © Her Majesty Queen Elizabeth II 2019

Plate 12: Postcard view of Matlock Bank (near) View in Lumsdale 1906 showing the Grinding Mill, launder carrying water to the Upper Bleach Works and a pipe carrying spring water across the brook to the Lower Bleach Works.

Plate 13: Photograph of Upper Bleach Works, 21 March 2017. © Alan Piper 2019

Plate 14: Postcard view of Garton's and other mills, Lumsdale, Matlock c.1900. Arkwright Society archive.

Plate 15: Lumsdale from the Wishing Stone Matlock c.1900. Publisher "Hawley" untraced.

Plate 16: Garton's Mill in a derelict state mid-20th century. Arkwright Society archive.

Plate 17: The last original Arkwright water frame at Helmshore Mills Textile Museum. © Alan Piper 2019

REFERENCES

Abingdon Area AHS (Archaeological and Historical Society) (undated) *Notes on Fulling and Fulling Mills* accessed 22.4.2019 at www.tinyurl.com/y3y2jk31

Anderson, J. (2000) *Derby Porcelain and the Early English Fine Ceramic Industry, c. 1750- 1830* Ph.D. University of Leicester.

Aquascience (2011) *Vegetation and Habitat Survey, The Middle Mill Pond in Upper Lumsdale in Matlock Derbyshire*, survey prepared by Dr. Nick Everall for the Arkwright Society.

Adam, W. (1838) *The Gem of the Peak or Matlock Bath and its Vicinity* London: Longman and Co; Derby: W and W Pike.

Adam. W. (1846) *Brief Remarks on the Geology of Derbyshire. A catalogue of the rocks, Marbles and Minerals of the County London*: Longman and Co. https://tinyurl.com/y2j4mmp7

Adam, W. (1861) *Dales, Scenery, Fishing Streams and Mines of Derbyshire* London: W. Kent and Co; Wirksworth: Joseph Buckley accessed 17.2.2019 at https://tinyurl.com/yy24ann6

Addy, S.O. (1888) *A Glossary of Words used in the Neighbourhood of Sheffield* London: Trubner and Co. accessed 15.4.2019 at https://tinyurl.com/y52x9mkb

Ainley, D. (2012) *Blinded by spectacle: disregard for human labour in a landscape of Joseph Wright of Derby, and a painter's response following modernism*. Digital and Material Arts Research Centre, University of Derby, accessed 17.5.2017 at https://tinyurl.com/y4al5yk8

Allen, R.C. (2009) *The British Industrial Revolution in Global Perspective* Cambridge: Cambridge University Press.

Annual Register (editor not known) (1775) *The Annual Register or a View of the History, Politics and Literature for the year 1771 2nd ed.* Pall-Mall, London: J.Dodsley accessed 14.3.2019 at https://tinyurl.com/y492d72x

Arkwright Society (2013) *Lumsdale Project Master Plan Cromford Mills*: Arkwright Society.

AS (Arkwright Society) archive; Sir Richard Arkwright's Cromford Mills, Cromford, DE4 3RQ.

Baggs, A.P., Kent, G H R., and Purdy, J.D. (1976) 'Escrick', in A History of the County of York East Riding: Volume 3, Ouse and Derwent Wapentake, and Part of Harthill Wapentake, ed. K J Allison. London. pp. 17-28. British History Online, accessed 30.5.2018 at https:// tinyurl.com/y4vtoxzr

Bagshaw, S. (1846) *History, gazetteer and directory of Derbyshire, with the town of Burton- upon Trent.* Sheffield: William Saxton, accessed 14.3.2019 @ https://tinyurl.com/y6k8ohga

Bailey, N. (1763) *An universal etymological English dictionary* London: Bailey, accessed 6.3.2019 at https://tinyurl.com/yyvtlmys

Baines, E. (1835) *History of the Cotton Manufacture in Great Britain* London: Fisher, Fisher and Jackson, accessed 14.2.2019 at https://tinyurl.com/yyav7b45

Band, S.R. (1996) 'An Ashover lead mining tithe dispute of the 17th century' Bull. PDMHS vol 13(1) 52-57 at https://tinyurl.com/y2u6ay9b

Bangs, J.D. (1946) *The Travels of Elkanah Watson: An American Businessman in the Revolutionary War, in 1780s Europe and in the Formative Decades of the United States.* Jefferson, North Carolina: McFarland and Co.

Barnatt, J., Huston, K., Mallon, D., Newman, R., Penny, R. and Shaw, R. (2013) 'The Lead Legacy: An Updated Inventory of Important Metal and Gangue Mining Sites in the Peak District' Bull.PDMHS vol 18(6) 1-112.

Bogart, D. (2017) 'The Turnpike Roads of England and Wales' in L. Shaw-Taylor, D. Bogart and M. Satchell (Eds) *The Online Historical Atlas of Transport, Urbanization and Economic Development in England and Wales* c.1680-1911 accessed 14.2.2019 at https:// tinyurl.com/y6jkeh3m

Bonser, G.G. (1948) *A History of Sutton-in-Ashfield* accessed 15.2.2019 at https://tinyurl.com/y5pa33h6

Bray, W. (1778) *Sketch of a tour into Derbyshire and Yorkshire.* London: B. White. Accessible at https://archive.org/details/sketchoftourinto00bray

Bray, W. (1783) *Sketch of a tour into Derbyshire and Yorkshire*, 2nd Ed. London: B. White accessed 26.6.2019 at https://tinyurl.com/yy9z82cj

Brewer, N. (1981) *Some aspects of the British coking industry in the twentieth century with special emphasis on plants in Yorkshire and Derbyshire*, Ph.D., Loughborough University,

Brooks, Rev. J. (1848) *Brief History of Hyde Chapel, Cheshire in The Christian Reformer Vol. IV* London: Sherwood, Gilbert and Piper accessed on 2.6.2019 at https://tinyurl.com/y57ls97o

Bryan, B. (1903) *Matlock, Manor and Parish*, London and Derby: Bemrose and Sons.

Budge, G. (2007a) 'Introduction: Science and Soul in the Midlands Enlightenment' *Journal for Eighteenth-Century Studies* vol 30(2) 157–160.

Budge, G. (2007b) 'Erasmus Darwin and the Poetics of William Wordsworth: "Excitement without the Application of Gross and Violent Stimulants"' *Journal for Eighteenth-Century Studies* vol 30(2) 279-308.

Burt, R. (1969) 'Lead Production in England and Wales, 1700-1770' *The Economic History Review* vol 22(2) 249-268

Canterbury Wills (1667) Prerogative Court of Canterbury Wills, 1384-1858 for William Woolley PROB 11: Will Registers 1660-1673 Piece 324: Carr, Quire Numbers 59-116 (1667).

Chapman, S. (1979) 'Financial Restraints on the Growth of Firms in the Cotton Industry, 1790-1850' *Economic History Review* vol 32(1) 50-69.

Chapman, S. (1981) 'The Arkwright Mills - Colquhoun's Census of 1788 and Archaeological Evidence,' *Industrial Archaeology Review* vol 6(1) 5-27.

Cole, A. (2010) *The Place-Name Evidence for a Routeway Network in Early Medieval England.* Deposited Thesis. Kellogg College, University of Oxford, accessed 26.6.2019 at https:// ora.ox.ac.uk/objects/uuid:f098ff71-7f78-45a8-b8a2-efd9c0e26345

Compiler unknown (1893) *The Matlocks and Bakewell, Famous Derbyshire Health Resorts.* Brighton: J.S.Rochard; reprinted by the Arkwright Society, 1984.

Cope, M. (2016) 'Derbyshire geodiversity, historical geotourism and the 'geocommercialisation' of tourists: setting the context of the Castleton Blue John Stone industry' *Proceedings of the Geologists Association* vol 127(6) 738-746

Crafts, N. (1985) *British Economic Growth during the Industrial Revolution* Oxford: Clarendon Press.

Crafts, N. (2017) 'The Industrial Revolution Revisited' in C. Wrigley (Ed.) *The Industrial Revolution and Industrialisation Revisited* Cromford: The Arkwright Society.

Crossley, D. and Kiernan, D, (1992) 'The Lead-Smelting Mills of Derbyshire' *Derbyshire Archaeol. J.* vol 102 6-47.

Croston, J. (1868) *On Foot Through the Peak* Manchester: John Heywood accessed 20.5.2019 at https://archive.org/details/onfootthroughpea00crosiala

Daniels, S. (1999) *Joseph Wright* London: Tate Gallery.

Davies, Rev D.P. (1811) *A New Historical and Descriptive View of Derbyshire.* Belper: S. Mason accessed 6.5.2019 at https://tinyurl.com/y2h7t473

Deane, P. (1965) *The First Industrial Revolution.* Cambridge: Cambridge University Press.

Defoe, Daniel (1724-27, reprinted 1927) *A Tour Thro' the Whole Island of Great Britain divided into circuits or journies* London: JM Dent and Co, 1927, accessed at http://www.visionofbritain.org.uk/travellers/Defoe/30

Derham. W. (1726) *Philosophical Experiments and Observations of the Late Dr. Robert Hooke and other Eminent Virtuosos in his Time.* London: W & J Innys accessed 6.3.2019 at https://tinyurl.com/y2fpyy3m

Dickinson, J., Gill, M and Martell, H. (1975) 'Lumb Clough Lead Smelting Mill, Sutton in Craven, Yorkshire' *British Mining, NMRS* vol 1, 5-17 accessed 10.6.2019 at https://tinyurl.com/y4rbawop

Dodd, A.E and Dodd, E.M. (1980) *Peakland Roads* 2nd ed. Ashbourne: Moorland Publishing.

Drabble, P. 1978. *Lumsdale* Unpublished manuscript, Cromford: Arkwright Society Archive.

Drabble, P. 1986. *Summary of Further Developments in Lumsdale Area* Unpublished manuscript, Cromford: Arkwright Society Archive.

Drabble, P. (1997) Lumsdale – *A Treasure of Industrial Archaeology* accessed 4.5.2019 at http://www.tansleyparish.com/TansleyVillage/lumsdale.html

Durtnall, M. *A Family History Website by Mike Durtnall* accessed 20.2.2019 at http://www.durtnall.org.uk/DEEDS/Derbyshire%201-100.html

Edwards, D.G. (1994) 'An Eighteenth Century Red Lead Production Record' Bull. PDMHS vol 12(4) 39-42, accessible at https://tinyurl.com/yybw5vnu

Ekwall, E. (1922) *The Place Names of Lancashire* Manchester: Manchester University Press accessed 17.2.2019 at https://tinyurl.com/y3gmkthq

Elliott, P. A. (2009) *The Derby Philosophers. Science and Culture in British Urban Society, 1700–1850* Manchester: Manchester University Press.

English Heritage (2011) *Strategic Stone Study, A Building Stone Atlas of Derbyshire and the Peak National Park* English Heritage.

Farey, J. (1811, 1813, 1817) *General View of the Agriculture and Minerals of Derbyshire, Drawn up for the consideration of the Board of Agriculture* Vols I, II, III. London: B McMillan, accessed 26.6.2019 at https://tinyurl.com/y5rh8jqv (Vol I), https://tinyurl.com/yyo8t6yw (Vol II), and https://tinyurl.com/y4tjtwkw (Vol III).

Felkin, W. (1845) *An Account of the Machine-Wrought Hosiery Trade, its extent and the condition of Framework Knitters* London: W. Strange; Nottingham: Allen, accessed 14.2.2019 at https://tinyurl.com/y2xclak4

Fiennes, C. (published 1888) *Through England on a Side Saddle in the Time of William and Mary, Being the Diary of Celia Fiennes* (1662-1741) with an introduction by Emily Wingfield Griffiths, London: Field and Tuer, The Leadenhall Press, accessed 14.2.2019
at https:// tinyurl.com/y5vug3qm

Fitton R.S and Wadsworth, A.P. (2012) *The Strutts and the Arkwrights* Matlock: Derwent Valley Mills Educational Trust, first published 1958 by Manchester University Press.

Fitton, R.S. (2012) *The Arkwrights Spinners of Fortune* Matlock: Derwent Valley Mills Educational Trust; first published 1989 by Manchester University Press.

Ford, T. D., (1967) 'The first detailed geological sections across England, 1806-1808' *Mercian Geologist* vol 2, 41-49.

Ford, T. and Torrens, H. (2001) 'A Farey story: the pioneer geologist John Farey (1766– 1826)' *Geology Today* vol 17(2) 59-68.

Fry, T. (2016) 'Basford Hall and the Hall Family' *The Thoroton Society of Nottinghamshire Newsletter* accessed 14.2.2019 at https://tinyurl.com/y3s525yp

Glover, C. and Riden, P. (1981) *William Woolley's History of Derbyshire* (c1712) Chesterfield: Derbyshire Record Society.

Glover, S. (1829) *The History, Gazetteer and Directory of the County of Derby Vol 1.* Derby: Mozley and Son, London, Longman and Co., accessed 14.2.2019 at https://tinyurl.com/y4ew4nae

Glover, S. (1830) *The Peak guide containing the topographical, statistical, and general history of Buxton, Chatsworth, Edensor, Castleton Bakewell, Haddon, Matlock, and Cromford with an introduction, giving a succinct account of the trade and manufactures of the county* Derby: Mozeley and Son, accessed 15.2.2019 at https://tinyurl.com/y28qcx3z

Glover, S. (1831) *The History and Gazeteer of the County of Derby: Drawn up from actual observation and the best authorities* Derby: Henry Mozley & Son accessed 24.6.2019 at https:// tinyurl.com/y63b577u

Glover, S. (1833) *History and Gazetteer of the County of Derby*, Vol.2; Stephen Glover, Derby accessed 14.6.2019 at https://tinyurl.com/y5jlhgtq

Harley, C.K. (2012) 'Was technological change in the early Industrial Revolution Schumpeterian? Evidence of cotton textile profitability' *Explorations in Economic History* vol 49(4) 516-527.

Harrod, J.G. and Co (1870) *1870 Postal and Commercial Directory of Derbyshire* London and Norwich.

Hey, D. (2010) *The Oxford Companion to Family and Local History 3rd ed.*, Oxford: Oxford University Press, accessed via https://tinyurl.com/y4q2onac

Hill, R. and Shackleton-Hill, A. (1988) *South Peak Archaeological Survey 1986-1988* (accessed at DRO).

Hills, R.L. and Pacey, A.J. (1972) 'The Measurement of Power in Early Steam-Driven Textile Mills' *Technology and Culture vol 13*(1) 25-43.

Home, F. (1756) *Experiments on Bleaching* Edinburgh: A. Kincaid and A. Donaldson accessed 14.2.2019 at https://tinyurl.com/y3xf4sh2

Hopkinson, G. (1958) 'Five Generations of Derbyshire Leadmining and Smelting 1729-1858' *Derbyshire Archaeological Journal* vol 78 9-24 accessed at https://tinyurl.com/yytw74ee

Hopkinson, G. (1971) 'Road Development in South Yorkshire and North Derbyshire, 1700-1850' *Transactions of the Hunter Archaeological Society* Vol 10, reproduced at https://tinyurl. com/y5c9578n accessed 2.3.2019.

Hoppit, J. (2018) 'Sir Joseph Banks's Provincial Turn' *Historical Journal* vol 61(2) 403-429, Cambridge University Press.

Humphries, J. and Schneider, B. (2019) 'Spinning the industrial revolution' *Economic History Review* vol 72(1): 126–155.

Hunt, R. (1859) *Memoirs of the Geological Survey of Great Britain, Mineral Statistics of the United Kingdom of Great Britain and Ireland for 1858 Part 1* London: Longman, Brown, Green, Longmans and Roberts accessed 14.2.2019 at https://tinyurl.com/y544y3os

Hunt, R. (1860) *Memoirs of the Geological Survey of Great Britain, Mineral Statistics of the United Kingdom of Great Britain and Ireland being Part 2 for 1858* London: Longman, Green, Longman, & Roberts, for HMSO, accessed 18.3.2019 at https://tinyurl.com/y3vn3k8d

Ince, T.N. (1824-1860) *Pedigrees*, transcribed by Palmer, J., Farrell, K. and Addis-Smith, S. 1999-2000 © John Palmer, accessed 11.4.2019 at www.wirksworth.org.uk/INCE.htm

Jamieson, A (1829) *A Dictionary of Mechanical Science, Arts, Manufactures, and Miscellaneous Knowledge* London: Henry Fisher, Son & Co. accessed 26.6.2019 at https:// tinyurl.com/y6jy6tfp

Jardine, L. (1999) *Ingenious pursuits: building the scientific revolution* New York: Doubleday.

Jardine, L. (2011) 'Britain and the Rise of Science' accessed 1.1.2019 at https://tinyurl.com/7sgd7jg

The Jurist (1839) *Reports of Cases determined in Law and in Equity during the year 1838* Vol. 2. London: S. Sweet and V & R Stevens and G S Norton accessed 17.2.2019 at https:// tinyurl.com/yym36xhk

Jones, P.D. (1980) 'The Bristol Bridge Riot and Its Antecedents: Eighteenth-Century Perception of the Crowd' *Journal of British Studies* Vol 19(2) 74-92, published online 1 January 2014.

Kiernan, D. (1989) *The Derbyshire lead industry in the sixteenth century*. Chesterfield: Derbyshire Record Society in association with the Peak District Mines Historical Society and the Derbyshire Archaeological Society.

Latimer, J. (1887) *The Annals of Bristol in the Nineteenth Century* Bristol: W.A.F. Morgan, accessed 26.6.2019 at https://tinyurl.com/yxpzzf9g

Lysons, D. and Lysons, S. (1817) *Magna Britannica*, Vol 5: Derbyshire, London: Cadell and Davies.

Mander, J. (1824) *The Derbyshire Miners Glossary, or an explanation of the technical terms of the miners which are used in the King's Field in the Hundred of High Peak* Bakewell: Minerva Press.

Martell, H.M. and Gill, M.C. (1990) 'Ore Hearth Smelting' *British Mining NMRS* No 41, 22-36 [translates *Voyage Metallurgique en Angleterre* written after a visit to Britain in 1823 by graduates of the School of Mines in Paris] accessed 15.2.2019 at https://tinyurl.com/yxvy6xzd

Martin, W. (1794) *An Attempt to establish Throughout His Majesty's Dominions An Universal Weight and Measure Dependant on Each Other, and Capable of Being Applied to Every Necessary Purpose Whatever* London: for William Martin accessed 6.3.2019 at https://tinyurl.com/y3hmyf38

Matthews, J.M. (1921) *Bleaching and Related Processes* New York: The Chemical Catalog Company accessed 14.2.2109 at https://tinyurl.com/yxzbvof2

Mavor, W. (1798-1800) *The British Tourists: Or, Traveller's Pocket Companion through England, Wales, Scotland, and Ireland. Comprehending the most celebrated tours in the British Islands*, Vol 2, London: E. Newbery.

Nightingale, B. (2003) 'The Loyd Entwistle Bank' *Entwistle Family History Association* accessed 28.7.2019 at http://www.entwistlefamily.org.uk/loyd-entwistle.html

McNeil, M. (2013) Darwin, Erasmus (1731-1802) *Oxford Dictionary of National Biography* accessed 17.3.2019 at https://tinyurl.com/y3nfxv3q

Moore, H. (1818) *Picturesque Excursions from Derby to Matlock Bath and its Vicinity being a Descriptive Guide to the most Interesting Scenery and Curiosities in that Romantic District*, Derby: H. Moore accessed on 13.6.2019 at https://archive.org/details/b22022636

Morris, M. (2010) *Lumsdale Conservation Area Character Appraisal,* accessed 1.4.2019 at https://tinyurl.com/yxfmhugy

Naylor, P. (2003) *A History of the Matlocks* Ashbourne: Landmark Publishing.

O'Connor, B. (undated) 'The Origins of the Fertiliser Industry' accessed 21.6.2019 at https:// tinyurl.com/y3pay7qt

O'Meadhra, C.E. (1970) *Industrial Archaeology Summer School; Lumsdale 1970.* Mill site excavation notes 9-14 August 1970 Cromford: Arkwright Society archive.

Palmer, J. (2006) *Wirksworth Website* accessed 5.4.2019 at www.wirksworth.org.uk

Peakdistrictonline 'Historic walk Around Belper, Milford And Blackbrook' accessed 14.2.2019 at https://tinyurl.com/yyz6w5w7

Pigot's *Derbyshire Directory* 1821-1822 London: J. Pigot and Co.

Pigot and Co.'s *National Commercial Directory, for 1828-9,* London and Manchester accessed 8.4.2019 at https://tinyurl.com/y3fn882a

Pigot and Co.'s *National Commercial Directory, for 1835,* London and Manchester accessed 8.4.2019 at www.genuki.org.uk/big/eng/DBY/Matlock

Pilkington, J. (1789) *A View of the Present State of Derbyshire* Vols 1 and 2, Derby: Drewry; London: Johnson.

Ploszajski, A. (2015) 'Material of the Month – Bone' *Materials World,* 3 August accessed 21.6.2019 at https://tinyurl.com/y5wups85

Post Office (1876) *Directory of Derbyshire, Lancashire, Rutland, Nottinghamshire 1876* London: Kelly and Co.

Price J.M. (1998) *The Imperial Economy, 1700-1776 in The Oxford History of the British Empire, Vol.2 The Eighteenth Century* New York: Oxford University Press. accessed 8.4.2019 at https://tinyurl.com/y2npp5ab

Raistrick, A. (1933) "The London Lead Company, 1692-1905" *Transactions of the Newcomen Society* vol 14(1) 119-162.

Raistrick, A. (1988) *Two Centuries of Industrial Welfare, The London (Quaker) Lead Company 1692-1905* Littleborough and Newcastle: Kelsall & Davis.

Randall, Dale B. J. (1983) *Gentle Flame: The Life and Verse of Dudley, Fourth Lord North (1602-1677)* Durham, NC: Duke University Press.

Rees, A. (1819) *The Cyclopædia, or, Universal Dictionary of Arts, Sciences, and Literature*, London: Longman accessed on 14.2.2109 at Vol 4 https://tinyurl.com/y5m4e4kw; Vol 22 https:// tinyurl.com/yxwccxev

Rhodes, E. (1824) *Peak scenery; or, Excursions in Derbyshire* London: Groombridge; Sheffield: Ridge and Jackson; Matlock: Mrs Mawe and Mr Vallance, accessed on 14.2.2019 at https://tinyurl.com/y67nl3qf

Rhodes, J. N. (1968) 'Derbyshire Influences on Lead Mining in North Wales in the 17th and 18th Centuries' Bull.PDMHS vol 3(6) 339-351 accessed 29.4.2019 via https://pdmhs.co.uk/ files/articles.php

Ritchie-Calder, Lord (1982) 'The Lunar Society of Birmingham' *Scientific American* vol 246(6): 136-145.

Rowe, J.D. (1983, reprinted 2018) *Lead Manufacturing in Britain: A History* London: Routledge.

Ruddy, J. (2017) *Lumsdale Mills Structural Report* Buxton: Capstone Consulting Engineers Ltd for the Arkwright Society.

Shaw, J.G. (1889, 3rd ed reprinted 2012) *History and Traditions of Darwen and its People* Blackburn: Heritage Publications accessed 17.2.2019 at https://tinyurl.com/y642ct5b

Slack, R. (1991) *Lands and Lead Miners, A history of Brassington* Chesterfield: Ronald Slack.

Slack, R. (2000) *Lead miners' heyday: the great days of mining in Wirksworth and the Low Peak of Derbyshire* Matlock Bath: The Peak District Mines Historical Society, accessed 1.3.2019 at https://tinyurl.com/y4bfsjss

Smith, M. (2018) 'The History of Two Dales in Derbyshire' *Derbyshire Life* 13 July.

Smith, Rev J. F. (Ed.) (1868) *The Admission Register of the Manchester Grammar School,* Vol 2, printed for The Chetham Society accessed 11.3.2019 at https://tinyurl.com/y6rashol

SPAS (South Peak Archaeological Survey) (1987) *Site Report for Lumsdale Paint Mill, Matlock 1/12/86- 7/1/87* Cromford: Arkwright Society archive.

Storm, A. (1982) *Eighteenth Century Paint Materials and The Painters Craft As Practiced In Louisbourg, Training Manual, Fortress of Louisbourg Report* H G 05 Chapter 1, accessed at https://tinyurl.com/y2enxp32

Strange, P. (2008) *Sir Richard Arkwright's Cromford Mill, The Archaeology 1969-2004* Cromford: The Arkwright Society.

Tann, J. (2015) 'Borrowing Brilliance: Technology Transfer Across Sectors in the Early Industrial Revolution' *The International Journal for the History of Engineering &Technology*, vol 85(1) 94-114.

Tvedt, T. (2010) 'Why England and not China and India? Water systems and the history of the Industrial Revolution' *Journal of Global History* vol 5(1): 29-50.

Tylecote, R. (2010) *A History of Mettalurgy*, 2nd ed. London: The Institute of Materials., accessed 27.4.2019 at https://tinyurl.com/y36wpmqj

Uglow, J. (2017) Lunar Society of Birmingham, Oxford DNB, accessed 3.4.2019 at https:// tinyurl.com/y9ro3pet

Walford, Thomas (1818) *The scientific tourist through England, Wales, & Scotland, in which the traveller is directed to the principal objects Antiquity, Art, Science and the Picturesque.* London: John Booth, accessed 14.3.2019 at https://tinyurl.com/y4l8fwky

Warner, Rev. R. (1802) *A Tour through the Northern Counties of England and the Borders of Scotland* London: J. and G. Robinson.

Warriner, D., Willies, L. and Flindall, R. (1981) 'Ringing Rake and Masson soughs and the mines on the east side of Masson Hill, Matlock' Bull. PDMHS vol 8 (2): 65-102 accessed on 1.3.2019 at https://tinyurl.com/y69x5d9r

Watson, R. (1785) *Chemical Essays,* Vol III, Essay VII "Of Derbyshire Lead Ore", Essay VIII "Of the smelting of lead ore as practised in Derbyshire", Essay X "Of Red and White Lead" London: T. Evans, accessed 2.5.2019 at https://tinyurl.com/y5grxucb

Watts, M and Watts, S. (2016) *From Quern to Computer: the history of flour milling, Post-medieval mills and milling 1540-1750* Mills Archive accessed 13.6.2019 at https:// tinyurl.com/yyxn7wbr

Weare, G.E. (1894) *Edmund Burke's Connection with Bristol, from 1774 till 1780*; William Bennett, Bristol, accessed 19.6.2019 at https://tinyurl.com/y3p7uxt7

Wheeler, J. (1836) *Manchester: its political, social and commercial history, ancient and modern* Whittaker, London; and Love and Barton, Manchester, accessed 19.6.2019 at https:// tinyurl.com/y3tku856

White, F. (1857) *History Gazetteer and Directory of the County of Derby* Sheffield: Francis White & Co., accessed 21.2.2019 at http://claycross.org.uk/White_Directory/index.html

Wigglesworth, G. (2011) *Asker Lane from Hassuk Kjar,* 3rd ed., accessed 15.2.2019 at https://tinyurl.com/y5mj47gs

Wild, C. (2017) *Archaeological Building Investigation and Assessment, Lumsdale Mills, Matlock, Derbyshire* Centre for Applied Archaeology, University of Salford.

Willies, L. (1969) 'Cupola lead smelting sites in Derbyshire 1737-1900' Bull. PDMHS vol 4(1) 97-115.

Willies, L. (1971) 'The introduction of the cupola "for smelting down" lead for Derbyshire' Bull. PDMHS vol 4(5) 384-94.

Willies, L. (1980) 'Technical and organisational development of the Derbyshire lead mining industry in the eighteenth and nineteenth centuries' Ph.D Thesis, University of Leicester, accessed at https://lra.le.ac.uk/handle/2381/35605

Willies, L. (1990) 'Derbyshire lead smelting in the eighteenth and nineteenth centuries' Bull. PDMHS vol 11(1) 1-19.

Willies, L. (1996) 'Prosperity and Decline in Derbyshire Lead Mining' Bull. PDMHS vol 9(5) 251-282.

Wood, A. (1993) 'Social Conflict and Change in the Mining Communities of North-West Derbyshire, c. 1600–1700' *International Review of Social History* vol 38(1) 31-58.

Wood, A. (1999) *The Politics of Social Conflict, The Peak Country 1520-1770*, Cambridge Studies in early Modern History. Cambridge: Cambridge University Press.

Woodcroft, B. (1854) *Titles of Patents of Invention, Chronologically Arranged from March 2, 1617 (14 James I.) to October 1, 1852 (16 Victoriæ)*, by Order of the Honourable the Commissioners of Patents, Printed by G.E. Eyre and W. Spottiswoode, London for The Queen's Printing Office, accessed 11.3.2019 at https://tinyurl.com/y5om3447

Worlidge, J. (1704) *Dictionarium Rusticum & Urbanicum: or, A Dictionary Of all sorts of Country Affairs, Handicraft, Trading, and Merchandizing.* London: J. Nicholson.

Wrigley, C. (2011) 'Out and about in Cromford Mill, Lea Mills and the Lumsdale Valley' *Historian* Issue 111: 26-31.

Wrigley, C. (2015) 'Introduction' in C. Wrigley (Ed.) *The Industrial Revolution: Cromford, the Derwent Valley and The Wider World* Cromford: The Arkwright Society.

Wrigley, C. (2017) 'Introduction' in C. Wrigley (Ed.) *The Industrial Revolution and Industrialisation Revisited* Cromford: The Arkwright Society.

Zupko, R.E. (1985) '*A Dictionary of Weights and Measures for the British Isles: The Middle Ages to the Twentieth Century*' Memoirs of the American Philosophical Society, Philadelphia Vol 168, accessed 28.6.2019 at https://tinyurl.com/y56ba8dg

NEWSPAPERS

Bath Chronicle and Weekly Gazette
Belper News
Bristol Mercury
Bristol Mirror
Chesterfield Herald
Derby Daily Telegraph
Derby Mercury
Derbyshire Advertiser and Journal
Derbyshire Courier
Derbyshire Times
Dundee Evening Telegraph
Hartlepool Northern Daily Mail
Lancashire Evening Post
London Gazette
Manchester Mercury
Nottingham Evening Post
Nottingham Review and General Advertiser for the Midland Counties
Pall Mall Gazette
Sheffield Daily Telegraph
Sheffield Independent

MAPS

1780 Enclosure map - Matlock

1791 Burdett's Map of Derbyshire by Peter Perez Burdett first published 1767, surveyed 1762-1767, published by George Snowden, London. Facsimile of 1791 edition by Derbyshire Archaeological Society 1975.

1835 George Sanderson's Map of the Country 20 Miles Round Mansfield.

1840 Ordnance Survey map 1" to 1 mile. Surveyed 1837-9. Revision 1860s published in facsimile David & Charles Newton Abbot 1970

1846 Tansley Tithe map - extracts in Morris (2010) at Fig. 4.

1849 Gratton, Joseph. Plan of the Parish of Matlock in the County of Derby surveyed in 1848 and 1849 (the Tithe Redemption map)

1876-1880 Ordnance Survey map 1:2,500 County Series accessed at old-maps.co.uk

1899 Ordnance Survey map 1:2,500 County Series accessed at old-maps.co.uk

1922 Ordnance Survey map 1:2,500 County Series accessed at old-maps.co.uk

1967 Ordnance Survey map 1:2,500 County Series accessed at old-maps.co.uk

INDEX

Allen, Obadiah 28, 193
Allwood family 193
Arkwright, Sir Richard 40, 42, 103-5
   patents 105, 114
   water frame 104
Arkwright, Richard, junior 99, 104
Arkwright Society
   conservation work 178-180, 186-7
   woodland management 184-6, 188-9
   See also Lumsdale Project

Bailey family 194
Bailey's Mill 91, 102, 132, 142
Barton, Thomas 92, 99-100
Barytes 27, 136-7
Bentley Brook 1-6, 32-4, 66, 89, 158-9
Bleach works
   Lower 18, 135, 158, 180, 188
   Upper 17, 135, 158

Bleaching 95, 123-8
   processes 123-8
   See also Farnsworths and Gartons
Bone Mill 7, 9-10, 55, 138-140
   cotton spinning 119-21
   lead smelting 56
   sources of bone 140
   uses for ground bone 139-40
Bonsall School 16, 58, 132
   lead smelters 16, 58-9, 69-70

Boot, Joseph 65
   Sybilla 67
Bowers Mill 62, 68
Bown or Bowne family 85-90
   John Bown 90
   Anthony Bowne 87-89
   William Bowne 89-90
Bray, William 31, 42, 70, 78, 98, 113
Brick 26
Bunting family 193

Calendering 94
Censuses 193
Chimney 9, 67, 135, 188
Cliffe, Robert 57-8
Coal 48, 61, 63, 72, 82
   seam 26, 72
Corn mills 85, 91-2, 94, 100-1
Cotton mills
   decline 121-2
   sources of cotton 28
   spinning 103-5
   water frame 104-5, 112, 117
   workers 191-5
Cozens, John Robert 44
Cromford Mills 103-4
Cupolas - see Lead smelting
   and Pond Cottages
Daily Mail in contempt 168
Darwin, Erasmus 40

Defoe, Daniel 2, 5, 42
Derwent Mills Ltd 173

Enclosures 55, 59, 65

Farey, John 3, 31, 36, 38, 61, 82
Farnsworths' bleaching works 128, 149-151, 173-4
  closure 165, 174
  lease from Garton 158-9
Farnsworth, Ernest Richard
  bleacher and inventor 157-161
  marriage and death 160
  purchase of Lumsdale estate 159
  sale of Lumsdale estate 165
Farnsworth, George Henry (Harry) 161-4
  High Court action 162-4
  sale of business to Richard Farnsworth Ltd 163
Farnsworth, James Richard 165-70
  claim to business 161, 165
  court martial 167
  fraud 170
  service career 166-8
Farnsworth, John 151-2
  local interests 151
  marriage 151
  purchase of Old Bank House 153
Farnsworth, Richard (b.1776) 149-150
  bleachworks 125-149
  expansion 149
  death 152
Farnsworth, Richard (b.1830) 152-6
  Co-Respondent 154-7
  death and will 156
  Hopewell House 153
  marriage 153
  Old Bank House 153
  See also Richard Farnsworth Ltd.
Fiennes, Celia 41
Flax 27
Fulling mills 88-93, 99
  process 92-3

Garton, John 129-134, 141-2
  connections 111, 133-4
  death 142
  employees 138, 194-5
  expansion of estate 130-133
  local interests 141
  marriage 129
  purchase of mills 59-60, 70, 132
Garton, Edward Hall 142-7
  Board of Guardians 146-7
  businessman and employer 144-5, 195
  death and sale of estate 147,158, 160
  expansion of estate 143
  farmer 143, 196
  local interests 145-7
Grinding Mill 14-15, 101, 179
Gritstone 24
  See also Millstones

Hall family
  of Basford 134
  of Horwich 134, 170
Hall, Edward 134, 147, 170
Harris, Wintour 108, 119
Historic England 187-8
Hodgkinson, George 56-7
Hurst, The 86

Investors 29, 49, 106, 111

Jones, Gamaliel 59, 118-9, 130-1

Lancaster, Duchy of 52-54
Lead 26, 46
  distribution routes 48-50
  pig and fother 46
  red 78-9
Lead smelting 45-48
  at Lummes Mill 53-5, 58
  cupola 61-3, 70, 79, 82-3
  decline 80-82
  ore hearth 50-1
  slag mills 71-73, 77

215

Leisure activities
　angling 174-6
　rambling 176-7
London Lead Company 62-3, 66
Longsdon, William 68
Lords of the Manor – see
　Manor of Matlock
Lowe, Thomas 110, 116
Lums Brook - see Bentley Brook
Lumsdale, origin of name 30-7
Lumsdale Conservation Area 180-2
Lumsdale House 135, 142, 159, 165
Lumsdale Project 4, 178-9, 184-5
See also Arkwright Society and
　Mills, Neville and Marjorie
Lumsdale Scheduled Monument 181
Lunar Society 39-40

Manor of Matlock 54-5, 67, 121
Marple, George 162-4, 166, 169
Midlands Enlightenment 39
Millstones 94
　French burr stones 95, 137-8
　gritstone 94
Mills, Neville and Marjorie
　gift to Arkwright Society 178-80
　purchase of valley 177
Milnes, John 70, 110-11, 119
　William 70, 110-11, 119

Nattes, Jean Claude 16, 44, 60, 98
Nightingale, Peter 55, 59, 65, 102, 114
Norman, George 55, 66, 68

Offspring Mill 10-11, 73
Oldknow, Samuel 115

Paint Mill 12-13
　Cupola 69-71
　　excavation and consolidation
　　71, 177-8, 180, 187
Parish Registers 106, 192
Paxton, Sir Joseph 91, 142
Peel, Robert 105, 125
Pond Cottages 8, 116

　cupolas 64-9, 82, 116
Ponds 6-9, 174-6, 184-5
　Lower pond 9, 19
　Middle Pond 8
　Upper Pond 6-8
Pre-industrial revolution 20

Quaker Lead Company -
　see London Lead Company
Quarries 24-5
　See also Gritstone

Reverberatory furnace -
　see Lead smelting - cupola
Richard Farnsworth Ltd 163

Sanderson, Matthew 74-7
Saw Mill 11-12
Simpson, Adam 97, 192
Smith, George 92
　John 91-2, 96
Society for the Protection of
　Ancient Buildings (SPAB) 187-8
Spencer, James 96-7
　Timothy 90-92, 96
Statham, John 57
　Thomas 54
Swettenham, James 55, 68-9

Tip (waste) 174
Toplis family 193
Turnor, Elizabeth 58, 69
Twigg, John 62, 64, 68

Visitors to Lumsdale 40, 183

Walk mills - see Fulling mills
Walker, Richard 96-7
Wall, George 64
　John 64
Waterfall 4, 17, 85, 184
Watts, Job 107, 112, 116
　William 108, 112, 119
Watts, Lowe & Co 18, 69, 105-17
　consortium 106-12

cotton mill description 18, 112-3
dissolution of partnership 116
purchase of Lums Mill 106
sale of mill 117-8
White, George 55, 68, 120
   Thomas 90-1
   William 86
White's Mill 55, 120
Whitfield, Joseph 49, 66-7
   Matthew Sparke 66-68
Wildgoose, John William 160
Wilson, Luke 92, 99-100, 119
Wingerworth 31, 45
Wolley, Adam of Riber 51-2
   Adam (b. 1758) 86, 111, 119-20
   William 53, 56
Wolley Manuscripts 30, 61, 85
Wood 25
   white coal 48
Woodward, Lydia 66-67
Wool 27
Workers 28, 138, 191-6
Wragg, Edward and Ann 154-7
Wright, Joseph 40, 43